THE POWER OF
RIGHT
BELIEVING

7 KEYS TO FREEDOM FROM FEAR, GUILT, AND ADDICTION

JOSEPH PRINCE

New York · Boston · Nashville

Unless otherwise noted, all Scripture quotations are taken from the New King James Version of the Bible. Copyright © 1982 by Thomas Nelson, Inc. Used by permission. All rights reserved.

Scripture quotations marked AMP are taken from the Amplified Bible. Copyright © 1954, 1958, 1962, 1964, 1965, 1987 by The Lockman Foundation. Used by permission. (www.lockman.org)

Scripture quotations marked KJV are taken from the King James Version of the Bible. Scripture quotations marked NASB are taken from the New American Standard Bible. Copyright © 1960, 1962, 1963, 1968, 1971, 1972, 1973, 1975, 1977, 1995 by The Lockman Foundation. Used by permission. (www.lockman.org)

Scripture quotations marked NIV are taken from the Holy Bible, New International Version. Copyright © 1973, 1978, 1984, 2011 by Biblica, Inc. Used by permission of Zondervan. All rights reserved worldwide. (www.zondervan.com)

Scripture quotations marked NLT are taken from the Holy Bible, New Living Translation. Copyright © 1996, 2004, 2007 by Tyndale House Foundation. Used by permission of Tyndale House Publishers, Inc, Carol Stream, Illinois 60188. All rights reserved.

Scripture quotations marked The Message are taken from THE MESSAGE. Copyright © by Eugene H. Peterson 1993, 1994, 1995, 1996, 2000, 2001, 2002. Used by permission of NavPress Publishing Group.

FaithWords
Hachette Book Group
1290 Avenue of the Americas
New York, NY 10019

www.faithwords.com

Printed in the United States of America

RRD-C

Originally published in hardcover by Hachette Book Group.

First trade edition: October 2014
10 9 8 7 6 5 4 3 2 1

FaithWords is a division of Hachette Book Group, Inc.
The FaithWords name and logo are trademarks of Hachette Book Group, Inc.

The Hachette Speakers Bureau provides a wide range of authors for speaking events. To find out more, go to www.hachettespeakersbureau.com or call (866) 376-6591.

The publisher is not responsible for websites (or their content) that are not owned by the publisher.

Library of Congress Control Number: 2013942949

ISBN 978-1-4555-5316-7 (pbk.)

This book is lovingly dedicated to my daughter
and friend Jessica Shayna Prince.

*Many daughters have done virtuously,
but thou excellest them all.*

—Proverbs 31:29 KJV

CONTENTS

PART 4
Win the Battle for Your Mind

PART 5
Be Free from Self-Occupation

PART 6
Have a Confident Expectation of Good

PART 7
Find Rest in the Father's Love

INTRODUCTION

During the last two decades, I have had the privilege of ministering to precious people from all walks of life. I have had the honor of meeting people in my congregation and at conferences around the world and hearing their stories. I can see them in my mind's eye even as I write.

Some of them brimmed with the exuberance that came with their release from condemnation. Others held back tears of gratefulness as they recounted addictions that had once shackled them with shame and the inability to do anything positive with their lives. For those whom I didn't get to meet in person, their letters and emails to me told their stories. Stories of liberation from a life of anxiety and depression. Stories of being rescued from the prison of fear. Stories of breaking loose from destructive habits.

I am deeply moved and humbled that God has used my messages, books, and television broadcast in some way to help these amazing individuals navigate their way to freedom.

But not all stories that I've come to know have had a happy ending. At least not yet.

As a pastor, I've also encountered many who are still struggling today. Some are bound by severe insecurities, trapped by eating disorders, or gripped by constant fears and recurring panic attacks.

Others have been held captive by years of chronic depression, fighting suicidal thoughts that strip them of their ability to function in their everyday lives. There are also those who are caught in a destructive cycle of addiction, some to alcohol and others to nicotine, drugs, or pornography. And sadly, some of these people are still desperately trying to claw their way out from under the burden of more than one of the above.

They all long for freedom and have tried everything, including psychological and psychiatric treatments. They have tried exercising their own willpower to the best of their abilities, only to find themselves even more entangled in their addictions and insecurities than they were before. Many have become financially drained from seeing psychiatrist after psychiatrist, doctor after doctor, counselor after counselor, spending thousands of dollars every month on consultation fees. They've taken all types of antidepressant and antipsychotic drugs, in addition to trying quick fixes of every imaginable kind. And they are no better.

Hearing stories like that always breaks my heart, and I remember asking myself this: What is the difference between those who have experienced their breakthroughs and those who are still trapped and bound by toxic emotions and addictions?

I believe the answer is simple but powerful: their *beliefs*.

Right believing always produces right living. When you believe right, you will live right.

You see, people are struggling to control their behaviors and actions because they don't have control over their emotions and feelings. They don't have control over their emotions and feelings because they don't have control over their thoughts. And they don't have control over their thoughts because they are not controlling what they believe.

Put simply, if you believe wrong, you will struggle with wrong thoughts. Those wrong thoughts will produce unhealthy emotions that will lead to toxic feelings of guilt, shame, condemnation, and fear. And those wrong feelings will ultimately produce wrong behaviors, actions, and painful addictions.

What you believe is critical. And wrong believing is the trigger that starts you on a path of defeat. It is what keeps you trapped and drives you deeper and deeper into paralyzing captivity.

The good news is there is a way out of this vicious cycle of defeat. *The Power of Right Believing* will teach you the powerful truths of God's Word to believe in His love for you. It will show you how God is for you and not against you. It will open your eyes to see how He is on your side, rooting for your success and propelling you toward your breakthrough with His love and tender mercies.

In this book, you will learn what God really sees when He looks at you as His beloved child, what it means to be completely forgiven, and how to have a confident expectation of good for your future and destiny in Christ.

You will read many amazing testimonies from people across America and around the world. Their lives were touched and transformed when they encountered the person of Jesus and allowed their minds to be renewed with right beliefs about their true identity in Christ.

To accelerate your learning experience, I have distilled the essence of the power of right believing into seven simple but practical keys that you can begin to apply every day in your life. These keys are easy and highly effective Bible-based principles that will calibrate your mind to develop positive habits for right believing. The seven keys are:

- Believe in God's Love for You
- Learn to See What God Sees
- Receive God's Complete Forgiveness
- Win the Battle for Your Mind
- Be Free from Self-Occupation
- Have a Confident Expectation of Good
- Find Rest in the Father's Love

My friend, if you are struggling with some of the issues I mentioned earlier, I believe with all of my heart that as you set aside some time to read this book, you'll find inspiration, hope, and encouragement to break free from the crippling grip of all that has held you back. I am confident that you'll find the freedom and power you need to live your life to the fullest.

God intended for you to live with joy overflowing, peace that surpasses understanding, and an unshakable confidence in what He has done for you. It's time to let go of the life of defeat and step into a life full of victory, security, and success. Forget about merely dealing with the symptoms—the guilt, fears, and addictions. We are going after the root! If you can change what you believe, you can change your life! Now that is the power of right believing.

PART ONE

BELIEVE IN GOD'S LOVE FOR YOU

CHAPTER 1

WHAT YOU BELIEVE IS POWERFUL

What you believe is powerful. If you can change what you believe, you can change your life! I have met many precious people who keep struggling to control their behaviors and actions. No matter how hard they try and how much effort, time, and resources they throw into the fight, like a beaten boxer they end up returning to their corners, their bodies defeated, morale crushed, and confidence shattered—trapped once again in guilt, fear, and addictions that simply refuse to go away.

Then the bell rings for the next round. The fight continues, and they unleash everything they have against their adversary. Left, right. Left, right. It seems like they are making progress. But then their opponent starts landing head shots, and each blow comes loaded with poisonous, condemning judgment:

> *Who do you think you are? Have you forgotten all those mistakes you've made?*
> *Things will never get better. You should just accept your lot.*
> *It's not going to work—you are just going to fail again!*
> *Nobody loves you. You are all alone.*

I've seen these deceptive tactics used too many times by the adversary. I've seen too many people try to move out from under the shadow of their past or break free from their addictions, only to end up succumbing to these lies about themselves, their identity, and their destiny.

That's the power of *wrong* believing.

Wrong believing puts people in a prison. Even though there are no physical shackles, wrong believing causes its inmates to behave as though they were incarcerated in a maximum-security penitentiary. They march inexorably to their dank cells of addictions. They allow themselves to be led into dungeons of destructive behaviors. They have convinced themselves never to dream of a better place, believing that they have no choice but to live in despair, frustration, and defeat.

Right believing, on the other hand, is a light that illuminates the path to freedom out of this prison.

> Wrong believing puts people in a prison. Right believing is a light that illuminates the path to freedom out of this prison.

God Wants to Light Your Way

Now before you dismiss this as yet another book that claims that everything will work itself out if only you could think positively, hang on. This is not about human psychology. This is about right believing that is birthed out of a very personal and intimate relationship with a loving Savior and founded upon His Word that brings life and illumination. The psalmist says it this way: "Your word is a lamp to my feet and a light to my path" (Ps. 119:105). The Message translation reads, "By your words I can see where I'm going; they throw a beam of light on my dark path."

My friend, God wants to throw a beam of light on your path today. Whatever you are struggling with currently, no matter how insurmountable your challenges appear, when you start believing right, things are going to start turning around for your good!

The breakthroughs you have been fighting to have for years can happen in a supernatural instant. I know this because I have counseled and prayed for many people who have told me about how their years of addiction to cigarettes, alcohol, or pornography just vanished when they allowed Jesus to come into their situations. They woke up one morning, and the desire for those things just wasn't there anymore!

If we're honest, we all have some measure of wrong believing in our lives. If you don't believe this, all you need to do is ask yourself, "Have I often felt anxious, worried, or fearful that the worst would happen to me and my loved ones?" My friend, these negative, exhausting emotions are merely flags that indicate what we truly believe about ourselves, our lives, and God.

When we are fearful and worried all the time, we are living as if we don't believe that we have a strong and able Shepherd who is tenderhearted toward us, who only leads us to good places, who protects us and lovingly watches over us. So if worrying or being fearful seems to be your natural default mode, what you need to do is to keep hearing and learning about how much God loves you and how precious you are to Him. The more strongly you believe this—

the more this truth gets a hold on the inside of you—the more it will change your thoughts and feelings and the less you will fall victim to unhealthy emotions and behaviors.

In varying degrees, we all have wrong beliefs in our hearts that need to be exposed to the truth of God's Word. That's why we need the Savior. Our wrong beliefs can only be demolished when they are exposed to His grace and the truth of His Word.

Knowing the Truth That Sets You Free

The very premise of this book is based on the oft-quoted verse that says, "And you shall know the truth, and the truth shall make you free" (John 8:32). This is a verse that has been widely used, even in secular literature. But what does it really mean? What *is* the truth that sets you free?

It is essential we recognize Jesus said this to the Jews of His day. These were people who at an early age grew up studying and learning the law. Yet these people, much like us today, still battled with fears, anxieties, sicknesses, and all kinds of oppression, bondages, and addictions.

So what is this truth that Jesus was talking about, this truth that if His hearers knew, would set them free of all these destructive things? Well, it clearly cannot be the law because these people were already well-versed in the law. They were already observing the law as best they could, yet they could not find freedom in the law. Freedom, my friend, can only be found in His grace. When you believe right in His grace and His love for you, the shackles of fear, guilt, and addictions will fall off.

Grace—Antidote for the Poisoned Mind

Grace is the truth that Jesus came to give us. His Word proclaims that "grace and truth came through Jesus Christ" (John 1:17).

In the original Greek, "grace and truth" are regarded as one item because the following verb, "came," is used in the singular. Grace and truth are one and the same thing. Grace is the truth that has the power to set you free from fear, guilt, and all addictions—"And you shall know the truth, and the truth shall make you free" (John 8:32).

It is the truth of grace and not of the law that brings you true freedom. The truth of the law only binds you. In fact, religious bondage is one of the most crippling bondages with which a person can be encumbered. Religious bondage keeps one in constant fear, guilt, and anxiety.

The good news is that grace came to set you free from the curse of the law. Grace is not a doctrine or theological subject. When Jesus talks about grace, He is talking about Himself. Grace is a person. Grace is Jesus Himself. "For the law was given through Moses, but grace and truth came through Jesus Christ" (John 1:17). The truth that has the power to fling wide open your prison doors is His grace. His grace is the antidote to counteract every poison in your mind! When you taste Jesus' love and savor His loving-kindness and tender mercies, every wrong belief begins to dissolve in the glory of His love.

When you taste Jesus' love and savor His loving-kindness and tender mercies, every wrong belief begins to dissolve.

I've seen this happen over and over again, everywhere I go proclaiming without apology the unadulterated gospel of grace and the unceasing love of our Lord Jesus. When a person starts to calibrate his or her believing so that he or she receives with gladness God's lavish, excessive, and superabounding love, destructive mind-sets or strongholds begin to shatter. And in a supernatural instant, he or she experiences liberation from destructive habits, fears, and bondages. You can't process His grace logically in your mind—it needs to be experienced in your heart!

My friend, your freedom is found in rightly believing in His love, His grace, and His favor in your life. When you believe right about His grace, you will begin to live right. Right believing always produces right living.

God's Grace Uproots Wrong Beliefs

I met a lady at a conference where I was speaking. I wish you could have seen Kate for yourself. She was a confident and attractive young lady, with a face radiant and glowing. So I couldn't believe it when she revealed to me that she had been delivered from more than four years of alcohol addiction!

She had been a corporate highflier, but the stress of work and the strain of maintaining her success and image drove her to consume at least one liter of alcohol a day as a means of escape. Before long, keeping up with the high-octane demands of her career became a constant struggle. Coupled with the self-imposed pressure to keep her veneer of success intact, this struggle pushed her deep into depression.

One thing led to another, and soon, besides being addicted to alcohol, Kate became dependent on a cocktail of strong antidepressants, tranquilizers, beta-blockers, and sleeping pills. She shared that she tried everything to beat the bottle. She made appointments with psychiatrists and psychologists, and even faithfully attended support groups for alcoholics. Through these endless appointments and meetings she experienced what she calls "a few bouts of recovery," but they only lasted several days at best.

One day, Kate's husband decided to take her on a holiday. This filled her with even more anxiety because she didn't know how she was going to get her secret alcohol "fix" while traveling with her husband. Now, she had tried over and over again to quit drinking and was all too familiar with how the withdrawal symptoms had defeated her every time. Her hands would tremble and shake so vigorously that she couldn't even hold a spoon to feed herself. She would feel faint and break out in a cold sweat and would constantly throw up and not be able to keep any food down.

All these symptoms would disappear with a drink or two, so she would sneak off to buy alcohol when she was supposed to be at the gym and guzzle hard liquor in secret when her husband was at work!

To the rest of the world, Kate appeared to have it all together. But she knew. She knew that she was trapped in the prison of alcoholism and there was no way out of this vicious cycle of defeat.

So after repeatedly trying to overcome her addiction without success, Kate was on the verge of giving up. But God had other plans. He led her to one of the leaders in my church who taught her to immerse herself in the Word and to keep praying in the Spirit. As she kept listening to my messages on God's grace, God began uprooting the wrong beliefs that had taken hold in her mind and replacing them with right beliefs.

When it was time for her to leave for the holiday, even though she was filled with trepidation and almost backed out of the trip at the last minute, she decided that she would go. She asked the Lord to help her keep her eyes on Him instead of trying to overcome the withdrawal symptoms. She was determined to enjoy her time with her husband and to give thanks to Jesus for every blessing, no matter how small.

Kate told me that throughout the trip, she just kept resting, praying in the Spirit, and listening continually to my messages on her iPod. To her amazement, she didn't suffer any symptoms. And you know what? It has been more than two years since that trip, and she has never taken another drop of alcohol. Hallelujah!

She admitted that while the thought of having a drink does come to her once in a while, she believes that God has given her the strength to resist the temptation. And by His grace, she knows that she will never give in to the bottle again!

My friend, in a supernatural instant, four long and treacherous years of addiction to alcohol disappeared for Kate. She didn't know it then, but God was freeing her from her addiction (and much more) by filling her with the Spirit as she looked away from her problem and kept her eyes on Jesus. She also shared how she had discovered recently that the answer to her drinking problem was in God's Word all this time: "And do not be drunk with wine, in which is dissipation; but be filled with the Spirit" (Eph. 5:18).

I applaud this young lady for having the courage to share her powerful story with me. I pray that her testimony will encourage, inspire, and give you hope.

A Jesus-Encounter Can Free You Supernaturally

You may be asking, "How can this be? How does four years of alcohol addiction just disappear like that? How could such a powerful craving just lose its hold in such a short time?"

The answer is simple but powerful.

Kate allowed God's love to invade her mind as she listened to grace-based messages on her iPod that were full of Jesus and His love. When you allow God's love to saturate your mind, it doesn't matter what wrong believing, fears, or addictions are keeping you bound. His grace will begin to break them down. That is what happens when you have an encounter with your loving Savior. Everyone who encounters Jesus never leaves the same. He came to set the captives free.

Listen to what Jesus says: "The Spirit of the LORD is upon Me, because He has anointed Me to preach the gospel to the poor; He has sent Me to heal the brokenhearted, to proclaim liberty to the captives and recovery of sight to the blind, to set at liberty those who are oppressed" (Luke 4:18).

My friend, I want to tell you that whatever you are oppressed with, Jesus came to set you free. It could be a debilitating physical condition, or like Kate, whom I met at the conference, you may be entangled in an addiction that has imprisoned you for years.

> *Whatever you are oppressed with, Jesus came to set you free.*

Whatever your condition, however long it has kept you bound—two years, ten years, thirty years—know this: *God can set you free in a supernatural instant.* He who created time isn't time-bound. He who in a fraction of a second turned water into the finest aged wine can bypass natural processes and accelerate your deliverance from any bondage!

I know of many people who struggled with addictions for decades. But once they had a supernatural encounter with Jesus, they just woke up one morning and found themselves free, with none of that familiar urge or desire to engage in their negative behavior anymore. Frank, who lives in the state of Maryland, wrote to me and shared how he was set free from drug addiction. He had been told that "once an addict, always an addict," and he had believed it.

But when he came to know the truth about the life-transforming love and grace of Jesus through one of my teaching resources, it just destroyed the chains that bound him. He shared, "Man, I could have jumped through the roof when I discovered that all I had to do was accept the finished work of Jesus and His grace! After thirty years of drug addiction, I thought that there was no hope for me. But praise Jesus, I am now drug-free, and I'm in a good grace-preaching church with my wife, who has also been set free of her drug addiction."

My friend, that is the power of right believing!

God's Truth Triggers Your Deliverance

The moment Kate and Frank began to hear and believe the right things about God, it triggered their deliverance in an accelerated fashion. Knowing the truth was the catalyst. Contrast this with those who focus on living right without paying attention to believing right. Sadly, they only experience transient breakthroughs to the extent their willpower, self-control, or discipline persists. But those who focus on and believe the truth about God experience lasting freedom effortlessly. Jesus certainly wasn't kidding or exaggerating when He said that knowing the truth sets you free.

Jesus has the truth that you need, that you've been searching for. He is *the* way, *the* truth, and *the* life (see John 14:6). In love, He willingly laid down His life at the cross to set you free. That's what this book is all about—transforming what you believe through the power of His sacrificial love and eternal truths. I've endeavored to make these truths as accessible and plain to see as possible for you. As you read the words, Scriptures, and stories of real people who have been set free by simply believing these truths about God and what He says about them, I pray that you will encounter God's grace like never before. And as you meditate on these truths, I am confident that you will be walking in freedom sooner than you think. Your liberation is at hand!

With God There Is Always Hope

Dear reader, I don't know what your hurt is today, and I don't know what exactly you are struggling with. I just want you to know that God loves you. No matter how many mistakes you have made in your life, no matter how dark, how dire, and how desperate the circumstances seem, I have a message for you: It's not over. Don't throw in the towel!

Maybe you are struggling with some dark thoughts right now. Perhaps even thoughts of suicide have crossed your mind. Well, I can tell you it isn't over. There is hope. There is help. God loves you so much. He wants to throw a beam of light on your path today, just like He did for Kate who was enslaved by alcohol for years. The mistakes of your past need not determine your future. God can give you a new beginning, a fresh start, and cause all things to work out for your good!

The mistakes of your past need not determine your future.

Pastor Prince, you don't understand. How can I expect God to help me since I'm not a "religious" person?

That makes two of us!

There is not a religious bone in my body. I'm not here to talk to you about a religion. I'm here to show you a God who is alive, who cares, who breathes, who loves, who in many ways has been misrepresented and misunderstood. There is so much wrong believing about who God is.

Presenting the Real God

I want you to put aside whatever you may have believed about God, whatever you may have heard about Him or seen about Him. Allow me, through this book, to introduce the real Jesus to you, for this is where it all begins. Not the religious Jesus you may have heard about growing up, but the real Jesus who walked along the dusty streets of Jerusalem and upon the raging waters of the Galilee.

He was the one whom the sick, the poor, the sinful, the down-and-out, and the outcast instinctively gravitated to and felt at ease with. He was God in the flesh, and He manifested God's tangible love. In His presence, those who were imperfect didn't feel fearful of Him or sense judgment or condemnation from Him. A far cry from what many of us have been taught about God.

Jesus kept His harshest words only for those who were perfect in their own estimation. If you look carefully at all the biblical accounts of Jesus, He really didn't get along well with the religious folks of His day, who were known as Pharisees. They paraded around, their noses in the air with a holier-than-thou attitude. Although they would never admit it, they were extremely arrogant and cruelly judgmental.

The Pharisees were critical, faultfinding, legalistic, pretentious, bigoted, and most of all, ignorant. They made loud claims about their piousness for God. Yet when they stood in the very presence of God Himself, they were too self-occupied to recognize Him. God was with them in the flesh, but they did not worship Him. Instead, they scorned Him and on many occasions even plotted to kill Him.

Unfortunately, their "descendants" are still around today! Perhaps you've encountered them and have felt the heat of their scorn, condemnation, and judgment.

But the God they speak of is not the God whom I personally know. You don't have to be "religious" to have access to the God whom I know. In fact, the less "religious" you are, the better. So I am asking you to throw out every idea, concept, and picture that you may have of a "religious" Jesus. The real Jesus didn't come to bring a new religion. He didn't come to be served and waited upon. No, He came to serve, and serve He did.

> *You don't have to be "religious" to have access to God.*

The real Jesus created the universe with one command and orchestrated the paths of each planet so that none would collide. He had every right to demand service from those He created, yet He supplied service. He kneeled down and with His own hands washed the grime and filth from His disciples' feet. Those same hands would later be pierced with coarse nails at the cross, and He would, with His own blood, wash us of the grime and filth of all our sins by taking them upon His own body. What a far cry from the condemning, judgmental, faultfinding God that many have portrayed Him to be!

Believe in a God of Grace

Many today believe in a "religious" God. They believe that God is against them when they fall short, that He is angry with them when they fail, that fellowship with Him is cut off when they make mistakes. They believe that God is perpetually unsatisfied with them, waiting impatiently to be appeased. They imagine a God who is constantly judging them for their weaknesses, shaking His head in abject disappointment at their mediocrity or never-ending failures. They believe that they are not good enough for God and will never be good enough for Him.

It's no wonder then that instead of running to the one true solution, they run in the opposite direction when they are hurting. So there is a great deception, a powerful, wrong belief about God that has trapped many in the vicious cycle of condemnation, guilt, fear, defeat, and addiction.

My friend, the God I know is a God of infinite grace. He is repugnant to the "religious," but gracious and irresistible to those who are hurting.

No matter what you are going through today, whatever addictions may be binding you, right believing can and will set you free. Start with believing this powerful truth:

> *God is a God of grace and forgiveness. He loves you very much, and He doesn't hold your mistakes against you.*

Begin to believe in His love for you and your entire life will be transformed. Right believing always leads to right living. If you can change what you believe, you can change your life!

If you can change what you believe, you can change your life!

CHAPTER 2

THE GOD WHO SEEKS THE SHUNNED

She waited patiently until the coast was clear. She didn't want to run into any of the other women who had made it painfully clear to her that her presence was repugnant to them. She could no longer stand the gossip, snide remarks, and disapproving eyes. Several weeks ago as she was nearing the well to draw water, the other women, fully aware that she was within earshot, began warning one another to keep their husbands far away from her.

"She's a seductress!" one had whispered loudly. "Do you know that she has had five husbands from other villages?"

Another woman had chimed in: "And the man whom she's living with now is not even her husband."

Nursing each other's insecurities, they began to make all kinds of baseless accusations about her.

"She's a loose woman!"

"She'll steal your husband in a heartbeat."

"Don't you be taken in by her innocent doe eyes and beguiling smile!"

Juicy variations of her "husband stealing" prowess had soon

spread throughout the village where she lived like a swarm of locusts, devouring every remaining shred of her dignity.

She had quickly become an outcast in the village. No one dared to befriend her. Since moving there, she had tried everything to keep her past under wraps. However, once the news broke, no one cared to hear her side of the story. She was pigeonholed as the woman with a shady past. The verdict was already in—she was a home wrecker! What else was there to know?

It had been weeks since she had spoken to anyone. Wild stories about why she had had five husbands spread virally through the village grapevine. To insulate herself and avoid further contact with the other ladies, she had devised a system. Since all the women would be at the well replenishing their water supply in the cool early morning, she would only make her daily visit to the well when the sun was at its apex. She would much rather bear the punishing blaze of the midday sun than the heat of their scorn and ridicule. Every day since then, she had come quietly to the well, meeting no one at all, and faded back into nonexistence after getting her fill of water.

Unbeknownst to her, on this day, as she was waiting patiently for the sun to rise to its peak, the Sun of righteousness was already by the well waiting for her.

A Savior Who Reaches Out to the Imperfect

You can actually read about this woman in the Gospel of John (see John 4:1–42). When you read her story or any story in the Bible, I encourage you to activate your imagination—not to change the meaning of the biblical accounts, but to draw out the essence of the details and gems that God has for your benefit. Put yourself in the narrative. These characters are not part of a fictional story. They are real people, with real challenges and a very real Savior!

There are no insignificant details in the Bible. It tells us specifically that it was about noon when Jesus was at the well waiting for the woman. It also records that Jesus was traveling from Judea to Galilee and that "He *had* to go through Samaria" (John 4:4 NLT, emphasis mine). The New King James Version says that "He *needed* to go through Samaria," and the King James Version puts it this way: "He *must* needs go through Samaria."

Had to. Needed to. Must. Words that speak not just of necessity, but underscore a steady resolve and even urgency!

Jesus' disciples must have been surprised when He said that He needed to go through Samaria. They had never taken that route before to Galilee. It was the custom of the Jews of that day to avoid any contact with the Samaritans, whom they perceived to be spiritually inferior. Jesus' disciples didn't know that He had deliberately scheduled a divine appointment with the woman at the well.

We know from the account found in John chapter 4 that this ostracized, lonely woman had a life-transforming conversation with Jesus at the well. But make no mistake—it wasn't she who sought out Jesus to talk to Him. It was the Savior who pursued the one whom others shunned. Do you know that He is still doing that today?

Do you have a past that you are ashamed of? Are you struggling to overcome something that you know is destroying you? Do you feel all alone and that no one understands the pain you are going through?

I want you to know that Jesus hasn't changed. As He was for

the Samaritan woman, the loving Savior is still your very present help in your time of need (see Ps. 46:1). He knows the suffering, shame, and struggles you are going through right now. And even if what you are going through is a consequence of bad life choices and mistakes of your own doing, He doesn't abandon and forsake you. No—a thousand times, no! He goes out of the way, just like He did for this woman in Samaria, to have a personal appointment with you, to restore and rescue you. The fact that you are reading this right now is a confirmation that Jesus is reaching out to you with His love, grace, and forgiveness. My friend, this is who Jesus is!

> *Jesus is reaching out to you with His love, grace, and forgiveness.*

He Comes to You in the Midst of Your Storm

The loving Savior comes to you at your point of need. When His disciples were out at sea, caught in a turbulent tempest and tossed by the waves, who came to them in their darkest hour? It was Jesus Himself. Jesus came in style, walking on the raging waters.

What does this tell you? That He is above the storms. He walks above—He is greater than—every adversity and opposition that you may be facing right now, and He comes to you to rescue you!

With the billowing waves beneath His feet, His first words to His disciples were, "Don't be afraid. Take courage. I am here!" (Matt. 14:27 NLT).

What comfort those words must have brought to the disciples

who were exhausted and shaking with fear. Storms are good at doing that to you. They overwhelm you. Wave after wave of relentless battering that knocks you off your feet till you don't know which side is up. Till every ounce of energy is used up and you feel so weak, abandoned, and lonely.

But don't go by those negative feelings and emotions, my friend. Live by the truth of God's Word, which encourages you to "be strong and courageous! Do not be afraid and do not panic... For the LORD your God will personally go ahead of you. He will neither fail you nor abandon you" (Deut. 31:6 NLT). Our God is a personal and loving God who is with you in your boat. He knows what storms are ahead and how to lead you to victory every time. He cannot fail you!

> *Our God is a personal and loving God who knows what storms*
> *are ahead and how to lead you to victory every time.*

The Good Shepherd Goes Ahead of You

Jenny, a lady in my church, shared that she went on a golfing holiday with her husband up in a mountainous area. That morning as they stood at the first tee, there was a light mist overhanging the beautiful and serene green golf course. She had been meditating on the Lord being her shepherd in Psalm 23 and felt so loved by Him as she took in the picturesque, pastoral landscape and the cool, clean mountain air. She pictured herself being led by the good Shepherd, Jesus, who makes her lie down in tender green pastures and leads her beside still waters.

Even though Jenny had never played on that course before, she ended up playing her best round of golf. How did that happen? It was because they had an experienced caddy with them, and she had benefitted from every bit of observation and advice that he had offered her. She wasn't a regular golfer and had been a little anxious about the challenges ahead, but the caddy had assured her confidently, saying, "Don't worry, I have thirty years of experience on this golf course. I have been all over this course, and I am familiar with every hazard and every trap that is ahead of you. I will show you what to avoid and where to aim." And by just heeding his guidance, her golf ball landed on every fairway and she played the best round of golf in her life!

My friend, you have more than just an experienced caddy in your life. You have the One who created the universe as the shepherd of your life! This shepherd has been to your future. He knows every hazard and every trap that is ahead, and He has laid out a path for you that is filled with His favor. And even when you make a mistake or take a wrong turn in life, He is still *with you* to *help* and *rescue* you. Look at what the psalmist says:

> *Yea, though I walk through the valley of the shadow of death, I will fear no evil; for You are with me; Your rod and Your staff, they comfort me.*
>
> —Psalm 23:4

The Door of Hope in Your Valley of Trouble

Notice from the verse that it was not the good shepherd who led the psalmist into the valley of trouble, as the psalmist says, "Yea, though *I walk* through the valley of the shadow of death…" Yet the Bible is so clear in stating that even if your trouble is due to your own willfulness, God is still with you. He has never left you, and He never will. He will never forsake you. You are precious in His eyes. Can you imagine living life with that kind of confidence, assurance, and peace? Then believe in no uncertain terms that God will *never* abandon you and leave you in the lurch!

In fact, the Bible says that God will turn the Valley of Achor into a door of hope for you (see Hosea 2:15). In the Hebrew, "Achor" means "trouble."[1] So even if you find yourself in the valley of trouble, you will not remain there for long. You will walk through it and not remain or camp there. God is opening a door of hope in your life today for you to step out of your darkness and into His marvelous light (see 1 Pet. 2:9). Things are going to get better. The breakthroughs that you have been waiting for are coming your way. Step through the door of hope and out of your valley of trouble today. Jesus is your door of hope! Believe in His love for you and allow Him to lead you to freedom.

> *Jesus is your door of hope! Believe in His love for you and allow Him to lead you to freedom.*

Some people think that when they fail, God leaves them and only returns when they get their act together. They think that they must clean up their lives and overcome all their struggles on their own before they can come before the presence of God. Well, I have a simple question for them: Do you clean yourself before you take a bath? Of course not!

God wants us to come to Him just as we are, with all our weaknesses, idiosyncrasies, wrong beliefs, hang-ups, and all our bondages, fears, and addictions. *He* is the bath! So don't try to clean yourself up before you come to Him. In the presence of His love, joy, and grace, you will find restoration, healing, and forgiveness. He will mend your life and transform you from the inside out. Right now, He is extending His hand of grace, love, and help to you. There is no shame in coming to Jesus just as you are. He who knows you perfectly loves you perfectly!

To Know the Truth, Go to the Source

But Pastor Prince, isn't God disappointed and angry with me for all my failings, mistakes, and sins? I'm too embarrassed to go to Him. I feel that I should sort out all this mess in my life before I can go back to church, read the Bible, and pray.

I understand how you feel. And I can tell you that you are not alone in those sentiments. Many believers that I have personally counseled feel exactly the same way. But the most effective way to address our problems and wrong beliefs is to go to God and find out the truth from His Word. In order to get our believing right, we need to first discover what the "right beliefs" are, based on the solid foundation of God's Word. We can't base our beliefs on feelings, circumstances, human conjectures, or what we may have heard someone say about God. We have to go to the source!

> *To get our believing right, we need to first discover what the "right beliefs" are, based on the solid foundation of God's Word.*

If you heard a rumor that someone you knew was saying horrible and negative things about you, don't believe it immediately. Go to the source first. Ask this person if this is what he or she really said or if this is what he or she really meant. Many people allow precious friendships and relationships to become fractured because they believe the rumors. They become bitter, angry, and disappointed without ever verifying with the person if he or she had actually said those nasty things.

In the same way, in the world we live in, there are all kinds of wrong beliefs perpetuated about God: "God is angry at you." "He is disappointed with you." "God is allowing all these negative things to happen to you because He's punishing you for your past sins."

Please do NOT believe all this baseless gossip about God! Such impressions of God have damaged many people's relationships with Him, and they live with a distorted perspective of who God really is. Instead of receiving His love, grace, and forgiveness, they become afraid, distant, and fearful of Him. Instead of allowing Jesus to come into their situations, they live their life running away, avoiding and hiding from Him. Come on, let's honor God and go to the source.

So what does the Bible—God's own Word—say about Him? Let me quote from one of my favorite psalms of David:

> The LORD is *merciful and gracious, slow to anger, and abounding in mercy . . . He has not dealt with us according to our sins, nor punished us according to our*

iniquities. For as the heavens are high above the earth,
so great is His mercy toward those who fear Him; as far
as the east is from the west, so far has He removed our
transgressions from us.

—Psalm 103:8, 10–12

Isn't this a beautiful psalm? Don't be thrown off by the phrase, "toward those who fear Him." Jesus defined the word "fear" as "worship" (see Deut. 6:13 and Matt. 4:10). So "those who fear Him" speaks of those who reverence and honor God in their lives. It is *not* the practice of being fearful or afraid of God. The whole context of this passage is about who and what God really is—gracious and merciful. And I strongly encourage you to memorize verse 10 if you can: "He has not dealt with us according to our sins, nor punished us according to our iniquities."

God Abounds in Mercy toward You

Let's get back to your earlier question: Is God disappointed and angry with you for your failures, mistakes, and sins? No! Read the above Scriptures again. The point here is that as a child of God, all your failures, mistakes, and sins have *already* been judged and punished on the body of Jesus at the cross! That's why God is no longer angry with you for your sins and He doesn't deal with you according to your sins. No, because of the cross, He deals with you according to His bountiful mercy and grace.

Just in case you missed it, the psalm repeatedly stresses that

God is merciful. It tells us that "the LORD is merciful" and goes on, almost immediately, to say again that He is "abounding in mercy." In the King James Version of the Bible, it says that God is "plenteous in mercy." I like the word "plenteous." It speaks of abundance, excess, and lavishness. His mercy toward you and me is plenteous. He abounds in mercy toward us!

My friend, God has exhausted His anger toward all your sins at the cross. The cross is an act of His love. If you ever doubt or question God's love for you, just turn your eyes to the cross. If God wants to deal with us and punish us according to our sins, He wouldn't have sent His Son to be scourged, beaten, and crucified, but He did! This is the good news of the gospel of grace. God sent His only beloved and precious Son to redeem us from the penalty and punishment of sin.

Now, can you imagine how far the east is from the west? You cannot think just in terms of the geographical boundaries of the earth. God is the Creator of the universe. So let me ask you again, how far is the east from the west? Are you getting this? The human mind cannot fathom the distance between the east and the west. There are frontiers in the cosmos and galaxies beyond our own that our most advanced telescopes cannot see. God thinks in infinite terms that our finite minds cannot wrap around. And this God of the infinite universe declares in the psalm that "as far as the east is from the west, so far has He removed our transgressions from us!"

Let us reason together. How can God still be judging and punishing you for your transgressions if He Himself has removed them? I can hear the chains of your wrong beliefs about God falling to the ground as you read this! This is what I call the power of right believing. You start to believe right when you start to believe in His love for you. The truth is, we can't go further if you don't first begin to believe that God is for you and not against you. The first key to right believing is to be established in His grace, anchored in His love, and secure in His mercy toward you.

> *You start to believe right when you start to believe in His love for you.*

From Self-Conscious to Savior-Conscious

Let's return to the story of the woman of Samaria, the one whom Jesus went deliberately to meet. This woman had a past that she was terribly ashamed of, which is why she came at noontime to draw water. She didn't want to meet anybody. What she didn't know was that Jesus was there and He wanted to meet *her*. He hadn't come all that way to embarrass, judge, or mock her. Read the account in John chapter 4 for yourself. Jesus drew her in with His love, grace, and compassion. She never felt exposed or ill at ease in His presence.

When she said that she had no husband, Jesus didn't call her out and humiliate her. Instead, knowing that she was self-conscious and insecure about her background, He commended her twice by saying, "*You have well said*, 'I have no husband,' for you have had five husbands, and the one whom you now have is not your husband; in that *you spoke truly*" (John 4:17–18, emphasis mine). He sandwiched what He already knew about her between two compliments! Jesus must have spoken to her with so much compassion and love in His eyes, and with no judgment or sarcasm in His voice, that it caused this woman to let down her defenses and open up to Him.

By the time she left His presence, this self-conscious lady who once feared meeting people was so occupied with Jesus' love and acceptance that she became an evangelist of Jesus and His grace. She went back to the village and testified about Jesus (to the very people she had been terrified of before), and the Bible records that "many of the Samaritans of that city believed in Him because of the word of the woman who testified, 'He told me all that I ever did'" (John 4:39).

In the same way, my friend, Jesus is not out to embarrass you today. He is here to meet you right where you are. He knows all that you have ever done and loves you with an everlasting love. Allow His love to change and transform you from within, just like it did for the woman at the well.

Perhaps like the Samaritan woman, you know what it's like to look for love in all the wrong places. Today Jesus offers you true intimacy that fully satisfies every aching need. He offers you a deep sense of rest that can only be found in His perfect and unconditional love. Perhaps you've had a past that has imprisoned you in shame and self-loathing. Perhaps you've allowed the things that you have done to convince you that you'll never have God's acceptance or love. If you've always only known or heard of a hard and judgmental God, a God who holds every misdeed you've committed against you, then I challenge you to encounter the real Savior who has already forgiven you and invites you to discover, taste, and experience His unfailing love.

It doesn't matter how ugly a mess your life may have spiraled down into. If you will open your heart to Jesus and allow His love to heal you, He can change the trajectory of your life and give you a fresh start and fulfilling future. Everything can change for the better when you begin to believe right about His love for you and learn to draw upon it!

> *Everything can change for the better when you begin to believe right about His love for you and learn to draw upon it!*

God Is Pleased When You Draw on His Love

Do you know that Jesus finds great joy when you draw on His love? Look at how the Samaritan woman's encounter with Jesus ended. When the disciples left Jesus at the well to buy food, He was weary and tired from the journey. When they came back, they were amazed to find Him refreshed, and they wondered if someone had brought Him something to eat. Jesus answered them by saying, "I have food to eat of which you do not know" (John 4:32).

What food was Jesus referring to here? He had not eaten or drunk anything. All He had done was minister to the woman from Samaria. In other words, Jesus found nourishment, strength, and joy when He ministered His love to her. You know, when you draw from men, they become depleted and weak. But the opposite is true of Jesus. When you draw from Him, He is strengthened, refreshed, and rejuvenated! Jesus wants us to know that He derives great joy and pleasure when we draw upon His love for us.

When the Samaritan woman asked Jesus why He (a Jew) would

ask her (a Samaritan) for a drink of water, this is what He said to her: "If you only knew the gift God has for you and who you are speaking to, you would ask me, and I would give you living water... Anyone who drinks this water [from the well] will soon become thirsty again. But those who drink the water I give will never be thirsty again. It becomes a fresh, bubbling spring within them, giving them eternal life" (John 4:10, 13–14 NLT).

Jesus is saying the same thing to you today: *If you only knew* who it is who comes to you in your darkest and weakest moments. *If you only knew* this gift of God who will never leave you nor forsake you, who has gone before you and who comes to you in the midst of your storms. *If you only knew* the One who reaches out to you even when you have failed and who doesn't hold your past mistakes or present failures against you.

Beloved, if you only knew this gift of God who offers the living water of His unconditional, endless love to you and you drink of that love, you will never thirst again. You won't need to look for love or acceptance in all the wrong places and have your heart broken and fearful about the future and your life derailed. You can wake up with a fresh expectation of good every day. Jesus was essentially inviting the woman to ask Him for the living water of His love. Will you do that today? Your life will never be the same again when you personally experience His love!

> *Your life will never be the same again when you personally experience His love!*

CHAPTER 3

"JESUS LOVES ME! THIS I KNOW"

I heard a story of a minister from Oregon who was assigned to provide counseling in a state mental institution. His first assignment was to a padded cell that housed deranged, barely clothed patients. The stench of human excrement filled the room. He couldn't even talk to the inmates, let alone counsel them—the only responses he got were groans, moans, and demonic laughter.

Then the Holy Spirit prompted him to sit in the middle of the room and for a full hour sing the famous children's hymn that goes, "Jesus loves me! This I know, for the Bible tells me so. Little ones to Him belong; they are weak, but He is strong." Nothing happened at the end of that first day, but he persisted. For weeks he would sit and sing the same melody with greater conviction each time: "Yes, Jesus loves me! Yes, Jesus loves me! Yes, Jesus loves me! The Bible tells me so."

As the days passed, the patients began singing with him one by one. Amazingly, by the end of the first month, thirty-six of the severely ill patients were transferred from the high-dependency ward to a self-care ward. Within a year, all but two were discharged from the mental institution.[1]

These simple words, "Jesus loves me! This I know," were first penned as a poem by Anna Bartlett Warner, an American writer born in 1827 in Long Island, New York. In 1862, the prolific hymn composer William Batchelder Bradbury set the words to the tune that we are familiar with today and added the chorus, "Yes, Jesus loves me!" The popularity of the hymn spread rapidly across America and to every continent in the world. It has been translated into many languages and quickly became one of the best-known and loved hymns of all time.

The hymn's ongoing popularity lies in its succinct elegance in unveiling Jesus' heart. It beckons one to recognize that no matter what challenges, failures, and misdeeds one might be dealing with, *the love of Jesus remains a constant.*

> *No matter what challenges, failures, and misdeeds one might be dealing with, the love of Jesus remains a constant.*

"Jesus loves me! This I know."

How so?

"For the Bible tells me so."

So simple, yet so powerful.

Whether we feel it or not, Jesus' constant love for us rests in the truth and on the foundation of His unchanging Word. It proclaims that His love for you and me is based utterly and completely on Him. On His promises, His work, and His grace.

God's Love for You Is Unconditional

Do you believe that God loves you today? No matter how many mistakes you've made in your life, I'm here to tell you beyond the shadow of a doubt that God loves you. He loves you with an everlasting love. Right now, regardless of the challenges you may be going through, I want to encourage you to see yourself walking under an open heaven, surrounded by His unmerited favor. Expect good things in your future. Believe in His love for you. Believe with all your heart that you are the apple of His eye and the delight of His heart. Believe that you are highly favored, greatly blessed, and deeply loved!

God's love for you is unconditional. It's a love that is so pure, pristine, and marvelous. It has nothing to do with your performance, but everything to do with who you are in God's eyes—His beloved. The emphasis of the old covenant of the law was all about your love for God, whereas the emphasis of the new covenant of grace is all about God's love for you. The sum total of the law under the old covenant is, "You shall love the LORD your God with all your heart, with all your soul, and with all your strength" (Deut. 6:5, see also Matt. 22:37, 40).

Let's be honest here. Have you ever met anyone who can love God this way? Of course not. Even David, whom the Bible describes as a man after God's own heart, didn't love God with all his heart, all his soul, all his mind, and all his strength. It's a human impossibility. The law was designed to show us that we are incapable of loving God perfectly.

Knowing that man wouldn't be able to fulfill His commandment to love Him with all his heart, all his soul, all his mind, and all his strength, do you know what God did? He demonstrated how only *He* could love us with all His heart, all His soul, all His mind, and all His strength when He sent His beloved Son, Jesus Christ, to redeem us from all our sins with His own blood. That is why the new covenant is all about God's love for you and not your love for Him! Under grace, God doesn't want you to focus your thoughts on, "Do I really love God?" That's not the focus of the new covenant. Under grace, God wants you to focus on *His* love for you. Therefore, the questions you should be asking yourself are:

> *"Do I know how much God loves me today?"*
> *"Do I really believe that God loves me right now?"*

You need to remind yourself of God's love especially when you have just failed. Do you believe that He loves you when you have just made a mistake? This is where the rubber meets the road. After you have failed, that is when what you really believe about God's love for you is tested. Do you really believe that His love for you is truly and indeed unconditional? Or has the unconditional love of God become merely a platitude that is no longer something real to you? I see this happen all the time. I hear people say, "God's love is unconditional!" But the moment they fail, all of a sudden the love they once said was unconditional becomes contingent upon their behavior.

Many believe that God loves them when they do right, but stops loving them the moment they do something wrong. I'm going to shatter that wrong belief into smithereens with the truth of God's Word!

While our love for God can fluctuate, His love for us always remains constant. His love for us is based on who He is and not based on what we do. I love just how confident and emphatic the apostle Paul is when he says, "For I am persuaded that neither death nor life, nor angels nor principalities nor powers, nor things present nor things to come, nor height nor depth, nor any other created thing, shall be able to separate us from the love of God which is in Christ Jesus our Lord" (Rom. 8:38–39). In the New International Version, it says, "For I am convinced..."

> *While our love for God can fluctuate, His love for us always remains constant. His love for us is based on who He is and not based on what we do.*

Are you *persuaded* and *convinced* the way the apostle Paul is that as a child of God, nothing, not even your sins, failings, and mistakes, can ever separate you from the love of God? Don't go by what you feel, think, or have been taught. God's Word proclaims in no uncertain terms that nothing can separate you from His love. Nothing means *nothing*! His love for you is not contingent on your immaculate performance. He loves you even in your failings. That's why it is called grace! It is the undeserved, unmerited, and unearned favor of God. If you can deserve God's grace, then it is no longer grace.

Power to Overcome Every Failing

The truth is, if you are able to receive His love afresh whenever you fail, you will have the power to overcome that failing in your life. Let's imagine a situation in which you have just lost your temper at your wife over a family situation. In your frustration and anger, perhaps you said some hurtful things that you know you shouldn't have, and a heated exchange of harsh and unkind words results. A cold war breaks out in the house, and your kids run for cover. Now you are feeling terribly guilty for what you started, and your conscience condemns you:

> *How can you speak that way to your wife?*
> *What kind of a believer are you?*
> *What a terrible example you are setting for your children!*

The more you dwell in guilt, the worse it gets and the more angry you become with your wife—it's all *her* fault that you feel so lousy and guilty now. Because of *her*, you believe that you are now cut off from God's love. You think—completely wrongly—that He is mad at you because you were mad at your wife. Why? Because while you may *know* about His unconditional love in your mind, you don't really *believe* in your heart that His love for you is truly unconditional.

My friend, if you could only see the truth that even in your anger, God still loves you perfectly. If you could see that the blood of His Son has already washed away that sin in your life. If you could grasp the fact that even in all your ugliness, He still sees you righteous in His sight and calls you His beloved. The truth is, if you truly knew how freely you have been forgiven and how unconditionally you are loved, it would be very hard for you to remain angry with your wife and keep up your end of the cold war. In fact, the opposite will happen.

As you feed on the Lord's beautiful love and lavish forgiveness even while you feel most undeserving, you'll end up doing whatever it takes to reconcile with your wife. Not only that, but whatever upset you to begin with also becomes infinitesimally small when you allow your heart to be embraced by the largeness of His love. It's no wonder the Word of God says, "Husbands, love your wives, *just as Christ also loved the church and gave Himself for her*" (Eph. 5:25, emphasis mine). You have no power to love your wife unless you have first experienced the unconditional love of Christ in your own life!

In the same way, the Bible exhorts wives to "submit to your own husbands, *as to the Lord*" (Eph. 5:22, emphasis mine). Don't you just love how practical the Bible is? We can so easily get upset over the smallest of things that arise in the minutiae of everyday domestic living. And it's only as we believe and submit to God's love that we let His love dissolve our fruitless frustrations over battles that are actually not worth fighting and find the strength to love, submit, and live in peace with our spouses.

Can you see? Our hang-ups are like a drop of water in the vast, blue ocean or a tiny speck of sand in an immense desert when contrasted with the love of God. His love consumes all your anger, frustrations, disappointments, and pain. His forgiveness envelops all your sins, failures, and mistakes. His grace gives you victory and power to overcome every sin, bondage, and addiction. That is why having a right belief about God's unconditional love for you is so vital to your relationship with Him.

> *His love consumes all your anger, frustrations, disappointments, and pain. His forgiveness envelops all your sins, failures, and mistakes.*

Completely and Irrevocably Forgiven

Beloved, you are completely and irrevocably forgiven. Because of His love for you, Jesus has already borne the punishment for your sins. This is why you can receive God's love afresh even when you fail and every time you fail. He has forgiven you. It's time for you to forgive yourself too! Don't for one moment think that He wants you to remain in guilt when you fail. The truth is, *the more guilty you feel, the more you are doomed to perpetuate that sin*. Unfortunately, there are religious folks who believe that when people fail or fall into sin, one needs to make them feel really bad about themselves and crush them with guilt and condemnation until they repent of their wrongdoing.

But this teaching is erroneous. In actual fact, the more people remain in guilt and condemnation, the more they will continue in their sin! You don't have to teach people to feel guilty and condemned. Their conscience condemns them whenever they fail. But here's the good news: God has provided an answer to the conscience that persistently calls for payment for all our transgressions. He sent His Son to ransom us with His own body and blood.

> *You can receive God's love afresh even when you fail and every time you fail.*

Today when your conscience condemns you and calls out for justice when you fail, see yourself cleansed, washed, and made righteous by the blood of Jesus. Activate your faith to see yourself righteous in God's eyes because of the precious blood of Jesus Christ. The conscience, which calls for punishment every time you fail, has in truth been silenced by the blood of the Lamb of God, who was punished and judged in your stead. Every time your conscience condemns you, take out and wave the receipt of your payment—the cross of Jesus! Keep seeing your sins washed by His precious blood. Guilt and condemnation stop where the blood of Jesus has been shed.

So when you fail, don't wallow in guilt and condemnation. That will only bring you to a slippery downward spiral toward defeat, depression, and destruction. Jesus didn't die on the cross to make the guilty guiltier. He didn't die on the cross to give the sick more diseases. He didn't die on the cross so that the condemned would be more condemned. Absolutely not! Jesus did not sacrifice Himself on the cross to justify those who are perfect and godly.

God Justifies the Ungodly

The Word of God clearly exhorts us to give up on our own self-efforts to be justified and to believe on Him "who justifies the ungodly" (Rom. 4:5). Be sure that you get this right. Who does God justify?

Did God die to justify the godly or the ungodly? My friend, He came to justify the *ungodly*—those who have failed, fallen short, made mistakes, and sinned. Have you failed? Made mistakes? Fallen short? Great, because it means that *you qualify for His justification*! Doesn't this truth just impart such hope and faith into your heart?

> *Guilt and condemnation stop where the blood of Jesus has been shed.*

Be encouraged to know this today: your failures qualify you to receive Jesus' love, forgiveness, and justification. Jesus didn't come to save those who are perfect (in their own eyes); He came to save and redeem those who are imperfect and ungodly. And when you just believe on Jesus who justifies the ungodly, your faith "is accounted for righteousness" (Rom. 4:5). This means that the moment you believe right, Jesus makes you righteous with His blood. What a secure foundation that is compared to having your righteousness contingent on your right doing! What a Savior we have in Christ!

Beloved, remember this the next time you fail: Jesus didn't die to make the guilty guiltier. He died to free the guilty from the torment of guilt, to heal those who are sick, and to make forever righteous those who have been condemned. Now that's the gospel. And let's not be apologetic or ashamed of the gospel, for it *is* the power of God unto salvation for all who believe (see Rom. 1:16)!

> *Jesus died to free the guilty from the torment of guilt, to heal those who are sick, and to make forever righteous those who have been condemned. That's the gospel.*

Jesus Loves the Sinner

Do you believe in a God who justifies the ungodly? Have you been hearing the true gospel of His amazing grace? Or have you been feeding your mind with human conjectures based on man's traditions and ideas about God that are not from His Word? Look at the Gospels. The corrupt tax collectors, the prostitutes, the foulmouthed fishermen, the lame, the blind, and the sick who encountered the love of Jesus were all forgiven, transformed, delivered, and healed. He never made a single one of them feel more guilty, more ashamed, and more condemned than He knew they already felt.

There is an account of a woman in the Bible who is described as "a sinner" (Luke 7:37). Many believe that she was a prostitute. When she came to Jesus, who was having a meal at Simon the Pharisee's house, Jesus allowed her to approach Him and worship Him with an alabaster box of ointment. The loving Savior knew who she was, but did not chase her away, humiliate her, or condemn her for her sins. Neither did He coldly tell her to get her life right before she dared step into His holy presence again.

The Jesus of the Bible had compassion for her and knew how guilty and deeply condemned she already felt. As she neared Jesus, she broke down in His presence and began weeping. Lovingly, she washed Jesus' feet with her tears and wiped them with her hair. She reverently kissed His feet and anointed them with the precious ointment that she had brought. It is said that this ointment would have cost her an entire year's wages, but without hesitation, she lavished it on Jesus' feet and worshiped Him.

On seeing this, the Pharisee was filled with indignation. He said to himself, "If this Jesus is the real deal, He would know that this woman is a great sinner. How could He allow her to come close to Him, let alone touch His feet?" (see Luke 7:39). He was disgusted at what he was witnessing in his own dining room. (Sadly, legalistic Christians today are a lot like this Pharisee.)

While Jesus welcomed the sinner and allowed her to worship and touch His feet, this religious Pharisee didn't even have an ounce of compassion for this woman who was weeping unceasingly, overwhelmed with Jesus' love and forgiveness toward her. Her shame and her tears meant nothing to him. As far as he was concerned, she deserved to be condemned. And if he had had it his way, she would not have been allowed to enter his house.

You can see from this biblical account that Jesus is the very antithesis of anyone or anything religious. His heart overflows with love and compassion for those who have failed. This was not a secret. Everyone who met and heard Jesus knew about His love.

This word spread far and wide from Jerusalem to Galilee, which was why sinners sought Him out instead of avoiding Him and running away from Him.

> *Believers who have been purchased with the blood of Jesus Christ should be bold, confident, and courageous to talk to God about their failings.*

Isn't it sad that today there are believers who have failed and are running away and hiding from God when sinners in Jesus' day had the confidence to seek Him out to find forgiveness, restoration, healing, and deliverance? Don't you think that something is amiss here? Believers who have been purchased with the blood of Jesus Christ should, of all people, be bold, confident, and courageous to talk to God about their failings and be reminded that they are still righteous in Christ even when they have failed.

You've Been Forgiven Much

Let's continue with the story (see Luke 7:40–46). Jesus, perceiving Simon the Pharisee's thoughts, asked him a question: "Imagine that there was a creditor who had two debtors. One owed a million dollars, and the other owed a hundred dollars. This creditor forgave them both. Now, who do you suppose will love the creditor more?"

Incredulous at the simplicity of the question, Simon replied, "I suppose the one he forgave the most!"

Jesus then said, "You are absolutely right! I came into your home, and you gave me no water for my feet. This lady has washed my feet with her tears and wiped them with the hairs of her head. You gave me no kiss, and this woman has not ceased to kiss my feet. You didn't anoint my head with oil, and this woman has anointed my feet with costly and precious ointment."

Now pay careful attention to what Jesus said next: "Therefore I say to you, her sins, which are many, are forgiven, for she loved much. But to whom little is forgiven, the same loves little" (Luke 7:47). What Jesus was saying is that those who know and believe how much God truly loves and has forgiven them will end up loving God very much. Simply put, those who have been forgiven much, love much. Those who have been forgiven little, love little. That's why the emphasis of the new covenant is not about your love for God; it is about God's love for you. If you know how abundantly God loves you and has forgiven you of all your sins, you will end up loving God—he who is forgiven much, loves much!

> *If you know how abundantly God loves you and has forgiven you of all your sins, you will end up loving God—he who is forgiven much, loves much!*

Do you see what I'm saying? Your love for God in the new covenant is birthed out of a genuine and authentic relationship with Him. It is not a groveling display that is birthed out of the fear of punishment or religious obligation. Under grace, we are able to love God because He first loved us. That is why people under grace become the holiest people you will ever meet. They are not holy because they fear punishment or because of their commitment to two cold tablets of stone. Their holiness flows out of their love relationship with Jesus! They have experienced His unconditional love for themselves in an intimate and personal way. Love transforms them. They just want to live lives that glorify and honor the name of Jesus. What the law could not do to transform God's people from the inside out, God did by sending His own Son, Jesus Christ!

Friend, we have all been forgiven much. The problem is, many don't know and don't *believe* this. Give up on your own self-efforts to be righteous. Give up on trying to overcome your own failings, mistakes, addictions, and bondages. Be like the woman with the alabaster box of precious ointment. When you fail, don't run away and hide. Come before His loving presence. Jesus already knows the guilt and condemnation that you are being tormented with. Come with boldness and confidence like this woman did. Feel free to weep in His sweet presence and simply worship Him. Pour out everything that is on your heart to Him. Don't worry, He will not heap more guilt, shame, judgment, and condemnation upon you. He will show you His nail-pierced hands and remind you of the cross. He will say to you, "Your sins are already forgiven. I have already paid the price for your sins at Calvary. Rest in My forgiveness and love for you."

I received a letter from a man, whom I'll just call Patrick, who struggled with sexual addictions for more than ten years. He knew it was wrong, but he couldn't break free from those addictions no matter how hard he tried. His conscience would plague him with reminders of his sins every time he tried to read the Word. This fed his belief that he wasn't good enough for God and that God didn't want anything to do with him because of his addictions.

This man lived in this realm of self-torture day after day. Then one day he read one of my books, *Destined To Reign*. Through the book, he came to discover and believe in Jesus' finished work at the cross. He said, "I just decided to rest in Jesus' finished work, His forgiveness, His victory, His grace, and His love, *and pornography and masturbation now have no power or dominion over me*. It truly is awesome especially because I had tried for more than ten years to get victory, and all it took was for me to know the truth and rest in Jesus' finished work. All glory to God!"

I don't know what guilt you may be struggling with today, but God does. You no longer have to live under the dictates of your conscience, which condemns you every time you miss the mark. See the blood of Jesus cleansing your heart, and be free from the prison of guilt to experience victory like this precious brother.

Abandon Yourself to His Love

My dear reader, the love of God is not a theological concept. Love is an emotion. God created us in His image with emotions, and one of the best ways to experience His love is by simply abandoning yourself to Him and worshiping Him. The Bible tells us that "worshipers, once purified, would have had no more consciousness of sins" (Heb. 10:2). When you no longer carry a sense of condemnation, when you believe that His blood has cleansed your sins, you become a worshiper enraptured with His love.

I encourage you to fill your heart with psalms, hymns, and spiritual songs that are full of God's love and grace. When your heart is full of Jesus, wrong beliefs will begin to be replaced by right beliefs. Destructive addictions will be replaced by new, positive habits. Fear, shame, and guilt will begin to dissolve in the warmth of His perfect love for you. His love is not an intellectual exercise. It needs to be experienced.

The psalmist calls out, "Oh, taste and see that the LORD is good; blessed is the man who trusts in Him!" (Ps. 34:8). Do you trust in His love for you? God wants you not just to have head knowledge of His love, but also to believe in and *taste* His love for yourself. It can't just remain in your mind or in the cerebral realm of logic; it has to be experienced in your heart.

> *No matter how many mistakes you have made, He has not given up on you!*

Today, believe with all your heart that God loves you. He is for you. No matter how many mistakes you have made, He has not given up on you! The first key to right believing is to believe in His unconditional love for you. Cast all your failings at His feet. Feel free to cry in His loving presence. Begin to see your fears, guilt, disorders, and dysfunctions fade away as you abandon yourself to His love and worship Him with these simple words:

Jesus loves me! This I know,
For the Bible tells me so.
Little ones to Him belong;
They are weak, but He is strong.

Yes, Jesus loves me!
Yes, Jesus loves me!
Yes, Jesus loves me!
The Bible tells me so.

PART TWO

LEARN TO SEE WHAT GOD SEES

CHAPTER 4

PLAY THE RIGHT MENTAL MOVIES

I can still remember what happened when I visited a lady from my congregation in the hospital. Heather had suffered a stroke that left the left side of her body completely paralyzed. As I prayed for her, she lifted her right hand in a gesture of prayer. Amazingly, her left hand followed suit, albeit slowly, but this was something that she had been unable to do following the stroke. By the grace of God, she was beginning to experience healing in her body, with sensations starting to seep back into her left arm.

Within a few moments, though, as she lay in the intensive-care ward, intubated and hooked up to incessantly beeping medical equipment, her left arm started to tremble with strain.

"Don't worry about praying for a breakthrough," I assured Heather. Smiling at her, I gestured to one of my pastors who was with me and told her, "Leave the praying to us."

Then, tapping my index finger on the side of my head, I told her, "But watch your mental movies. Make sure that you play the right movies in your mind."

What did I mean by that? I was telling her to see what God sees and ignore all the *sounds, scents, and sights that her natural senses were picking up in the hospital environment.* I was encouraging her to fill her mind with mental images of herself being healthy, strong, and basking in the love of her family at home. I didn't want her to keep seeing all the worst-case scenarios in her mind.

Then I said to her, "It takes a thought to heal a thought."

It was a word that I had received in my spirit for her. For some reason, I just felt like the enemy had succeeded in planting a wrong thought or mental picture in her mind, and that had to be removed and replaced with the right thoughts, pictures, and beliefs that are based on the unchanging Word of God. Shortly after our meeting, Heather was discharged from the hospital and her condition improved.

Learn to See as God Sees

Learning to see what God sees is a powerful key in right believing. It involves replacing your wrong beliefs with right beliefs based on God's Word. When Jesus saw the man with the withered hand, He didn't just see the withered hand, He saw that there was more than enough grace for that hand to be made completely whole. Jesus said to the man, "Stretch out your hand!" The man did as told, and his hand was completely restored and made as whole as his other hand (see Mark 3:1–5).

Learning to see what God sees involves replacing your wrong beliefs with right beliefs based on God's Word.

Now, you don't say "stretch out your hand" to someone whose hand is obviously shriveled and disabled unless you see differently. Jesus sees differently from you and me. That's why we need to go back to God's Word and learn to see what He sees. When Jesus sees a disease, a lack, or someone trapped in fear, guilt, addiction, and sin, He doesn't just see the problem. He sees God's healing, grace, and power superabounding in that area of weakness.

You too can change what you believe by seeing beyond what your natural eyes see. Press in to see what God sees. In your very area of lack, struggle, or challenge, see His superabounding grace all around your current situation. Jesus says to you today, "My grace is sufficient for you, for My strength is made perfect in weakness" (2 Cor. 12:9). Give all your weaknesses, failings, and mistakes to the Lord Jesus and see Him transform your weaknesses into strengths.

> *In your very area of lack, struggle, or challenge, see His superabounding grace all around your current situation.*

What you believe is powerful, so are you going by what you see or what God sees? You may not be able to stop negative thoughts from passing through your mind or unhealthy emotions like fear gripping your heart, but you can definitely anchor your thoughts and emotions on the unshakable Word of God. You can certainly ensure that you believe right regarding what God says about you in His Word, which contains His precious promises to you. The more you learn and believe right about His love and what His Word says about your situation and your life, the more your thoughts will line up with His thoughts about you. You'll begin to develop thoughts of peace and not of evil, thoughts of hope and a bright future (see Jer. 29:11).

The apostle Paul says, "And do not be conformed to this world, but be transformed by the renewing of your mind..." (Rom. 12:2). You see, God doesn't want us to think the way the world thinks, or see the way the world sees, and be bound by all sorts of fears, worries, and unhealthy habits. He wants us to renew our minds. How? By believing and meditating on the real truths found only in His Word so that we can experience transformation and wholeness in every aspect of our lives.

The word "renewing" is the Greek word *anakainosis*, which is defined by Thayer's Greek Lexicon as "a renewal, renovation, complete change for the better."[1] I like the word "renovation." Our minds certainly need a complete overhaul by the Word of Christ!

Who's Your Interior Decorator?

If you are going to overhaul and *renovate* your mind, whom are you going to hire as your interior decorator? Don't let your morning newspapers, negative friends, or social media channels be your interior decorator. Don't be conformed to this world!

So many of us are entangled with the information, ideas, and thoughts of this world. We live in an era where we have at our fingertips access to massive amounts of information and knowledge. Need to know something in a jiffy? Just Google it on your smartphone. Yet this mass accumulation of knowledge has not made us freer or happier. People are more connected than ever before, but have never felt more alone, isolated, and cut off.

Be careful also not to let the devil be the interior decorator for your mind. You can just imagine him choosing the dreariest drapes, grimmest upholstery, and ghastliest furnishing to adorn the different rooms of your mind. The color palette for your walls and ceilings would be selected from his favorite Pantone range of gloomy gray to depressive black. His mission is to keep your thoughts dark, pessimistic, and defeated. If you are defeated in your mind, then for him, the battle is already won.

Don't Get Coiled Up in Fear

When I was out grocery shopping with my wife one day, a man came up to me and introduced himself. He shared with me how he had been listening to my messages for many years and had been attending our church regularly. Derek was a successful business owner. Business was brisk—doors of opportunities were opening and all his sales numbers were trending upward.

But it wasn't always so.

In the early days, the stress of running a fledgling business consumed him. Derek shared that during those days, as was his daily routine, he picked up the newspaper one morning and read an article about how somebody that was of his gender and age had suddenly died of a heart attack. He couldn't explain it, but from the moment he read the news article, it was as if the air in his living

room started to thin, and he began experiencing respiratory difficulties. Fear had begun to coil itself around his heart like a python.

Constriction is a well-documented method used by various
snake species to gradually kill their prey. Interesting research has
been conducted on how some constrictors kill their prey. Contrary
to popular opinion, the snake does not crush and break its victim's
bones to kill it. Instead, a constricting snake like a boa or python
kills its prey by suffocation. It uses the momentum of its strike to
throw coils around its victim's body. Then it squeezes (each time its
prey exhales) and squeezes until its victim can breathe no more.[2]

However, while studying why some prey die faster than it would
be possible through suffocation, some researchers have hypoth-
esized that the constriction pressure causes a rise in the pressure
in the prey's body cavity that is greater than what its heart can
counter, resulting in cardiac arrest. While research on this theory
is still ongoing, it is scientifically proven that certain snakes can
exert enough pressure for this to be plausible. For example, a green
anaconda has a constriction strength of $6kg/cm^2$ which effectively
equals a total strength of 4,000kg![3]

How is all this relevant for our study on the power of right
believing?

You see, our adversary is a crafty old serpent. It would be prudent for us to understand his strategy against us, for as the Bible
says, "lest Satan should take advantage of us; for we are not ignorant of his devices" (2 Cor. 2:11). His methods have not changed,
and while he has no real power because Christ has disarmed him at
the cross (see Col. 2:15), he knows that he can use negative thoughts
to incite fear in our hearts.

Establish Your Heart in God's Love

The Word of God also draws a direct correlation between fear and heart conditions. In describing events in the end times, Jesus said that fear will cause men's hearts to fail. However, He encourages believers, "Do not be terrified; for these things must come to pass first..." (Luke 21:9), asserting His firm control over everything that will happen in the future. Assuring us why there is no need to be afraid, He adds, "Look up and lift up your heads, because your redemption draws near" (Luke 21:28).

Only a revelation of His perfect love can drive out all fear.

God wants our hearts to be at peace, to be at rest. His Word tells us, "A peaceful heart leads to a healthy body" (Prov. 14:30 NLT). Peace comes when our hearts and minds are anchored on His *love* and not on fear. And only a revelation of His perfect love can drive out all fear. I will use many different Bible verses over the course of this book, but I strongly encourage you to commit this one Scripture to memory. It will be a source of great spiritual, physical, and mental comfort to you for the rest of your life:

> *There is no fear in love; but perfect love casts out fear, because fear involves torment. But he who fears has not been made perfect in love. We love Him because He first loved us.*
>
> —1 John 4:18–19

Notice how God's Word states in no uncertain terms that fear involves torment.

My friend, God is not your tormentor—the devil is. God is not the author of fear—the enemy is. Fear and security cannot coexist. Can you truly love someone you fear? Of course not. Fear always leads to insecurity. So God doesn't want you to fear Him. In fact, Jesus defined for us the fear of God as the *worship* of God—not fear that carries the idea of being punished by an angry God. (I talk more about Jesus' definition of the fear of the Lord in chapter 15.) The truth is, God wants you to receive His perfect love, complete acceptance, and abounding grace. If you have received any teaching that contradicts this, just remember, *there is no fear in love*. And God *is* love (see 1 John 4:8, 16). Fear is the strategy of the enemy, not God. The devil uses fear to torment you and manipulate your thoughts, just like he did with the man I had met.

> *Fear is the strategy of the enemy, not God.*

How Fear Enters

Derek had been innocently reading the morning newspaper, and just like that, fear struck like a preying python and exerted its grip on his heart.

It began with breathlessness, and then the poor man started to experience all kinds of evil imaginations. In his mind's eye, Derek would see himself entering his warehouse alone to pick up some inventory (something that he was used to doing), but he would have mental pictures of himself getting badly hurt in the process, with nobody ever knowing that he needed medical attention.

Day by day, Derek felt the constricting pressure of fear tightening its grip on his heart. He became obsessed with how he would get hurt and die until he was afraid to go anywhere alone.

Needless to say, he went into a downward spiral as his mental oppression worsened. Images of himself getting hurt played over and over again in his mind like a horror movie in perpetual slow motion, and he would suffer major bouts of debilitating anxiety attacks.

As his breathing difficulties increased, Derek checked himself into a hospital, convinced that he was severely ill. But after numerous tests, the doctor told him, "You don't have a heart problem. You have an anxiety problem. Please give up your bed for someone with a real heart problem." Once a strong and healthy individual, Derek had folded and collapsed under the pressure of the serpent's constriction.

Turn on the Light of God's Words

Thankfully, a volunteer who serves as an usher on Sundays in our church invited Derek to attend one of our care group gatherings. Derek shared with me that the leader of the care group encouraged him to get into God's Word every morning and pray in the Spirit for thirty minutes every day as he drove to work.

"I would listen to your messages over and over again in my car," Derek said as he related his testimony. "In one of your messages, you said to focus on the Word of God and not on my problems. And that was exactly what I did! I began turning away from those dark thoughts and allowing the light of Jesus' words to come into my situation."

My friend, do you believe that God's thoughts are greater than the devil's thoughts? Do you know that His light is greater than any darkness? Imagine walking into a room that is pitch-dark. When you flick on the light switch, does the darkness consume the light, or does the light drive away the darkness?

For this precious brother, his breakthrough began when he turned on the light of God's Word and allowed it to shine upon him and his situation. He realized that he was afraid of being alone because of his irrational belief that for some reason he would get hurt and die. And he began to realize that it was a clear lie from the pit of hell. He shared that one of his favorite verses that gave him both courage and comfort during that dark season was the Lord saying to him, "I will never leave you nor forsake you" (Heb. 13:5). He would speak this verse whenever he was fearful and then tell himself, "The Lord is my helper; I will not fear" (Heb. 13:6).

Equipped with God's Word, Derek began playing the right mental movies in his mind. Every time the anxiety attacks came and every time the evil imaginations began to replay in his mind, he would wield these Scriptures like a weapon against the onslaught of the serpent's attack. Over and over, he would proclaim, "I will never leave you nor forsake you. The Lord is my helper; I will not fear."

The more he said that, the more the grip of the serpent began to loosen and weaken. He found that he could breathe freely again and his heart no longer felt constricted. Strengthened by the Word, he began to see the Lord with him always. He began to see himself full of health and protected from harm as he went about his work. Derek was completely healed and released from all his fears as he began to replace the wrong mental movies that he had been playing in his mind with the right ones.

What mental movies are you playing in your head today? Are they thoughts of defeat and despair or thoughts of victory and favor? Faith is simply saying what God says about you and seeing what God sees in you and your situation.

Replace Negative Thoughts with God's Thoughts

Remember what I shared earlier about how it takes a thought to heal a thought? Unlike the world, which teaches you to empty your mind to achieve peace, God's way is to fill your mind with fresh, powerful, and redeeming thoughts.

> *It takes a right belief to replace a wrong belief. You need God's truth to replace the enemy's lies that have kept you in bondage.*

The apostle Paul tells us, "Fix your thoughts on what is true, and honorable, and right, and pure, and lovely, and admirable. Think about things that are excellent and worthy of praise" (Phil. 4:8 NLT). So it's not just trying to blot out bad thoughts with your willpower. It takes a thought to replace a thought. It takes a right belief to replace a wrong belief. You need God's truth to replace the enemy's lies that have kept you in bondage.

My friend, if a wrong, bad, or negative thought is lodged in your mind today and you can't seem to shake it, stop trying! Perhaps you're lying in a hospital bed and can't help but think of the worst-case scenario. You're attempting to suppress it, but it's not working. Well, stop! Stop trying to erase it from your mind. That just won't work. What you need to do is replace that destructive thought with a thought that's from God. That's the only way to deal with a wrong thought and begin the healing process. Start to meditate on truths like, "Surely Jesus has borne my sicknesses and carried my pains. The chastisement for my wholeness fell upon Him, and by His stripes I am healed. With long life He will satisfy me" (see Isa. 53:4–5 and Ps. 91:16). Play mental movies of yourself getting well, being discharged from the hospital, having fun with your kids, or going on a nice holiday!

Keep Your Thoughts on Jesus

You need the truth of God's Word to uproot any wrong belief. Get into His Word, and get into His thoughts. If you find your mind drifting into anxious thoughts over the smallest things, memorize and quote this verse: "You will keep him in perfect peace, whose mind is stayed on You, because he trusts in You" (Isa. 26:3).

You need the truth of God's Word to uproot any wrong belief.

Whenever I feel stressed or worried about something, I pull away from life's hustle and bustle and simply meditate on God's promises. Sometimes I like to drive to a quiet park, and as gentle anointed music plays in my car, I feed on and speak His Word, allowing it to permeate my spirit: "God's Word declares, 'You will keep him in perfect peace, whose mind is stayed on You.'" And I tell the Lord, "Yes, Lord, it is You who will keep me in perfect peace. Perfect peace comes from You. I just need to rest in Your grace and keep my mind on You. I don't need to think about what to do about this challenge. As I trust in You and keep my mind stayed on You, You will lead me and guide me. My trust is not in my own strength, but in You and You alone, Jesus."

What am I doing here? Instead of allowing stress and worry to get to me, I'm training my heart to see how God sees my challenges. The bigger God becomes in my heart, the smaller my challenges become. In fact, many times when I just relax and keep my mind on the Lord, His peace and wisdom begin to flow in me, and the challenge that I was previously so worried about becomes minute and inconsequential in the presence of Almighty God.

Are you faced with an insurmountable circumstance today? See what God sees, and let His peace drive out your anxiety. Let His wisdom direct your thoughts.

Which Ground Is Your Heart?

The key to seeing what God sees is to base your beliefs on His sure and unshakable Word. Unfortunately, not everybody believes in what God's Word says about them. Jesus shares this in the parable of the seed and the sower (see Matt. 13:3–9, 18–23).

> *The key to seeing what God sees is to base your beliefs on His sure and unshakable Word.*

In this parable, a sower sows seeds that fall on four types of ground. The sower here is a picture of someone sharing God's Word. The ground is a picture of how the hearer receives the Word. You'll notice in this parable that the sower doesn't control the type of ground the seeds of God's truth fall onto. You and I have to decide for ourselves how our hearts receive the Word of God. Do we want to see what God sees, or do we choose to see things our way?

The parable starts with the seeds of God's Word falling by the wayside. This means that even before the Word can go deep into the hearer's heart, it is stolen by the enemy through his own doubt and unbelief. For example, you may be reading this book right now and thinking, "God can never love me. I have made so many shameful mistakes. I will never be able to break out of my addictions. This is my life, and nothing can change that." If that is you, I just want to encourage you to be open and receptive to God's superabounding grace as you pore over what is written in this book. Open your heart, and let His love fill and heal you. Let it restore your faith. God will never hurt you. He will never force His way. You have a choice to either let His words of life come into your heart, take root, and establish you in His grace, or to allow His words to fall by the wayside.

Keep Hearing about God's Goodness

The parable then goes on to talk about the stony ground. This speaks of hearers who hear God's Word and receive it excitedly, thinking, "Wow, God forgives me and accepts me for who I am. That's cool!" However, they don't have the grace foundation to hold the Word in their hearts. The moment their conscience condemns them with guilt, they forget everything they have learned about God's unconditional love for them and spiral rapidly back into defeat and condemnation.

That's why it is so vital to keep on listening to messages that are full of what Jesus has done for you at the cross and to fill your heart with His new covenant truths. "Let the word of Christ dwell in you richly in all wisdom, teaching and admonishing one another in psalms and hymns and spiritual songs, singing with grace in your hearts to the Lord" (Col. 3:16).

When you allow Jesus' words to dwell abundantly in you in all wisdom, the seeds of His truth, His love, and His forgiveness will germinate and take root in your heart. When adversity comes, your belief in God will not easily be uprooted and stolen by the enemy. When the voice of condemnation comes, your heart is fortified with God's truth, garrisoned by His grace, and armed with the everlasting blood of Jesus. You'll be a believer against whom "no weapon formed...shall prosper, and every tongue which rises against you in judgment you shall condemn" (Isa. 54:17). Guilt and condemnation will not be able to penetrate your heart when you are cognizant of your righteous identity in Christ. Once the enemy's lies about you are exposed in the light of God's truth, they are rendered obsolete and can no longer torment your mind.

> *Guilt and condemnation will not be able to penetrate your heart when you are cognizant of your righteous identity in Christ.*

Prioritize the Word over Material Pursuits

The next ground, thorny ground, speaks of people who hear God's Word, but instead of believing it, their hearts are consumed with the cares of this world. To them, God's truths are not practical. It's just spiritual mumbo jumbo, and they are more interested in how to make more money and in other transient material pursuits. As a result, they lead extremely stressful lifestyles, fretting over money and never seeing good fruits manifesting in their lives.

Do you know that there are a lot of people in the world who have plenty of money, but in reality are poor when it comes to possessing what really matters? I like to say it this way: there are a lot of "poor" people with plenty of money. You can buy sleeping pills with money, but you cannot buy sweet sleep. You cannot buy peace for your mind, forgiveness for your heart, and health for your body. Don't make the pleasures of this world and making more money your only goals in life and end up living in constant stress, fear, and anxiety. The Bible asks, "For what will it profit a man if he gains the whole world, and loses his own soul?" (Mark 8:36). Jesus loves you, and He can remove every thorn of anxiety in your heart if you let

Him. Rest in Jesus your provider. He is the shepherd of your soul, and in Him there is no lack (see Ps. 23:1).

Choose to Be Good Ground

The final ground in the parable is what this book is all about. This ground speaks of people who believe in the power of right believing, people whose hearts are open, receptive, and ready to receive all that God has for them. It speaks of people who are ready to allow His Word to take root in their lives.

As you read this book, I want to encourage you to see yourself as good, fertile ground. Don't let the precious Word of God fall by the wayside because of unbelief. Don't be the stony ground that is easily shaken the moment opposition shows up. Also, don't allow His promises over your life to be choked by the cares of this world. Be good ground—a receptive heart that is anchored in God's grace. As you nourish yourself in His Word and see what He sees, you will surely see your thirtyfold, sixtyfold, and hundredfold breakthroughs in every area of your life!

CHAPTER 5

SEE YOURSELF AS GOD SEES YOU

My team received a very encouraging email from Ron, one of our key ministry partners. Ron shared how he had a dear friend named Tyler, whom he went to grade school and became best buddies with. Tyler was from a good Christian family, was great at sports, and was living the "American Dream."

After college, however, Tyler started hanging out with the wrong crowd at work and developed a severe drug and drinking problem, which in turn led to a series of devastating mistakes. Within a twenty-four-month period, Tyler had lost everything he held dear in his life. Ashamed and miserable, Tyler dropped out of church and almost gave up on life, God, and grace. But God, in His grace, was still reaching out to Tyler (through Ron), as Ron related this story in his email:

> One night, while jogging at a park and listening to a message by Pastor Prince, I felt God prompting me to send Tyler a text message. I felt that God wanted me to ask Tyler, "What does God see when He looks at you?"

So while running, I texted him exactly those words. After a long time, I received his text reply:

Tyler: "Are you serious?"
Ron: "Yes."
Tyler: "Well...I'm sure it's not good."
Ron: "Jesus."
Tyler: "What do you mean?"
Ron: "I mean, when God looks at you, He sees Jesus!"
Thirty minutes later, I got this message:
Tyler: "Thanks, man, you don't know how badly I needed to hear that!"

Would it bless your heart to know that the text Ron sent Tyler is the very message God wants you to receive today? I believe that like Tyler, thousands upon thousands of believers go through life believing God's love for them depends on their actions. So many honestly believe that God is ashamed of them because of their mistakes and failures. They have either not heard or have forgotten that Jesus didn't only pay for our sins, but He also took all of our shame. Somewhere along the way, we have lost sight of how God's grace abounds "much more" (Rom. 5:20). We have underestimated the measure of His grace!

> *Jesus didn't only pay for our sins, but He also took all of our shame.*

What Do You Really Believe?

My friend Ron was listening to one of my messages about our righteous identity in Christ when he felt led by the Lord to send his buddy Tyler that thought-provoking question, "What does God see when He looks at you?" I think it's a great question, and if you were to answer this question honestly today, it would reveal what you really believe in your heart about God.

Most people, when things are going well, believe that God is well pleased with their behavior and conduct. However, they believe all that changes when they fail and make mistakes. It could be losing their cool on the road, visiting a website they shouldn't have, or saying hurtful words to someone they love. At that moment of failure, they believe when God looks at them, He sees nothing good. They believe He is angry and disappointed with them and wants to punish them for their failures.

What hope is there in the belief that when you do right, you are blessed, but when you fail, you are cursed? This was exactly how the old covenant of the law worked. The old covenant was an imperfect system. Notice how in the book of Hebrews, God Himself found fault with that covenant and sought to replace it: "For if that first covenant had been faultless, then no place would have been sought for a second... 'Behold, the days are coming, says the LORD, when I will make a new covenant...'" (Heb. 8:7–8).

Heard about the New Covenant of Grace?

My friend, I am here to announce to you that God has already made a new covenant. The new covenant that He instituted is the covenant of grace that you and I get to enjoy today. It's a covenant in which He declares, "For I will be merciful to their unrighteousness, and their sins and their lawless deeds I will remember no more" (Heb. 8:12). Hallelujah!

God can be merciful to all your unrighteousness and remember your sins no more because the payment for your sins has already been made in full upon the body of Jesus at the cross. Therefore, when God looks at you today, He doesn't judge, esteem, and measure you according to your imperfections. He sees you in the Beloved—He sees you in Christ, and He sees the blood that has been shed for you by His dear Son.

When God looks at you today, He sees Jesus. Because of this, His thoughts toward you are thoughts of loving-kindness, forgiveness, blessings, and favor. Jesus paid an immensely heavy price on the cross so that you can live life completely accepted and unconditionally loved by God. Knowing and believing this will make all the difference in how you live your life—no matter what is staring you in the face.

But Pastor Prince, I don't deserve this love from God!

You are absolutely right! If we go by what we deserve today, all of us (myself included) deserve to be punished for our sins. Do you know that the punishment for sin is not simply a slap on the wrist? This isn't something we can sugarcoat—the wages of sin is death (see Rom. 6:23). In other words, if you and I go by what we deserve, the punishment we deserve for our sins is death. And even then, our deaths can never pay adequately for our sins because our blood isn't sinless blood. That's why I like to remind people who desire to be justified by their own righteousness that it's simply impossible. All of us owe a debt we can never pay.

The good news is that Jesus bore the death sentence on our behalf at the cross. Did He deserve to be crucified on the cross? Absolutely not! He chose the cross so that His sinless blood could cleanse us from all our sins. The cross stands—for all eternity—as a declaration of Jesus' everlasting love for us. At the cross, Jesus was suspended between heaven and earth as the sacrifice for our sins. He bore every punishment that we deserved. He absorbed every penalty the law demanded for our sins.

> *The cross stands—for all eternity—as a declaration of Jesus' everlasting love for us.*

Only Believe

Do you know why Jesus chose the cross? John 3:14–15 gives us the answer: "And as Moses lifted up the serpent in the wilderness, even so must the Son of Man be lifted up, that whoever believes in Him should not perish but have eternal life."

He went to the cross so that whoever *believes* in Him can receive the gift of eternal life.

Whoever *believes*. That is all you need to do to step into the inheritance that was purchased for you with the blood of the Son of God. Believe in HIM. Believe in Jesus. Believe in what He has done for you at the cross. Believe that all your sins have been imputed to Him and all His righteousness has been imputed to you. Believe in the divine exchange. Believe in His love. Believe that all your sins have been punished at the cross and that through Jesus you have received the gifts of righteousness and eternal life.

There is so much to glean from John 3:15. Look at that verse again. Tell me, who qualifies for salvation? The Word of God doesn't say, "Whoever obeys Him perfectly." It doesn't say, "Whoever never fails again." And it certainly doesn't say, "Whoever keeps all His commandments." It simply says, "Whoever *believes* in Him." Whoever believes in Him will not perish but have eternal life. The only action needed on your part is to believe!

Pastor Prince, how can simply believing *in Jesus make me righteous? There must be something more that I must* do *to earn and deserve God's love for me.*

Don't write it off just because it sounds simple, and don't underestimate the power of right believing. When you believe right—when you believe that you are made righteous through Jesus—you will end up producing the fruits of righteousness. The apostle Paul refers to "the fruits of righteousness" in Philippians 1:11, and he specifies that they are "by Jesus Christ." When you set your eyes on Jesus and Jesus alone as the source of your righteousness and forgiveness, you will end up producing the fruits of righteousness, holiness, and moral character.

Indeed, the Bible tells us it is when we don't see or have forgotten that we have been cleansed from our old sins that we end up lacking in self-control, godliness, and brotherly love (see 2 Pet. 1:5–9). Can you see how when you believe right, you will end up living right? So make Jesus, His forgiveness, and His love the center of every part of your life!

> *Make Jesus, His forgiveness, and His love the center of every part of your life!*

Lifting Jesus Higher

Grammy Award–winning songwriter and renowned worship leader Israel Houghton is a dear friend of mine. After hearing my message at a conference about making Jesus the center of our lives, he told me that he was inspired to write the song "Jesus at the Center," which he cowrote with Adam Ranney and Micah Massey. This song has become an anthem sung by Christians all around the world. Whenever I meet Israel, he jokes that he is seriously considering writing me a royalty check because every time he hears me preach about Jesus, he gets inspiration for a new song.

Well, Israel, if you are reading this, I ain't seen nothing in my mailbox yet, my friend.

Of course, I'm just kidding! I am truly glad that more and more, the name of Jesus is lifted up all around the world. In fact, on one of my trips to Israel, I met Adam Ranney. He shared with me how my ministry had impacted him because Christ is always given center place. All this really encourages me because more than two decades ago, I received a mandate from the Father to bring His Son back to the church.

It's sad, but there are some churches where you'll hear all about how you should conduct yourself, but you don't hear the name of Jesus. You don't hear about the cross, and you don't hear about how you are made righteous in Christ. You don't hear how God sees you in Christ today. That is why I am so excited and blessed to know that the glorious name of our Lord Jesus is being exalted and lifted up more and more all around the world. That's what I live for!

People call me a grace preacher, and they are right. But above all else, my passion is just to be someone who points people to Jesus! I know that when the beauty, perfection, and love of Jesus are unveiled in people's lives, their lives will be transformed, and they will never be the same again. Self-help books point you to what you must do. My messages and books are all about Jesus helping you— pointing you to Jesus and what He has done for you!

It doesn't matter how many times you've failed. When you make Jesus the center of your life, God will cause His blessings, favor, and grace to flow into your situation. That addiction that you have been battling with will be no more. That heavy load of guilt and condemnation that you have been carrying around for years will be lifted off your shoulders. That eating disorder, that bitterness, and that paralyzing fear will all be consumed in the person of Jesus!

Shielded in Christ

When you begin to see what God sees, your life will never be the same again. I've said this before but it bears repeating: When you became a believer, God no longer saw you as you! When He looks at you today, He sees Jesus. You are now *in* Christ. When I teach this in my church, I like to illustrate it like this: I take an ordinary ballpoint pen, place it in the middle of my Bible, and close the Bible.

"Can you see the pen now?" I ask my congregation, holding up my Bible. No, they can't. All they can see is the Bible. The pen is now completely hidden in and shielded within the pages of the Bible.

In the same way, the moment you accept Jesus, you are shielded in Christ. When God looks at you today, He doesn't see you with all your flaws and imperfections. He only sees His darling Son, Jesus! His Word says, "to the praise of the glory of His grace, by which He made us accepted in the Beloved" (Eph. 1:6). That refers to you, my friend. By God's abundant and lavish grace—His unmerited favor—you are accepted and approved in Jesus, the Beloved!

What this means is that God is no longer assessing and judging you based on your merits. It is no longer about what you have done or *not* done. His love for you is not contingent on your actions; it is contingent on Jesus. No matter what mistakes you have made, He sees you washed in the blood of His beloved Son.

Because you are in Christ, having a blessed future is not contingent on how much you strive to be perfect or how hard you work at changing yourself. It is contingent on the person of Jesus. It is not about whether *you* deserve to be blessed, favored, and victorious. The question is, does *Jesus* deserve to be blessed, favored, and victorious?

The Bible proclaims, "as He is, so are we in this world" (1 John 4:17). Does Jesus deserve to be blessed, favored, and victorious? Then so do you! This is what being in Christ Jesus means. It means that today, God assesses you and sees you based on the perfection of Jesus Christ. Jesus' righteousness is your righteousness. In fact, the Bible explains that because Jesus, who knew no sin, became sin for us, we are now the righteousness of God in Christ (see 2 Cor. 5:21).

> *Does Jesus deserve to be blessed, favored, and victorious? Then so do you! This is what being in Christ Jesus means.*

Your Righteousness Is a Gift

"Righteousness" is a legal term. It means to have right standing before God. *Vine's Expository Dictionary of Biblical Words* defines righteousness as "that gracious gift of God to men whereby all who believe on the Lord Jesus Christ are brought into right relationship with God."[1] In other words, your right standing before God is based upon Jesus' right standing before God.

Today, you are as righteous as Jesus because your righteousness is from Him. He purchased it for you at the cross. When you received Him as your Lord and Savior, He took away all your unrighteousness once and for all and gave you *His* gift of righteousness. This righteousness is something that you can never obtain or achieve through your right doing; it can only be *received* by your right believing in Jesus.

And do you know what happens when you receive this gift of righteousness? The Bible declares that "those who receive abundance of grace and of the gift of righteousness will reign in life through the One, Jesus Christ" (Rom. 5:17). Hey, when you reign, your addictions don't. When you reign, sicknesses don't. When you reign, fear, depression, and every obstacle that is obstructing you from living your life to the fullest will be torn down and flushed out.

Believe Right about Your Right Standing in Christ

There is so much teaching today on right doing, but the answer is found in believing right about your right standing in Christ. This is why it is so important for you to remember this: your righteousness (right standing) before God is a *gift*.

So many people are struggling today because they are trying, through their own obedience, efforts, and abilities, to earn their right standing before God. Out of the sincerity of their hearts, they believe that by performing more good deeds, by becoming more obedient, by giving up more for Jesus, by praying and serving God more, God will bless them. Please hear me out here. I am all for doing all of that. But if you believe that these things will earn you righteousness, that's when it becomes a problem.

As good as all the above sounds, when people fail to be obedient (which they will), when they fail to give up more for Jesus (which they will), and when they don't pray "enough," read the Bible "enough," and serve in church "enough," they will begin to consciously or unconsciously disqualify themselves from God's love, presence, and blessings. And who determines what is "enough," anyway? The accuser of the brethren will take every opportunity to condemn believers for *never* doing "enough." When that happens, they will begin to fall into the trap of guilt, inferiority, condemnation, and shame.

That is the problem. When someone bases their relationship with God on their own merits, they will always fall short. That's the old covenant way—do right, and God will bless you; do wrong, and you will be cursed. Unfortunately, man has no ability to deserve God's blessing through his actions. Even under the old covenant, no one was blessed because they obeyed God perfectly. They were blessed because of the temporary righteousness that they received through the blood of bulls and goats. The blood from these animal sacrifices was merely a shadow of the blood that Jesus would finally shed at the cross to purchase for us the gift of everlasting righteousness. Do you see? Then and now, right standing with God cannot be merited; it is a gift from Him, based on His unmerited favor.

> *Right standing with God cannot be merited; it is a gift from Him, based on His unmerited favor.*

Seeing the Finished Work Brings God's Blessings

The team that runs my television ministry received an email from a precious lady in Texas. Nancy discovered my ministry via television and began to really have a personal revelation of God's goodness and how righteous she was through Christ's finished work.

Writing to me about how God's grace has not just impacted her life but the lives of her entire family, she shared:

> *When I first saw you on television five years ago, I was rather skeptical. However, something about you was different. I knew in my spirit that you were teaching the true gospel. So I began watching your sermons every day, sometimes twice a day. The more I watched, the more I saw the wisdom of God on you, and the more I wanted to have a relationship with God and Jesus.*
>
> *At that time, I was at a low point in my life and I was about to give up on my marriage. I was even questioning my faith and God. I didn't realize how much I'd kept God in a box and only involved Him in certain areas of my life because I thought He was judging me.*
>
> *When I finally heard the truth about the gospel, I ran with it! Never will I look back because you have taught me the true freedom that Jesus died to give me. Praise God! Once the veil was removed, I realized how righteous I really am, and God just started blessing my socks off!*
>
> *My marriage has turned around and is now growing stronger. We're going on the twelfth year in our marriage, and I thank God for the four beautiful and healthy daughters He has blessed me with. God has also promoted my husband in his career and given him a salary increase. In addition, God has recently upgraded us to an amazing neighborhood and even opened the doors to*

a charter school for two of my girls. He has given us so much favor because at least five hundred people are on the waiting list for this school!

And that's not all. About a year ago, when I was watching you teach in Israel, I told the Lord quietly in my heart, "Lord, I want to go to Israel. I don't know how I ever will, but I want it." I never thought about the trip again until early April this year when God dropped a free trip to Israel into my lap and opened every door for me to go!

My heavenly Father has shown me that I am His daughter and that He is willing to take care of every need for the rest of my life! I did nothing to deserve it! My light is shining, and everybody wants to know what it's all about.

I can't tell you how much it warms my heart to hear real stories from people like Nancy and to know how Jesus has transformed their lives and their walk with Him. I am so thankful to folks like her who take the time to write to us and share how the revelation of God's forgiveness and His gift of righteousness has freed them to believe and receive His provision for every need.

We receive emails every day from people all around the world, sharing with us how hearing about God's love and grace through our broadcast, books, and media resources has completely revolutionized their lives and restored hope for their future. And we love hearing from them because this is what it's all about—life transformation in the precious people that Jesus died to redeem!

See What Really Happened at the Cross

Once, the Lord showed me a vision of what happened at the cross. I saw how all the sins of the entire human race (lies, deceit, envy, bitterness, adultery, addiction, bondage, murder) and all the consequences of sin (fear, sicknesses, guilt, disease, and condemnation) swirled around Jesus like evil spirits and demons, laughing heinously, taunting and tormenting Him. Jesus became like a magnet for all sin and of His own volition accepted all this sin into His own body.

You and I will never be able to imagine the excruciating pain that tore through His body at the cross. Every malignant cancer, every tumor, every sickness, and every disease also came upon Him at the same time. He who knew no sin took upon Himself the mountainous weight of all men's darkest and foulest sins. He took it all Himself.

The Word says that "He Himself took our infirmities and bore our sicknesses" (Matt. 8:17). "Himself"—a singular, reflexive pronoun that signifies the exclusion of you and me. Since He Himself has taken the full punishment, judgment, and condemnation for all sin, you and I are excluded from every punishment, judgment, and condemnation for all sin when we receive Him as our Savior.

But the story did not end there. Jesus did not die on the cross in the middle of receiving upon Himself all of humanity's sins. He took it all and accepted it all in His body. Then the fire of God's judgment was unleashed upon His own precious Son, and only when every last sin had been punished did Jesus cry out, "IT IS FINISHED!" moments before breathing His last breath (see John

19:30). Can you see that? Jesus held on at the cross until every single sin that you have ever committed and will ever commit was punished in His own body. That is why we call what Jesus has accomplished at the cross a "finished work."

See as God Sees

Now, what is your part today? Your part is to believe with your heart and confess with your mouth that Jesus Christ is the Lord of your life and that all your sins have been paid for at the cross. If you believe that all your sins have been forgiven, sin will have no more power over you. You don't have to walk around with "a mountain of sin" on your shoulders anymore because this "mountain of sin" was laid squarely on the shoulders of another—Jesus. He Himself has already paid the price for your sins, so stop condemning yourself!

> *Jesus Himself has already paid the price for your sins, so stop condemning yourself!*

Today, when you look into the mirror, what do you see? Do you see yourself trapped in all your failings, mistakes, and sins? Or do you see what God sees?

My dear friend, when God sees you today, He sees Jesus. Use your eyes of faith and believe that as Jesus is, so are you. In God's eyes, you are righteous, you are favored, you are blessed, and you are healed. You are freed from all sin, all pangs of guilt, all forms of condemnation, and every bondage of addiction!

CHAPTER 6

YOU ARE IRREVERSIBLY BLESSED

Like a sniper, Balaam ascended the mountain looking for the best vantage point to fire a crippling curse at God's people. He had been hired by the mobster Balak, who was growing increasingly intimidated by the children of Israel encroaching on his turf.

Balak had witnessed what Israel had done to another mob family, the Amorites. He didn't want to take any chances and was making a preemptive strike to defend the honor of his family and protect their legacy in the plains of Moab at any cost.

Balaam had a reputation for being a highly reliable assassin-for-hire. It was said that whomever Balaam blessed was blessed, and whomever he cursed was cursed. Armed with this knowledge, Balak had solicited the professional hit man's services to drive his enemy, Israel, from his territory.

But as Balaam and Balak stood in a high place overlooking the encampment of the children of Israel, a strange phenomenon occurred. When Balaam opened his mouth to curse, he ended up blessing the people of Israel! Nervous and infuriated, Balak cried out, "What have you done to me? I took you to curse my enemies, and look, you have blessed them bountifully!" (Num. 23:11).

Anxious to see his enemies cursed and out of his territory, Balak brought Balaam to another high place and demanded that he reload and try once more to shoot curses at Israel. Again, instead of curses, blessings flowed out of Balaam's mouth.

Now, listen closely to what Balaam said, for God had said that He would put His words in Balaam's mouth (see Num. 22:35): "Behold, I have received a command to bless; He has blessed, and I cannot reverse it. He has not observed iniquity in Jacob, nor has He seen wickedness in Israel. The LORD his God is with him, and the shout of a King is among them" (Num. 23:20–21).

In Christ, You Are Irreversibly Blessed

These are precious words, and they reveal how God sees you and me today. Do you know that when He blesses you, no one—no prophet, no sorcerer, and no devil—can reverse it? You are irreversibly blessed! You can never be cursed! No generational curse or any other curse can come upon you because God has already blessed you! That includes being redeemed from the curse of the law as recorded in Galatians 3:13: "Christ has redeemed us from the curse of the law, having become a curse for us (for it is written, 'Cursed is everyone who hangs on a tree')."

When God blesses you, no one can reverse it.

When your enemies say negative things about you out of envy, jealousy, and fear, or if there are people spreading nasty lies about you to assassinate your character, know this: the Lord is your defender. It is God who gives influence to words, and He can cause their words to fall to the ground. He can even, as we have just read, turn their curses into blessings. You don't have to get all flustered, agitated, and angry. Just know that the Lord is on your side and that when He has blessed you, no one can reverse it. Amen!

I want this right belief to sink deep into your heart: *in Christ Jesus, you are irreversibly blessed.* No matter how dire your circumstances may seem right now, put a smile on your face and a spring in your step. Whom the Lord has blessed, no one can curse! God is going to see you through this storm. Things are going to turn around for your good. You don't have to live in disappointment, discouragement, and despair. As you see in the biblical account of Balaam, if God is on your side, who can be against you?

Believe God Watches Over You

There's another truth I want you to see in the story of Balaam. Notice that the children of Israel did nothing to defend themselves against Balak. In fact, they were completely oblivious to how God was watching out for them, and yet He defended them.

In the same way, you can rest knowing that God is your defender. The psalmist reminds us that "He who keeps Israel shall neither slumber nor sleep. The LORD is your keeper; the LORD is your shade at your right hand. The sun shall not strike you by day, nor the moon by night. The LORD shall preserve you from all evil; He shall preserve your soul. The LORD shall preserve your going out and your coming in from this time forth, and even forevermore" (Ps. 121:4–8).

What a promise! God watches over you and your loved ones, and He never takes a break. You are protected from every danger at every moment of the day.

> *God watches over you and your loved ones, and He never takes a break.*

Know What God Doesn't See

Let me give you even more reason to rejoice as we learn to see what God sees. Let's go back to the words that God placed in Balaam's mouth: "He has not observed iniquity in Jacob, nor has He seen wickedness in Israel" (Num. 23:21). Let's pause for a moment. Was there iniquity in Israel? (When God used the word "Jacob" here, He was referring to all the children of Israel.) Was there any sin in Israel? Or was everybody in the encampment perfect?

If you were to zoom in from the top of the mountain into the encampment of Israel, you would probably hear all kinds of murmuring and complaining against Moses and his leadership. Surely there were some who had trouble keeping their tempers, and perhaps there were one or two who were coveting their neighbors' donkeys. It's not hard to imagine that a wide variety of imperfections, sins, iniquities, and wickedness was present in the camp. But the question is, did God see it?

Look at Numbers 23:21 again. Notice that God did *not* say there was no sin or iniquity in His people. He simply said He did not see it. Similarly, He is not saying that there is no sin in you. What God says is, "I don't see it."

Wait a minute, how can an unbendingly holy God not see sin in me?

My friend, it is because those same holy eyes saw all your sins punished in the body of Jesus Christ. Your sins were punished into nonexistence.

In the Israelite encampment, even though there were iniquities, sins, and wickedness, God did not see any of them because the blood of bulls and goats, which they offered up to the Lord daily, covered the children of Israel. How much more true that is for us today, we who are washed clean forever by the blood of the Lamb of God, Jesus Christ, our beautiful Savior.

Under the old covenant, the Israelites enjoyed a *temporal* covering through the animal sacrifices, but for us, the atonement and payment for all our sins by Jesus Christ is *eternal*. That is why God does not observe sin and iniquity in you nor has He seen wickedness in you. When God looks at you today, He sees you as a righteous, forgiven, healed, favored, blessed, accepted, and beloved son or daughter because of the cross of Jesus. Now, do you see yourself as God sees you?

When God looks at you today, He sees you as a righteous, forgiven, healed, favored, blessed, accepted, and beloved son or daughter because of the cross of Jesus.

Perfected in Christ

I believe that we struggle to believe this truth because we know ourselves so well, too well, in fact. We are so acutely aware of every little flaw in our physical and emotional makeup. We know, remember, and replay in our minds the sins, failings, and mistakes we have made. Mistakes that we made ten or even twenty years ago are still fresh in our minds as if they were made yesterday.

I once saw some women being interviewed on television who, when asked what their best features were, had a really hard time coming up with an answer. However, when asked to name the features they disliked about themselves, they unanimously said, "Oh, where do I start?" and they went on and on about every part of themselves—their hair, their noses, their ears. They could even find something about their shoulders they didn't like.

Our propensity to zoom in on flaws doesn't end at just our looks. Have you noticed how our attention is drawn to even minute flaws in anything we look at? Just imagine standing before a big whiteboard. Instead of seeing the broad expanse of the clean, white surface, we're very likely to find and focus on the tiny black speck at the bottom left corner of the whiteboard if there is one there. Our natural minds are just so inclined to latch onto the negative and imperfect. Correspondingly, we have a tendency to focus on and condemn ourselves for even our smallest flaws instead of focusing on how God really sees us—perfect in Christ.

Jesus, the Source of Our Faith

This is why it takes faith to believe that God sees you righteous. It takes faith to believe that He does not see you in your sins, that He does not observe sin or iniquity in you. It takes faith to believe that He means what He says when He says, "For I will be merciful to their unrighteousness, and their sins and their lawless deeds I will remember no more" (Heb. 8:12). It takes faith to believe that God will not remember your failings and mistakes!

But Pastor Prince, my sins are staring right at me. How can I have faith to believe that God doesn't see them?

My friend, the key to faith is found in looking to the source of faith—Jesus. As the Bible says, "fixing our eyes on Jesus, the author and perfecter of faith" (Heb. 12:2 NASB). Your faith to believe is found in Jesus! The Amplified Bible puts it this way: "Looking away [from all that will distract] to Jesus, Who is the Leader *and* the Source of our faith [giving the first incentive for our belief] and is also its Finisher [bringing it to maturity and perfection]."

> *The key to faith is found in looking to the source of faith—Jesus.*

In other words, turn your eyes away from your own flaws, imperfections, failings, and mistakes, and just fix your eyes on Jesus. The more you see Jesus and His finished work, the more faith arises in your heart to believe that all your sins are truly forgiven. You can start on a clean slate and have a brand-new beginning in Christ. The old is gone, and the new has come!

The Power of Beholding Jesus

You may be thinking to yourself, "But that sounds so impractical. How can my life change just by fixing my eyes on Jesus?"

Well, it didn't seem that impractical when Peter fixed his eyes on Jesus. *He walked on water!* Only when he turned away and looked at the boisterous waves did he begin to sink.

Similarly, when we fix our eyes on Jesus and make Him the center of our lives, we will be transformed supernaturally and walk above the churning waters of guilt and condemnation. However, when we turn our eyes away from Jesus and start to look again at the waves of our failures, mistakes, and sins, we will, like Peter, begin to sink into the raging tempest of guilt and condemnation. But even when that happens, you can take heart because Jesus will be right there to pull you out and rescue you, just like He did for Peter.

I believe that Jesus is doing that in your life right now. Is there something that you have done in your past that you just can't seem to shake off, that seems like weights around your feet holding you

down? Today is the day for your breakthrough. Learn to see what
God sees by fixing your eyes on Jesus.

You need to understand that what you see or how others see you
is not as important as how *God* sees you. Many people think that
God sees them in their sins and is just waiting to pounce on them
to punish them. This wrong belief produces wrong living. If you
see God this way, you can't help but be in constant fear, insecurity, and anxiety over your past sins. Today, make a decision to turn
your eyes to Jesus, for He has already made you righteous with His
blood!

> *What you see or how others see you is not as important as how*
> *God sees you.*

In fact, the more you behold Jesus, the more you are transformed from glory to glory. The Bible tells us that "we all, with
unveiled face, beholding as in a mirror the glory of the Lord, are
being transformed into the same image from glory to glory, just as
by the Spirit of the Lord" (2 Cor. 3:18). Fixing your eyes on Jesus is
the greatest holiness. Many think they have to *do more* in order to
be more holy, accepted, and loved by God. The truth is, when you
behold Jesus more and see His love, His forgiveness, His abundant
grace, and His gift of righteousness purchased for you with His
own blood, you will be transformed supernaturally.

Holiness is a by-product of seeing Jesus in His grace. When you
see Jesus and receive His love and grace every day, your heart is
transformed inwardly. This is not outward behavior modification.

This is real change that is sustained by a heart touched by His grace and by an emancipated conscience that is forever freed from guilt. This is when that addiction begins to drop from your life. This is when that fear begins to dissolve in His perfect love, and that condemnation arising from your past mistakes is cleansed by His precious blood. What a life! This is the life that God wants you to experience. Can you see it? Can you see what He sees?

> *Holiness is a by-product of seeing Jesus in His grace.*

You Are Precious in His Eyes

I want to show you another aspect of how God sees you today through a beautiful truth hidden in the breastplate of the high priest of Israel. The Bible gives us very detailed information about what the high priest wore in the days of ancient Israel and there are no insignificant details in the Bible. Today, Jesus is our High Priest, and when we examine the breastplate, we will see something powerful about the way the Lord sees His people.

Notice in the following illustration that there are twelve stones on the high priest's breastplate. The names of the twelve tribes of Israel are engraved on each of the stones. For example, "Judah" is engraved on the sardius stone set in the first row, and "Gad" is engraved on the diamond set in the second row.

The high priest of Israel: The names of the twelve tribes of Israel are engraved on twelve precious stones found on his breastplate.

These twelve stones represent God's people today. Notice how God depicts His people, you and me, as precious stones. He didn't use common rocks and pebbles that are in abundance in Israel. He deliberately chose very costly, rare, and precious gems such as sapphire, topaz, emerald, amethyst, diamond, onyx, and jasper to represent you and me (see Exod. 39:9–14). Also, of all the garments donned by the high priest, the breastplate is closest to the heart. This speaks of how much the Lord values you and His desire to keep you close to His heart. In His eyes, you are very costly, precious, and loved. If you have ever been told that God sees you as a dirty, rotten sinner, then know that it's a lie from the pit of hell!

I would also like to draw your attention to the fact that the names of the tribes of Israel were not merely written on the gems. The Bible tells us that they were *engraved* (see Exod. 39:14). This means that once you become a believer in Jesus, your name is forever engraved in His Book of Life. If your name were only written, you might think that it could easily be erased or blotted out. But the truth is that Jesus has *engraved* your name on a precious stone, and He keeps it close to His heart.

Can your name ever be blotted out of its place on God's heart? Just look at what Jesus promises those who are born again: "He who overcomes shall be clothed in white garments, and I will not blot out his name from the Book of Life; but I will confess his name before My Father and before His angels" (Rev. 3:5). Beloved, through Christ Jesus you are an overcomer, and in Christ Jesus, you are eternally secure. Rest in the assurance that your name will not be blotted out from the Book of Life. It will remain engraved on stone and close to God's heart for all eternity!

You Are an Overcomer through Christ

Now, how do you become a "he who overcomes"? Don't let anyone twist this verse to make it all about you. Many wrong beliefs are birthed out of man-centered teachings that focus on what man has to do, or in this case, what man has to overcome by himself through his own works. Make sure that what you believe is Christ-centered teachings that focus on what Jesus has done and continues to do in your life.

Let Scripture interpret Scripture when in doubt. In this case, a few chapters later, Revelation 12:10–11 tells us, "for the accuser of our brethren, who accused them before our God day and night, has been cast down. And they overcame him by the blood of the Lamb and by the word of their testimony."

How do you overcome the devil, who comes to accuse and condemn you for your mistakes? By the blood of the Lamb that washes you from all unrighteousness, and by the word of your testimony that Jesus Christ is your Lord and Savior! Heaven and eternal salvation have nothing to do with your self-efforts. It's all about your belief in Jesus and everything that He has done for you at the cross. No one goes to heaven by his own righteousness. We are ALL qualified only by the blood of the Lamb!

> *Heaven and eternal salvation have nothing to do with your self-efforts. It's all about your belief in Jesus and everything that He has done for you at the cross.*

Whenever your guilty conscience or the accuser of the brethren, the devil, condemns you for your mistakes, keep this beautiful picture that God paints of us in His Word in your mind. See and believe in your heart that you are, like the gems on the high priest's breastplate, precious in His eyes and close to His heart. It's not about how you see yourself, how your spouse sees you, or how your relatives, friends, and coworkers see you. The most important thing is to first learn to *see how God sees you.*

Gems Sparkle under Light

Perhaps for years you have seen yourself as someone who is weak, someone who easily succumbs to guilt, anxiety attacks, or addictions. Today is the day to turn your eyes away from yourself and your weaknesses. Learn to see what God sees. He sees you in Christ Jesus, through the lens of the cross and through the precious blood that was shed for your redemption. Flush out all your wrong beliefs and see yourself as a precious gem, dearly beloved and close to God's heart.

Let me ask you this: When you realize how valuable and precious you are in His eyes, does that make you want to go out and sin or to continue living in sin?

Of course not!

On the contrary, your thoughts will run more along lines of, "Hey, this is not how a believer, who is precious to the Lord, behaves. A precious diamond doesn't belong in the mud, grime, and filth of sin. It's unbecoming of a diamond. The rightful place of the diamond is close to God's heart where it sparkles and shines."

Knowing your true, righteous, and precious-to-God identity in Christ will elevate you from every addiction, bondage, and sin. It makes you want to walk and live the high life as a child of the King. Holy living, good character, and true morality are birthed out of seeing how God sees you today. If you see yourself as a dirty, rotten sinner, that wrong belief will keep you bound, and you will end up behaving like a dirty, rotten sinner. I wrote this book to tell you that is *not* you! God sees you in Christ. When He sees you, He sees the cross, and through the cross you look beautiful. Therefore, don't be afraid of God's truth and light.

> *God sees you in Christ. When He sees you, He sees the cross, and through the cross you look beautiful.*

Do you know what happens to precious stones when light shines upon them? They sparkle and radiate with beauty. The truth is, light is a gem's best friend because it brings out the best qualities of the precious stone. In the same way, as you are reading this right now, do you know that the light of God's grace and truth is shining on you? It's not here to condemn you, but to cause you to sparkle brilliantly and bring out your best qualities. It's a light that shows the perfection of the work of Jesus in making you completely clean. It's not a light to be feared. Grace brings out the best in you because grace always produces holiness. The more you receive God's love and grace, and see how He sees you, the more you will arise from every area of defeat and shine gloriously for Jesus like the precious gems on the high priest's breastplate.

It's All about the Cross

There is an amazing secret hidden in the story of Balaam. Do you know what Balaam saw from the mountaintop when he was trying to curse God's people? He saw this:

The Israelite encampment that Balaam saw formed a picture of the cross of Jesus.

What do you see? That's right! It's the cross of Jesus!

The Bible gives very specific details on how the twelve tribes of Israel set up their encampment and the number of people in each tribe (see Num. 2:2–32). We read that the camp of Judah (comprising Judah, Issachar, and Zebulun) on the eastern side of the encampment is the largest camp among them, and you can see from the illustration that it forms the longer, bottom extension of the cross. I told you that there are no insignificant details in the Bible—everything points to the person of Jesus. Isn't this amazing? I love it when the cross of Jesus is revealed!

This means that when Balaam was trying to curse God's people, he actually caught a glimpse of how God sees His people—through the cross, through the sacrifice of His Son. Of course, Balaam didn't understand the significance of the cross, and neither did the children of Israel at that time.

But you and I do.

My friend, when God looks at you today, He sees the price His beloved Son paid at the cross to ransom you from all your sins. He sees you in Christ. In His eyes, you are forgiven, righteous, precious, beautiful, valuable, and close to His heart. It's time to see yourself as God sees you!

PART THREE

RECEIVE GOD'S COMPLETE FORGIVENESS

CHAPTER 7

RECEIVE HIS FORGIVENESS AND REIGN

Even after being in active ministry for more than two decades, I am still amazed when I see just how hard people are on themselves. I believe this can be traced to their wrong beliefs about God. When you believe erroneously that God is hard on you for your failures, you will inevitably be hard on the people around you, and most of all, you will end up being really hard on yourself.

People who are hard on themselves cannot forgive themselves for the mistakes they've made in the past. Sadly, they end up punishing themselves, whether they know it or not. Some end up physically cutting and hurting themselves. Some binge on food or fall into substance abuse. Others indulge their sexual appetites and spiral out of control, hurting not only themselves but also their loved ones, all because they respond to an instinct to punish themselves, albeit unconsciously.

It's a vicious cycle of defeat. The more they can't forgive themselves, the more they hurt themselves with all kinds of behaviors and the more they end up bound by various destructive addictions.

This leads to even more guilt, which in turn drives them to punish themselves even more—and the cycle continues.

Release Your Failings to Jesus

That is why I believe the root cause of many sinful habits, fears, and addictions can be traced to condemnation. I want to talk to you today about going after condemnation as the root to help you receive God's forgiveness in those areas so that you can break out of your cycle of defeat and step into a new cycle of victory.

Are you living with some unresolved guilt and condemnation today? I have great news for you. When you realize that God's heart is not in condemnation but in forgiveness, your entire life can be turned around for His glory! I have personally witnessed so many lives transformed when they just take a small step of faith to believe in His grace and receive His forgiveness in their lives.

> *When you realize that God's heart is not in condemnation but in forgiveness, your entire life can be turned around for His glory!*

Instead of punishing themselves for their mistakes and disqualifying themselves, these people began to correct their beliefs and receive God's forgiveness by seeing Jesus taking on their punishment. They began to see their Savior qualifying them to receive every blessing from God for their marriages, families, and careers.

Right now I want to encourage you to release the built-up guilt and condemnation for whatever mistakes you've made over the years to the Lord.

Would you pray this prayer with me?

> *Lord Jesus, I don't want to live this way anymore. Today I release all my failings, sins, and mistakes into Your loving hands. And I receive Your forgiveness right now into my heart. Thank You for Your precious blood that washes me whiter than snow. Right now I stand in Your righteousness, favor, joy, and peace. In Jesus' name, Amen!*

It's a simple but powerful prayer. I encourage you to pray this prayer every time you fail and experience guilt and condemnation in your heart. Stop punishing yourself—your answer is found at the cross of Jesus. I promise you that when you turn to Jesus and remind yourself just how forgiven and righteous you are in Christ every time you fall short, you will start living like the forgiven and righteous person Jesus has made you.

God Loves You Perfectly

God is a God of forgiveness. He knows you perfectly and still loves you perfectly. We are slaves to the idea that if someone sees our flaws, they won't love us anymore. Well, while that may be true in human relationships, God is not like that.

God sees all our imperfections, failings, and flaws on Jesus at the cross. Our sins and ugliness do not turn Him off. In fact, to

Him they are occasions to demonstrate His grace and forgiveness through the blood of His Son, who has removed all our sins efficaciously at Calvary.

> *God knows your weaknesses better than you do, and He loves you just the same.*

So don't be embarrassed about your flaws, mistakes, and imperfections. God knows your weaknesses better than you do, and He loves you just the same. His Word reminds us that Jesus is not someone "who cannot sympathize with our weaknesses." Instead, Jesus was tempted in all points, yet He was without sin (Heb. 4:15). He understands every temptation and every trial that you are going through. He is not disappointed with you, and He is not waiting for you to live up to a set of dos and don'ts before He forgives and loves you. The Bible says, "But God demonstrates His own love toward us, in that while we were still sinners, Christ died for us. Much more then, having now been justified by His blood, we shall be saved from wrath through Him" (Rom. 5:8–9).

Did you get that? *When* did God love you?

That's right, *when you were still a sinner.* Before you even knew Him, when you were still in sin, He already loved you. How much more today, when you have been cleansed by Jesus' blood and made righteous! Having received Jesus' righteousness, you are righteous forever. Even when you fall into sin, your sins don't make you a sinner again.

When you fall short today, you are still the righteousness of God. This is because your righteousness comes from Jesus. In the same way that a beautiful butterfly cannot morph back into a caterpillar, once you have been made righteous by the blood of Jesus, you cannot morph back into a sinner. Knowing your righteous identity in Him then gives you the power to overcome every sin, every addiction, and every bad habit!

> *Knowing your righteous identity in Him then gives you the power to overcome every sin, every addiction, and every bad habit!*

You Are Righteous in Christ

The wrong belief that many believers have is that they become sinners again whenever they fail. So they live their Christian lives in insecurity and condemnation. Sometimes they think they are righteous, sometimes they think they are sinners. They wrongly believe that their righteousness is dependent on how they perform that day. This leads to a severe identity crisis. It's no wonder they are not seeing the breakthroughs that Jesus has already purchased for them at the cross!

My friend, find your righteous identity in Jesus. Born-again believers who have been washed by the blood of Jesus don't enjoy living in sin, any more than sheep enjoy wallowing in mud. Now, when a sheep falls into mud, is it still a sheep? Of course it is! It doesn't suddenly become a pig that enjoys mud. The sheep may be in the mud, but it is uncomfortable in that mud, hates the mud, and can't wait to be washed clean from this mud.

I am writing to people who are genuinely looking for a way out of their fears, guilt, bondages, addictions, and habits. I am writing to sheep who hate living in fear, hate being bound by guilt, and hate being trapped in addictions and habits they know are destroying them, but don't know how to find freedom. And I'm here to tell them this: the grace of God is the answer. Grace is not a license to sin; it is the *answer* to overcoming sin!

> *Grace is not a license to sin; it is the answer to overcoming sin!*

What about that person I know who calls himself a believer, but lives like the devil?

It's not our part to judge who is a believer and who isn't. There are people who profess to be "believers," but there is no evidence in their lives that they are. Just because a person goes to church doesn't make that person a believer, any more than going to McDonald's makes you a hamburger or going into a garage makes you a car!

The good news is, while you can't judge if someone else is truly a born-again believer, you can surely know if *you* yourself are born again.

Just ask yourself this: Do you believe in your heart that Jesus Christ is your Lord and Savior? If your answer is yes, then you are a born-again believer made righteous by the blood of Jesus, and you can have eternal assurance that heaven is your home!

You are saved and made righteous by grace through faith. As a believer, you will still make mistakes, you will still fail, and you will still be tempted. From time to time, you will fall into sin. But having sinned doesn't turn you back into a sinner. You have been purchased and redeemed by the blood of Jesus, and in Christ, you are still the righteousness of God even when you fail. Why? Because your righteousness is not a result of your right doing—it is a result of your right believing. It is a gift of God, not something you can earn through your obedience, right doing, and sinless perfection. That is why you can have eternal security, knowing that you are saved by Jesus and not by your own works!

At the cross, Jesus redeemed you from all your sins. But do you know that Jesus didn't redeem you from ever being tempted and sinning again? Don't believe me? Name me one believer that you know today on this planet who is never tempted and who never sins.

I rest my case.

Can you see this? If we are saved and made righteous today by our own works and right doing, what hope do we have? Praise God that our unshakable hope of salvation is found in Jesus and Jesus alone!

The Power to Overcome Sin

Unfortunately, in many places today all you hear is more teaching on right doing, right doing, and more right doing! But I believe what we need is more teaching on right *believing*. What we need to do is keep pointing people to Jesus, His grace, His finished work, and His forgiveness. I have no doubt then that their right believing will produce right living. They will become people whose hope is not in the righteousness *they* can produce, but in the *gift of righteousness* from Jesus Christ and what *Jesus* can produce in them.

I can show you thousands of believers who are experiencing

victories over temptation, over guilt, over addiction, and over sin. My ministry team has received emails and letters from my congregation as well as from believers all around the world who received their breakthroughs over sin when they found their righteous identity in Jesus.

These are believers who know they are not made righteous by their own works, but made righteous by the blood of Jesus. They are believers under grace, where sin has no power in their lives. Once they come under grace, they begin to live out Romans 6:14, which says, "For sin shall not have dominion over you, for you are not under law but under grace." These are believers who, when tempted in their mind to sin, are already receiving the forgiveness of God in their hearts, therefore stopping sin in its tracks before the sinful thought can even mature into a sinful action.

Let me share with you a testimony I received from Lucas. This precious brother shared:

> *Even though I was raised in a Christian home with parents who are both totally dedicated to Jesus, I fell into drug abuse. I tried attending church, but listening to the sermons made me feel like I just couldn't confess my sins enough, repent enough, or hate my sins enough to get God's forgiveness.*
>
> *Then one day a very dear friend gave me a copy of your book* Destined To Reign. *The book rocked my spiritual world. I saw that sin was not the issue. The issue was not understanding the grace of my wonderful Lord and Savior. When I saw the finished work of Jesus,*

> *I realized that God is not up there with a big stick wait-*
> *ing for me to mess up so that He can beat me with it.*
>
> *As I continued reading your book and feeding on the*
> *gospel of grace, I was set free from a five-year drug addic-*
> *tion in just five days! And I know it's all through the*
> *sweet, sweet grace of Jesus being revealed in my life.*
>
> *Thank you, Pastor Prince, for your book, resources,*
> *and sermons. I want to know this God of grace more, and*
> *I want my family to also know Him as a God of grace*
> *and not a God of law who condemns His children. I have*
> *never known a loving God as I do right now!*

Can you see how powerful living with a consciousness of Jesus' forgiveness can be? Sin has no dominion over your life when you are under grace. Sin cannot take root in your life when you are established in God's forgiveness. Receiving His forgiveness puts you in a cycle of victory over sin, whereas those who receive condemnation for every wrong thought in their mind enter into a never-ending cycle of defeat. Do you see the difference?

Forgiveness Is Received, Not Achieved

There is absolutely nothing you can do to earn God's forgiveness. Forgiveness is received, not achieved. If you are trying to earn your own forgiveness and thinking that God is constantly mad at you, I am here to tell you that is not the heart of God. That is Christian religion. Christian religion is a never-ending treadmill based on our own efforts to try to earn God's forgiveness, God's approval, and God's acceptance. Have you been there before? If that is you, listen to the words of Jesus:

> *"Are you tired? Worn out? Burned out on religion? Come to me. Get away with me and you'll recover your life. I'll show you how to take a real rest. Walk with me and work with me—watch how I do it. Learn the unforced rhythms of grace. I won't lay anything heavy or ill-fitting on you. Keep company with me and you'll learn to live freely and lightly."*
>
> —Matthew 11:28–30, The Message

"The unforced rhythms of grace." I like that phrase. What it means is that there is an ease and enjoyment when you walk in His grace. This is in contrast to the struggle and strain found in self-effort. There is such rest when you know there is nothing you can do to earn His forgiveness. Give up on your own self-righteousness, which the Bible describes as "filthy rags" (Isa. 64:6), and with open arms and an open heart, receive His forgiveness!

> *There is such rest when you know there is nothing you can do to earn His forgiveness.*

The key to getting out of a cycle of sin and defeat is to receive and to stop beating yourself up. Receive and stop punishing yourself because your sins have already been punished on the body of another—His name is Jesus, our beautiful Lord and Savior. No wonder the gospel is called the *good news*.

Obligation Versus Relationship

When you understand God's grace and forgiveness, you will understand the difference between obligation and relationship. Under the new covenant of grace, the motivation for right living has been changed. Under the law, right living is done out of religious obligation. Under grace, everything we do today is birthed out of an inward motivation that flows directly from a love relationship with Jesus.

> *Under grace, everything we do today is birthed out of an inward motivation that flows directly from a love relationship with Jesus.*

My friend, God is not a legalist. He doesn't want you to read His Word just because He said so. He wants you to experience His love and spend time in His Word because you *want to* enjoy His sweet presence. The outward action can be the same: Two persons can be reading the Bible. However, one can do it out of religious obligation, while the other is inwardly motivated by God's love. One does it to try to earn God's forgiveness and acceptance; the other does it because he knows that he has been forgiven. One does it out of legalism; the other does it out of relationship. The reality is, when you don't read the Bible, you should not be feeling guilty; you should be feeling hungry.

Recently, I had lunch with an itinerant minister who asked me, "Is it legalistic for pastors to ask husbands in their congregation to love their wives and to instruct wives to submit to their husbands?" I could tell from his manner that he was expecting me to say, "Of course it is not legalistic." So he was stunned at my response when I said, "Yes, it is!" and when I added, "The Bible doesn't tell us to do that."

I explained that as ministers, we need to teach the entire verse, which actually says, "Wives, submit to your own husbands, as to the Lord," and "Husbands, love your wives, *just as Christ also loved the church and gave Himself for her*" (Eph. 5:22, 25, emphasis mine). The emphasis is on Jesus' love for us. Everything we do today under the new covenant of grace springs from our love relationship with Jesus. His love needs to first work in us.

You see, it is a question of motivation. How would you like your husband to say to you, "God says that I should love you and that we should talk more, so let's go out for dinner tonight"? Then he sets a timer on his phone and says, "Alright, lady, your time begins now." Hey, no self-respecting woman would accept that, right? You want your husband to take you out for dinner not because he has to, but because he *wants* to.

That's why the Word of God doesn't simply exhort husbands to love their wives and then stop there. It goes on to teach husbands just how to go about doing so—the power to love comes when husbands first experience how Jesus loved them and gave Himself for them.

Transformed by His Love

Men, when you feed on the love of Jesus, your fuel tank of love for your wife and for your kids will never run empty. Think about His love. Close your eyes and see your Savior giving up everything at the cross for you. When you tank up on His love in your heart, your wife becomes the direct beneficiary of that overflowing love from Jesus. A man who experiences Jesus' love, just loves! A man who experiences Jesus' forgiveness, just forgives! We have the power to love and forgive because He first loved and forgave us.

> *We have the power to love and forgive because He first loved and forgave us.*

That is how we become transformed in His image. You want to be more patient? Meditate on just how patient Jesus has been with you all these years. You desire to be more forgiving toward your wife? Then saturate yourself with thoughts of His forgiveness for every failing you have. Think about how He was right there to pick you up each time you fumbled, with no judgment and no condemnation, only love. "For a righteous man may fall seven times and rise again" (Prov. 24:16).

That's right, my brother, however you may have fallen, Jesus sees you as a righteous man, clothed with His own robes of righteousness, and nothing is going to keep you down. You may think it's all over, but it isn't. God's not done with you. His plans and His purposes for your life have not yet been fulfilled. His love for you has never wavered.

All your imperfections are swallowed up by His perfect love. You may have made mistakes, but it's never too late to receive His forgiveness and receive courage and strength from Him to do the right thing—go back to your wife, seek her forgiveness, and trust the Lord to reignite your love for one another and bring about healing and restoration to your marriage. Your answer is found in the person of Jesus. He will fix you up and cause all things to work together for good and to His glory. Receive His forgiveness and let Him guide you.

> *Your answer is found in the person of Jesus. He will fix you up and cause all things to work together for good and to His glory.*

Grace Exceeds the Law

When you center your heart and life on Jesus and His forgiveness, you will exceed even what the law demands of you. The law says, "Thou shall not covet," but it cannot command you to be generous. Only grace makes you generous. The law says, "Thou shall not commit murder," but it cannot put love and forgiveness in your heart for someone who has wronged you. Only the love and forgiveness of Jesus can do that in your heart and transform you to love and forgive your enemies and those who have hurt you. The law says, "Thou shall not commit adultery," but it cannot put passion, love, and forgiveness in your heart for your spouse. Only Jesus can!

In every way when you are under grace, not only will you fulfill the commands of the law, you will end up unconsciously and effortlessly exceeding all the demands of the law! That is what God means when He says about the new covenant, "I will put My laws in their mind and write them on their hearts; and I will be their God, and they shall be My people" (Heb. 8:10). These laws that God writes in our minds and on our hearts are not the Ten Commandments. They exceed the Ten Commandments. They pertain to the royal law of love that flows from the heart of Jesus and fills our minds and hearts. Truly, "love is the fulfillment of the law" (Rom. 13:10)!

What are you filling your heart with today—with condemnation or with God's forgiveness? Beloved, I encourage you to receive His forgiveness and stop punishing yourself. It is the key to not just breaking the cycle of sin and defeat in your life, but to living a life full of love, peace, hope, and victory.

Remember, he who is forgiven much, loves much, and he who is loved most, loves best!

He who is forgiven much, loves much, and he who is loved most, loves best!

CHAPTER 8

FRESH GRACE FOR EVERY FAILING

Not too long ago, I was driving out for lunch with Wendy, and for some reason, every time she made a passing comment, I found myself snapping irritably at her or making an unnecessarily provocative remark. Every reply of mine had a bite to it, and as you can imagine, the car journey fell into silence pretty quickly. Later during lunch, being the patient lady that my wife is, she asked me, "Darling, is there any reason you are so irritable today?"

Have you had one of those days, where your wife has to ask you a question like that? Well, that was one of those days for me. In case you didn't know, we ministers of God don't have "arguments" with our wives; we merely have "intense discussions"! I'm just kidding. Of course there are occasional disagreements in the Prince household. It's certainly not the norm, but it does come up from time to time, especially when Wendy fails to see my "wisdom." Can I be real here? Can I be vulnerable with you and share with you my infirmities?

You know, people sometimes run into me on the streets when I am wearing just my jeans, a casual shirt, and a baseball cap. When they suddenly recognize me, they are astonished and exclaim, "Pastor Prince, you look so different from how you look on your book covers!" Well, of course I look different. Do you honestly think that I go around wearing a three-piece suit or a tuxedo every day?

Relax. I am just having fun and poking holes at how some ministers like to portray themselves as always holy and perfect—every strand of hair in place, appearance and behavior always immaculate. That's not me. I enjoy being open, authentic, and transparent. I like being the same person on and off the platform. Whether I am standing behind the pulpit or lounging in a café with you, I'm the same person. I love the Word, I love people, and I love pointing imperfect people to Jesus. And I am the first on that list of imperfect people. Even as I am writing this book, I am preaching to myself too from God's Word.

Now, getting back to my story about that lunch with my wife and why I was so irritable that day, let me say, for the record, that I am generally really good company, so what happened that day was out of character. Of course, as in all things, my wife was the direct "beneficiary" of this bout of irritability. And though I was still not in the best frame of mind, my response to my wife's question that day was a really good one, if I may say so myself.

I said, "Darling, I don't know what is wrong with me, but if you see this happening again, please let me know, alright?" And just in case you have some outlandish illusions of me as a husband, let me say that is also *not* the way I respond all the time. I'd rather not get into the details since we have more important matters to discuss in this chapter, but you catch my drift.

My brother, when it comes to learning to love our wives and

being more attentive, caring, and gentle, none of us has arrived. Like any of you husbands, I'm also learning and growing. Praise Jesus for His abundance of grace and the gift of no condemnation!

Could Guilt Be Creeping In?

Wendy's question—"Darling, is there any reason you are so irritable today?"—made me reflect upon the source of my bad temper with her that day. Could it be fatigue? I thought about whether I had a good rest the night before. I had slept well. I had even managed to sleep more hours than I normally would have.

Then I remembered. Earlier that day I had a little encounter with a relative. It was nothing serious, but I had been questioning the tone of my voice and even the choice of my words. I had not said anything that was inappropriate, but still, I had begun judging myself, thinking, "Maybe I should have just let it go. Perhaps I shouldn't have said that. This person is a relative, after all."

These were the thoughts that were circling in my head. I was justifying my actions and my words in my mind, but at the same time, I was also unconsciously beginning to feel guilty. Then, later in the day, I was on the phone correcting someone from my team who had made a rather serious blunder. As I put down the phone, I thought to myself, "Was I too hard?"

It was following this incident that I took my wife out for lunch, and you already know what happened when I was with her. All Wendy did was make small talk. She wasn't the relative, and she wasn't the person I had corrected over the phone. She was an innocent (and if I may add, beautiful) bystander at the wrong place at the wrong time! Do you know what I mean?

I realized then that I was so irritable because I was actually feeling guilty. I didn't necessarily do anything wrong, but I just allowed that little bit of guilt to creep into my heart and unconsciously allowed condemnation to come in. My friend, when you are walking under a cloud of judgment, you can become a really unpleasant person to be around. Trust me, I know what I am talking about. I thank God that when Wendy asked me the question, He gave me that moment of clarity where I could see the condition of my heart.

Praise Jesus for a discerning and perceptive wife who didn't take my remarks personally and knew something was not right with me. That was why I told her to let me know the next time she noticed such behavior from me because even if you are an author of books about God's grace and forgiveness, there can be moments where condemnation creeps into your heart and you are completely oblivious to it. All day long you can feel lousy, and all your answers have a sting in them. That's not the abundant life, and you know what it all comes back to? It comes back to having a constant sense of God's forgiveness over your life. Instead of taking in and harboring all the guilt, condemnation, and judgment, we need to stand secure in our perfect forgiveness in Jesus.

There is a redeeming quality to being forgiveness-conscious, as opposed to being conscious of your failings, sins, and mistakes. When you are forgiveness-conscious and see your failings on the cross of Jesus, you receive power to break out of your irritability, impatience, and short-temperedness with others. You receive power to break out of your eating disorders, addictions, and anxieties!

When you realize that we don't deserve God's forgiveness and grace yet He gives it to us anyway, this revelation of His unmerited favor changes us from within. It dissolves the knots of anger and impatience in us that have built up over the years and frees us to enjoy God's love and to show it to others.

> *When you realize that we don't deserve God's forgiveness and grace yet He gives it to us anyway, this revelation of His unmerited favor changes us from within.*

Grace Is Not Merely Empowerment

The key, therefore, is to receive His grace as unmerited favor and believe that same unmerited favor is what transforms you. There is a teaching going around where grace is defined as "divine empowerment." Be careful about defining grace as merely empowerment—that is diluting and reducing what grace truly is.

Grace produces divine empowerment, but in and of itself, the essence of grace is His undeserved, unmerited, and unearned favor. When are you in your most undeserving state? When you have failed. Unmerited favor means that when you have failed and are in your most undeserving state, you *can* receive Jesus' favor, blessings, love, and perfect acceptance in your life. Let me tell you, when you understand and receive grace as God's unmerited favor, not only will you be empowered, you will be healed, and you will be changed from the inside out.

So be careful what you hear and believe about grace. God's grace is not a transaction for you to do more and perform more (because you have received more power). No, it is a genuine heart encounter with a Savior who loves you more than you can imagine. It's not about what *you have to do*, but it's all about what *Jesus has done*.

The real danger with defining grace as just divine empowerment is that we can unconsciously flip grace around and instead of seeing it as God's work in our life, we make it our work. From being centered on what Jesus has done, the erroneous definition of grace as "empowerment" swings it to being about what *you* must do and how *you* must perform now that you have received this grace, this "divine empowerment." Can you see this? With such a definition of grace, the onus to live the Christ life falls back squarely on your shoulders.

My friend, make sure that what you believe in your heart always points you back to Jesus and Jesus alone and not to yourself. Remember, it is all about His work, His doing, His performance, and His love in our lives. It never points back to you. Don't be hoodwinked by those who move away from the pristine definition of grace as God's unmerited favor and end up making it all about you and what you need to do. That's not grace. Grace is God's doing—from inception and all the way to the end.

> *Grace is God's doing—from inception and all the way to the end.*

Let the Bible Define Grace for You

Did you know that when you read the Amplified Bible, there is a parenthesis next to the word "grace" whenever it appears, and what's in that parenthesis defines grace as God's unearned, undeserved, unmerited favor? For example, in John 1:17, it says this: "For while the Law was given through Moses, grace (unearned, undeserved favor and spiritual blessing) and truth came through Jesus Christ." In another Scripture, Romans 5:17, it says that "those who receive [God's] overflowing grace (unmerited favor) and the free gift of righteousness [putting them into right standing with Himself] reign as kings in life through the one Man Jesus Christ (the Messiah, the Anointed One)."

So every time you hear the word "grace," think about Jesus' unmerited favor. Don't allow someone else to change the purity of God's grace in your life. They will quote you definitions of grace from various dictionaries, but at the end of the day, those are man's definitions. I don't know about you, but I want the Bible's definition of grace. Man's definitions of grace will never equal God's. It's best to let Scripture interpret Scripture.

Now, just how does the Bible define grace? Paul, the greatest apostle of grace, describes it very clearly in Romans 11:6: "And if by grace, then it is no longer of works; otherwise grace is no longer grace. But if it is of works, it is no longer grace; otherwise work is no longer work."

Do you see it? In grace, there is no place for man's works, pure and simple. For those who teach that grace means "empowerment," they tend to skew it toward man's works and man's performance. That's not true grace. Remember that true divine empowerment comes from Jesus, not you.

The New Living Translation renders Romans 11:6 this way: "And since it is through God's kindness, then it is not by their good works. For in that case, God's grace would not be what it really is—free and undeserved." I love that—His grace is *free* and *undeserved*! When you truly experience this free and undeserved favor and love from God, you don't have to worry about performing. His love and unmerited favor within you will flush out all the wrong thinking and wrong believing, and you will produce good works. You will produce results. You will produce true fruits of righteousness that are lasting, sustainable, and enduring!

God's Unmerited Favor Brings Effortless Change

I'd like you to picture a strong and healthy tree. A strong and healthy tree does not worry about producing fruit or getting rid of the dead leaves on it. As long as the tree receives the right amount of sunshine, water, and nutrients, it will have healthy sap flowing in it that is brimming with all the right nutrients and that naturally pushes out all the dead leaves. And as long as its inward life—its healthy sap life—keeps flowing, new leaves will spring forth on this tree and good fruits will naturally grow and flourish on all the branches.

My friend, as you begin to receive the sunshine of God's favor and take in the water of His Word—as you begin to feed on Jesus' forgiveness in your life and your righteous standing in Christ, the dead leaves of guilt, fear, addictions, and every type of disorder will begin to be pushed out by the new life of Jesus within you. The transformation you will experience, when it is not based on your own discipline and self-control, is truly effortless. It is no longer, "How will I overcome this anger problem?" or "How will I beat this cigarette addiction?" or "How can I curb this habit of overeating when I am stressed and insecure?" Instead, it becomes, "How will *Jesus* in me overcome this anger problem, this cigarette addiction, this habit of overeating?"

The fruits of your success will be effortless. One by one, the addictions, dysfunctions, and negative emotions will begin to drop off from your life like dead leaves, and new leaves (new positive thoughts and attitudes), new flowers (new desires and dreams), and new fruit (new behaviors and habits) will begin to flourish in your life.

> *As you begin to receive the sunshine of God's favor and feed on Jesus' forgiveness and your righteous standing in Christ, the dead leaves of guilt, fear, addictions, and every type of disorder will begin to be pushed out by the new life of Jesus within you.*

Jesus said, "Abide in Me, and I in you. As the branch cannot bear fruit of itself, unless it abides in the vine, neither can you, unless you abide in Me. I am the vine, you are the branches. He who abides in Me, and I in him, bears much fruit; for without Me you can do nothing" (John 15:4–5). I want to encourage you to abide in His grace—His undeserved, unmerited, and unearned favor for your life.

Your Ledger Is Clean

It's so important that you understand, believe, and abide in the truth of God's unmerited favor and His forgiveness in your life, even when your behavior is not perfect. Why? Because it frees you to enjoy your relationship with God, to enjoy spending time with Him, and to expect good from Him. It frees you to enjoy peace and rest on a daily basis, good relationships with others, and a life of wholeness. It frees you to confidently expect a bright future.

Imagine for a moment that you are a businessperson. Through some bad decisions and some things beyond your control, your business got into serious debt. Because of this, you've made a habit of avoiding your company's ledger. You know that when you open it, all you're going to see is red, and all that red is a screaming reminder of how much you owe and how unhealthy a state of affairs your business has gotten into. You can't help thinking about the ledger, but the more you think of it, the more it fills you with dread.

In the same way, if you keep believing and thinking that there is still unsettled debt between you and God in your account with Him, you can't breathe easy. You become consumed with thoughts of how to pay off your debt. In fact, just the thought of red in your ledger makes you afraid to go to Him or expect His help for anything.

But say a good friend who loves you finds out about your business debt, and of his own free will and out of his own pocket, he pays off the debt. He does it because, as your good friend, he doesn't want you carrying this burden of debt anymore. Furthermore, knowing that you can't ever pay this debt on your own, he doesn't want you to even try to pay him back.

Now (after you've gotten over this incredible news), you're not afraid of your ledger anymore. You can breathe easy again. You can throw off your despair and laugh and look forward to life again. You no longer become afraid at the very thought of your ledger. In fact, you'd be quite happy to look at your ledger because it shows you how you are now debt-free and how good your benefactor is.

Likewise, once you understand that you are completely forgiven, you will no longer be afraid or defensive when your mistakes, faults, and failures are exposed. Rather, you will find your security, peace, and assurance in the Lord's love for you. You are perfectly forgiven and righteous through Jesus' finished work.

My friend, this is what Jesus has done for you, and much more. Being who He is, the Son of God, He is an overpayment for your sins. And He didn't just cleanse you of your entire life of sins, but He also gave you His very own righteousness and favor. Why? So that you can be free to enjoy being with God and receive all His blessings, with no more consciousness of debt standing in the way. The extent to which you can live life with a confident expectation of good is the extent to which you abide in this truth that your sins have totally been forgiven at the cross and that there is no red in your ledger.

> *The extent to which you can live life with a confident expectation of good is the extent to which you abide in this truth that your sins have totally been forgiven at the cross.*

Once in a while, though, because of the force of habit, you may wake up fearful that you're back in debt. But all you have to do is open your ledger and look at it. It will show you how debt-free you really are, no matter what you feel. Similarly, should you ever experience days when you doubt that God has forgiven you, all you have to do is open the Word of God and see in it how the price has been fully paid, the judgment executed, and every bit of condemnation already meted out on the body of Christ!

Fresh Grace for Every Failing

Can I give you an assignment today? Every time you fail, whether you lose your temper at your spouse or fall back into an addiction that you are trying to beat, I want to challenge you to be forgiveness-conscious and not sin-conscious. Come into God's presence every single time you fail and say:

> *Dear God, thank You that even right now, Your forgiveness and Your perfect love are raining all over me because of Your Son's finished work in my life. Take away every lingering sense of ugliness, guilt, and condemnation in me. I believe with all my heart that right now when You*

> *look at me, You see me in Christ Jesus. I am clothed in*
> *His robes of righteousness, favor, and blessings. Thank*
> *You for Your abundance of grace and Your gift of righ-*
> *teousness in my life. Through Jesus, I will reign in this life*
> *over every sin, addiction, and failure.*

My friend, every time you fail, there is fresh grace from Jesus to rescue you. Every time you fall short, confess your righteousness in Jesus by faith. I know you probably won't *feel* particularly righteous, and that is why you need to say it by faith.

> *Every time you fail, there is fresh grace from*
> *Jesus to rescue you.*

I have received so many testimonies of breakthroughs from people around the world who, even as they succumb to their addictions, would confess, "Even right now, I am the righteousness of God in Christ," and eventually found freedom from their bondages. It could be a smoking addiction or an alcohol or pornography addiction. Michael, a brother in Australia, happily shared, "I have just given up smoking by following what you've taught in your books and DVDs (about being conscious of and confessing my righteousness in Christ) whenever I was tempted to smoke. I have also been set free from twenty years of drug and alcohol abuse and am free of paranoid thoughts. I couldn't give them up through my own efforts, but through Christ I have."

The more these people confessed and saw themselves as righteous in Jesus, even in the midst of their failings, the more they came to see their true identity in Christ. The dead leaves began to fall, and they came to the place where they didn't have any desire to ever smoke another cigarette, drink another drop of alcohol, or visit another pornographic website. New leaves, new flowers, and new fruits unconsciously and effortlessly sprang up in their lives. Grace put an end to the barrenness and torment of winter and ushered in perpetual spring for them.

Beloved, if you are grappling with something right now, stop struggling and start receiving. Start receiving the abundance of the Lord's unmerited favor. Start receiving the free gift of His righteousness. Start receiving the cleansing power of His forgiveness. There is nothing for you to do but to soak it all up and to allow His resurrection power to drive out every symptom of death and decay in your circumstances and in your life. Jesus says to you today, "Now it shall spring forth; shall you not know it? I will even make a road in the wilderness and rivers in the desert" (Isa. 43:19).

> *If you are grappling with something right now, stop struggling and start receiving.*

Stop allowing the enemy to heap condemnation upon you in all the areas that you have fallen short. You are in Christ—completely accepted, irrevocably forgiven, and totally loved. Believe this and receive His forgiveness and love to overcome every sin. The time for your rejoicing is here, for your Savior has come to save you!

CHAPTER 9

EXPERIENCE FREEDOM FROM CONDEMNATION

She had struggled frantically when she was suddenly yanked from the bed and hauled into the streets by men from the temple. But she was no match for the rabble that had seized her, and her bare feet now struggled to find their footing as she was roughly shoved from all directions. Cold fear hammered deafeningly in her heart, almost drowning out the scornful taunts of the people drawn into the streets by the commotion.

She had sinned, and she knew what was coming. A few months earlier, she had witnessed a woman trying to crawl away as, one after another, heavy stones were violently hurled at her by the scornful mob called upon to execute God's justice. She still remembered how she had to choke back the bile that rose in her throat when she saw the mangled body of the bloodied woman after her executioners had finally dispersed. She never imagined that she would one day face the same fate. She had never set out to commit adultery. She knew that it was a mistake to meet him alone. It was a terrible mistake, and now it was too late. According to the Law of

Moses, capital punishment was the price for adultery. There was no escape.

Dragged into the temple precinct like a rag doll, she vaguely recognized the fragrance of the offerings being made on the bronze altar. Though she didn't understand the significance, the smell had always given her comfort as a child growing up in Jerusalem. Snatches of her father telling her that God would rain His blessings down upon their family as the smell of the sacrifice ascended to heaven flashed in her mind's eye, just before the mob of religious Pharisees abruptly stopped and threw her before the feet of a man they called Teacher.

She knew her trial had begun, that this man must be her chief executioner, the religious judge who would officially sentence her to death before they dragged her out of the city to be stoned. Shivering uncontrollably, she bowed her head and tried to cover her eyes with her hair as best as she could so that she could not see the clamoring crowd converging around her as they all awaited her sentence.

Then her merciless accusers fired the first salvo: "Teacher, this woman was caught in adultery, in the very act. Now Moses, in the law, commanded us that such should be stoned. But what do You say?" (John 8:4–5). Anticipating further humiliation, she braced herself for the condemning words of judgment that she was sure would come from the teacher.

But she heard nothing except a deafening silence. It was as if the teacher had not heard the accusatory charges read against her. Then, from the corner of her eye, she saw the teacher stooping down and writing with His finger on the ground. The Pharisees, poised with rocks in their hands and infuriated by this delay, demanded, "What do you say, teacher? Do we stone her now?"

The teacher stood up before them, and she heard a voice so resounding with majesty that her breath caught in her throat. Articulating each word with a perfect blend of authority and compassion, He declared, "He who is without sin among you, let him throw a stone at her first" (John 8:7). And then He stooped to the ground once more and resumed writing as though the leaders of the synagogue were not even there.

His words bewildered her. Who *was* this teacher? Why was He defending her, a sinful woman and an adulteress? Was *this* the man from the small village of Nazareth that everybody was talking about? The man who heals the blind and makes the lame walk again? The man whom they say hates legalism and loves sinners? Is this the man? *Who* is this man? As these questions whirled around in her frightened mind, she heard the sound of her salvation.

Thud.

Thud.

Thud.

The rocks that would have battered her to death fell impotent to the ground. One by one, the sandals of those who had dragged her to the temple turned and moved away. The crowds that had gathered also began to disperse, since it became clear that there would be no spectacle.

After some time, all she could see were the teacher's sandals. He lifted her head, and she saw His face for the first time. It was a face of compassion and love. A face that glowed with acceptance and assurance. She let her pent-up tears flow as He asked her, "Woman, where are those accusers of yours? Has no one condemned you?" (John 8:10). Throughout her ordeal, no one had spoken to her. *She* had not mattered. All that had mattered was that she had done the deed and that it warranted her death. But now her accusers had left, and the man who had rescued her was speaking to her and looking at her as if she *mattered*.

Gratefully, she breathed, "No one, Lord!" She knew beyond a doubt that this teacher was no ordinary teacher. That is why she addressed Him as "Lord" and not "teacher" like the Pharisees did. He *was* the Jesus everyone was talking about. Then she heard the words that she would never forget for the rest of her life: "Neither do I condemn you; go and sin no more" (John 8:11). As she made her way home, she recounted these words to herself over and over again, "Neither do I condemn you; go and sin no more." He had saved her life, and she knew that it would never be the same again.

The Power of No Condemnation

Jesus demonstrated something very important in the account of the woman caught in adultery. What enables someone to have the power to overcome sin? The threat of the law obviously didn't stop the woman from committing adultery. But receiving Jesus' acceptance—knowing that even though she deserved to be stoned to death, He did not condemn her—*that* gave her the power to "go and sin no more."

Let's take a step back to examine what Jesus did. Jesus saved the woman righteously. He didn't say, "Don't stone her. Show mercy to her." What He said was, "Let he who is without sin cast the first stone." And on their own accord, the Pharisees and religious mob all left one by one.

Notice how, after that, Jesus did not ask the woman, "Why did you sin?" No, what He asked was, "Where are those who accuse you? Has no one condemned you?" It seems as if Jesus was more preoccupied with the *condemnation* of the sin than the sin itself. He made sure that she walked away not feeling the condemnation and shame. Let's not reverse God's order. When God says something comes first, it must come first. What God puts first, man cannot put last. God says "no condemnation" comes first, and then you can "go and sin no more."

Christian religion has it in reverse. We say, "Go and sin no more first, then we won't condemn you." What we need to understand is that when there is no condemnation, people are empowered to live victorious lives, lives that glorify Jesus. This is where our empowerment comes from. Grace produces an effortless empowerment through the revelation of no condemnation. It is unmerited and completely undeserved. But we can receive it—this gift of no condemnation—because Jesus paid for it at the cross.

> *When there is no condemnation, people are empowered to live victorious lives.*

Truth be told, none of us could have cast the first stone at this woman. We have all sinned and fallen short. Our confidence today is not in our ability to keep God's laws perfectly, but in the only one, Jesus Christ, who is the fulfillment of the law itself. In Christ, we are all on equal ground. If a brother or sister gets tangled in sin, our place is not to judge them, but to restore them by pointing them to the forgiveness and gift of no condemnation that is found in Jesus.

The only person who is without sin and could have exercised judicial punishment on the woman was Jesus. Only He was qualified to cast the first stone, and He did not. Jesus was in the flesh to represent what was in God's heart. It wasn't judgment. His heart is unveiled in His grace and His forgiveness. I like to say it this way when describing what happened as the Pharisees waited to stone the woman: The Pharisees *would* if they *could*, but they could not. Jesus *could* if He *would*, but He would not. That's our Jesus!

The Law Cannot Condemn You Today

Interestingly, the Bible is silent on what Jesus wrote on the ground with His finger. But I believe that when He stooped down, He was writing the Law of Moses. I have been to Jerusalem many times. During one of my visits many years ago to the temple precinct where Jesus would have met this woman, the Lord opened my eyes to see that the floor of the temple precinct was made of hard stone. This means Jesus was not writing on dirt ground. He was writing with His finger on stone.

When Jesus wrote with His finger on the ground, He was writing on stone, not dirt ground.

Then, in a flash, I saw that Jesus was writing *the law* on stone. He was effectively saying to the Pharisees, "You presume to teach Me about the Law of Moses? I am He who wrote the law." Jesus wrote twice on the ground with His finger, thus completing the typology, as we know that God wrote the Ten Commandments with His finger twice.

The first set of the Ten Commandments was destroyed by Moses when he saw the Israelites worshiping the golden calf at the foot of Mount Sinai. God then wrote another set on stones and gave it to Moses for it to be placed under the mercy seat in the ark of the covenant. I had never heard anyone preach this before—it was a fresh revelation straight from heaven. I love it when the Lord opens my eyes to see His grace!

We are forgiven because He was judged. We are accepted because He was condemned!

Do you know why it's so exciting to know what Jesus wrote on the ground that day? It's so significant because it shows us that the very author of God's perfect law does *not* use the law to judge and condemn us today. And it's not because God simply decided to be merciful on us. No! It's because Jesus Himself fulfilled all the righteous requirements of the law on our behalf and took upon Himself every curse and stroke of punishment for our sins on His own body at the cross. We are forgiven because He was judged. We are accepted because He was condemned!

Forgiveness and Healing Go Hand in Hand

There is another reason we can rejoice in the knowledge that Jesus has borne the punishment that was due us: forgiveness and healing go hand in hand. The Bible says that He who never broke a single law of God "…was wounded for our transgressions, He was bruised for our iniquities; the chastisement for our peace was upon Him, and by His stripes we are healed" (Isa. 53:5). Do you see how healing and the price for our forgiveness are so closely intertwined in God's Word?

Many today are struggling to heal themselves from their sicknesses, diseases, mental dysfunctions, and addictions. I want to announce to you today that our part is to *receive* forgiveness from

Jesus and to believe that we are forgiven every single day. The more forgiveness-conscious we are, the more easily we will experience healing and liberty from every bodily ailment, mental oppression, and destructive habit.

One of my favorite psalms goes like this: "Bless the LORD, O my soul; and all that is within me, bless His holy name! Bless the LORD, O my soul, and forget not all His benefits: Who forgives all your iniquities, who heals all your diseases" (Ps. 103:1–3). Now which comes first? The consciousness that all your sins are forgiven precedes the healing of all your diseases!

And the operative word here is *all*. Some of us are comfortable with receiving partial forgiveness in certain areas of our lives. But we refuse to allow Jesus' forgiveness to touch some dark areas— areas that we can't let go of and that we can't forgive ourselves for. Whatever those mistakes may be, I encourage you to allow Jesus to forgive you of *all* your sins and receive healing for *all* your diseases. My friend, let the past go. Let the mistakes go. Allow yourself to be free, and learn to forgive yourself by receiving with an open heart Jesus' total and complete forgiveness.

Jesus further reinforced this correlation between forgiveness and healing in His encounter with the man paralyzed with palsy. It was obvious that the man's great need was to be healed in his body. Desiring his healing, his four friends had even removed the tiling of the roof and lowered him down on a stretcher to get him to Jesus. But what was Jesus' first statement to him? Jesus said, "Son, be of good cheer; your sins are forgiven you," before healing him by saying, "Arise, take up your bed, and go to your house" (Matt. 9:2,

6). Jesus knew that the man needed to receive forgiveness for all his sins before his body could experience total healing.

What are you paralyzed by today? Fear? An addiction to anti-depressants? Anxiety attacks? Perhaps it's some bodily sickness? Whatever your challenge, your answer is found in receiving a fresh revelation of just how much you are forgiven in Christ and believing that you are no longer under condemnation (see Romans 8:1)!

> *Your answer is found in receiving a fresh revelation of just how much you are forgiven in Christ and believing that you are no longer under condemnation.*

The Transforming Power of Believing the Gospel

I want to share with you a wonderful praise report from Pat, who lives in Ohio and wrote me this email:

> *Amazing changes in my life have started ever since I fed on the truths you taught. I now have a joy and appreciation for life that I never had since my teen years (and I am in my fifties). I have a permeating peace that manifests in every area of my life—from parenting to my finances to my health.*
>
> *Initially, when I started listening to you, I did not believe what you taught regarding holiness, fullness of*

blessings, and righteousness through faith in the finished work of Christ. When I got sick and bedridden, I continued to watch you as I was unable to do more. You supported your teachings with Scriptures and evidence from the Old Testament. I began to realize that what you were teaching was true. I began to read the Gospels and epistles with an enlightened mind and could clearly see that you were presenting the gospel.

Once I embraced these truths, my physical condition began to change. I had been suffering from a spinal cord and disc injury for which there was no cure. Spine specialists refused to operate on me unless I came to the stage when part of my body became paralyzed, which is the usual course of events. I had been in a state of pain and was physically incapacitated for more than two years.

Since feeding on your teachings, I have regained use of my body and most of the previously excruciating pain has subsided. Now I am able to relax and be confident and trust in the willingness and availability of the power and grace of God to heal me. This came as a result of increased faith, the elimination of condemnation, an understanding of the Holy Communion, and an increased awareness of God's love for me.

I have also been freed from a ten-year habit of smoking cigarettes. I used to only smoke at night just before going to bed in order to calm my nerves. I tried for years to break the habit but could not. I always felt so guilty for having such a weakness. But once I realized that God did not hold my weakness against me and that He accepted me unconditionally and would still bless me, I let go of all the worry and struggle over my habit. I began to experience peace and rest.

A few months later, I was able to quit smoking. It's as if the habit was effortlessly removed from my life, like it just dropped off me. I know that it was the Spirit of God working in me to perfect me and give me the power to no longer crave for cigarettes.

Truly, my life has been transformed. The gospel is what this world is hungry for and much in need of. I have been a believer for more than twenty-five years and have never heard it presented the way you teach it. Thank you for everything. Keep awakening the world to the love and grace of God, as well as the hope of salvation, blessing, and glory in Christ Jesus!

Only Receive

Dear reader, you too can experience this victory. It's time to stop hurting yourself. Jesus was hurt for all your sins. It's time to stop beating yourself. Jesus has taken all your beatings at the cross. It's time to stop cutting and punishing yourself because Jesus has received all the cutting and punishment on your behalf. It's time to stop asking yourself if you have done enough to earn God's forgiveness and acceptance. His forgiveness and grace are undeserved—they cannot be achieved; they can only be received. Have you ever given loved ones a gift for Christmas or for their birthday? All you want them to do is to take it from you and enjoy it. That's exactly how God wants you to receive His love and gift of no condemnation today.

> *Stop asking yourself if you have done enough to earn God's forgiveness and acceptance. His forgiveness and grace cannot be achieved; they can only be received.*

Look to the cross today and say:

> *Thank You, Jesus, for loving me. Today I receive Your complete forgiveness in my life, and I forgive myself for all my sins, mistakes, and failings. I release them all into Your loving hands. I declare that in You, I am completely forgiven, free, accepted, favored, righteous, blessed, and healed from every sickness and disease. Amen!*

The more you let the waterfall of God's forgiveness and unmerited favor wash over you like this every day, the more you'll receive His health for your body and soundness for your mind. Whatever may have happened in the past, and whatever may be staring you in the face now, I encourage you to remember and believe that God loves you and has forgiven you. Now begin to enjoy His love and let His grace work in you and for you, to bring you to a place of greater health, emotional strength, peace, and enjoyment in life.

PART FOUR

WIN THE BATTLE FOR YOUR MIND

CHAPTER 10

WIN THE BATTLE FOR YOUR MIND

I trust that you have been enjoying this journey of discovering the power of right believing. We have looked at how vital it is to believe in God's love for you and talked about the importance of seeing what He sees. We have also explored the impact of being forgiveness-conscious as opposed to being perpetually guilt-conscious.

Now that you are midway through this book, I want you to be aware that as you begin practicing some of the keys that we have been discussing, you'll experience some battles in your mind that will challenge your beliefs. Be encouraged to know that you don't have to be afraid of these battles. I will show you in the following chapters how to win the battle for your mind through right believing. My friend, the battle is not without (in your external circumstances), it is within. It is fought and won in the battlefield of your beliefs and thoughts.

Wrong beliefs and thoughts will keep you defeated.

Right beliefs and thoughts will launch you toward your breakthrough.

That is why Jesus said, "And you shall know the truth, and the truth shall make you free" (John 8:32). Truth sitting on your coffee table doesn't set you free. Truth lodged comfortably on your bookshelf doesn't set you free. You may have a copy of the Holy Bible sitting stately in your impressive custom-built mahogany library, but it will not set you free.

It is the truth that you *know* and *believe* that has the power to set you free. That is what this book is all about. It is about imparting to you truths from God's Word to shape your believing. The more your believing becomes aligned with the truth of His Word, the more you will experience His freedom, grace, favor, forgiveness, and blessings.

> *Wrong beliefs and thoughts will keep you defeated.*
> *Right beliefs and thoughts will launch you toward*
> *your breakthrough.*

There are many people who are actually living in defeat and bondage today even though they may not be aware that they are living in bondage to anything. In some ways they have grown accustomed to their bondages. Let me explain this further. Are there areas that you are now feeling fearful and anxious about? The very areas you are fearful and anxious about indicate the presence of wrong beliefs in your life that God wants you to be freed from. Replace those wrong beliefs with right beliefs based on God's Word, and you will eradicate those fears and anxieties. Right believing is the key that unlocks the treasures of God in your life. You see, the grace, favor, blessings, and forgiveness have always been there, but when you begin to believe right, you begin to *access* the fullness of His love and finished work on Calvary's hill. Every benefit of the finished work is already yours. It already belongs to you. Jesus has already paid the price. The hindrance then between you and your victory is your wrong beliefs. The battle has to do with your beliefs. This is why when you start believing right, you will step into your breakthrough.

> *It is the truth that you know and believe that has the power to set you free.*

The Enemy's Strategy

The enemy knows that if he can control your thought life, he can manipulate your emotions and feelings. For instance, if he can make you entertain thoughts of guilt, failure, and defeat, you will begin to feel lousy about yourself, physically weak, and even depressed.

Our emotions are flags that indicate to us what our thoughts are. Thank God for emotions. They tell us if something is terribly wrong with our thoughts. Many of us are not cognizant when our thinking slides down a slippery slope to fear, doubt, pessimism, and anxiety. However, God has designed us in such a way that we can quickly recognize our thinking through our emotions.

Try this: whenever you begin to sense negative emotions like fear, worry, guilt, and anger, stop and ask yourself, "What am I thinking?"

Your emotions follow quickly at the heels of your thoughts. If your thoughts are negative, you will naturally produce negative emotions. Conversely, if your thoughts are positive in Christ, you will produce positive emotions.

That is why there is a battle for your mind. The devil wants to keep your thoughts negative so that he can keep you defeated. He is a master of mind games, and he doesn't play fair. When he first tempted Adam and Eve in the garden, he made them doubt God's motives by lying to them and insinuating that God was deliberately withholding something good from them. He made God appear stingy, when in reality God was protecting them. The devil's strategy hasn't changed—he is still using lies, accusations, guilt, and condemnation to ensnare believers today and to make them doubt God's perfect love, forgiveness, and superabounding grace.

Many years ago, when I was fairly new in the ministry, together with another pastor, I prayed for a lady who was oppressed by the devil. She was not a believer. While we were praying for her, all of a sudden the woman growled menacingly in a deep male voice, "*I want her mind!*" Whoa! It was the first time I had prayed for a demon-possessed person and the demon actually spoke back! I remember it vividly till this day. Well, we prayed for her and cast the demon out of her.

Now, please don't worry, as a believer in Jesus, you can *never* be possessed by the devil. He can oppress you mentally. But he can never possess you. I shared my experience with this woman to unveil to you the enemy's strategy. He wants your mind! He wants to keep your mind negative, oppressed, depressed, and pessimistic. He wants you to remain in wrong belief, knowing that as long as you continue to believe wrong, you will continue to live wrong. There is a battle for your mind, and we win it through the power of right believing.

> *There is a battle for your mind, and we win it through the power of right believing.*

Jesus Is Greater

It is important that you be established in this truth. You don't have to be afraid of the devil because "He who is in you is greater than he who is in the world" (1 John 4:4). Jesus, who is in you, is greater than the devil in this world. No matter what the enemy's evil tactics are, he will not prevail against you in this battle. The devil is a defeated foe. Greater is He who is in you than all the negative thoughts the enemy can throw at you. Greater is He who is in you than the feelings of guilt and inadequacy. Greater is He who is in you than every accusation that is leveled against you.

Stand strong on this declaration: "No weapon formed against you shall prosper, and every tongue which rises against you in judgment you shall condemn" (Isa. 54:17). Wow! No weapon formed against you shall prosper. The Bible doesn't say that you will not experience any challenges or be faced with any attacks. But it does promise that when trials come, you can be confident in the certainty that they shall not prosper against you.

Do you know why you can stand firm on this promise today? In the very same verse, God goes on to declare that "This is the heritage of the servants of the LORD, and their righteousness is from Me" (Isa. 54:17). This protection is your heritage. God does not protect you because of your right doing; He protects you because your righteousness is from the Lord Himself!

Notice that the weapon against you could have *already been formed*, which means that a weapon may already have been conceived, prepared, and aimed at you. Don't be afraid. Whatever this challenge or weapon may be, know beyond any doubt that it shall not prevail against you. This is God's promise to you today—*no weapon formed against you shall prosper.* Not because your behavior is perfect, but because your standing in Christ is perfect. Your victory is firmly secured through Jesus' finished work, which is your heritage in Christ.

Pulling Down Strongholds

As you meditate on Bible promises that proclaim God's truth over your life, you are already beginning to win the battle for your mind. It's not a coincidence that Jesus was crucified on Golgotha, which actually means "Place of a Skull" (Matt. 27:33). Your breakthrough has to begin in your mind first. The Word of God tells us:

> *For though we walk in the flesh, we do not war accord-*
> *ing to the flesh. For the weapons of our warfare are not*
> *carnal but mighty in God for pulling down strongholds.*
> —2 Corinthians 10:3–4

This battle for your mind is not waged externally. Our weapons are not physical or tangible. Our weapons in this battle are not nuclear warheads, machine guns, or grenades. Our weapons are the weapons of right believing, and they are mighty in God for pulling down strongholds that have kept us bound. Strongholds cannot be destroyed with physical weapons; they can only be utterly torn down by rightly believing in the truth of God's Word.

> *Strongholds cannot be destroyed with physical weapons; they*
> *can only be utterly torn down by rightly believing in the truth*
> *of God's Word.*

The devil can only sow wrong thoughts in your mind, but he cannot control what you believe! When you start to believe right, every lie and wrong thought will melt away like butter on a hot, sunny day. Lies can imprison and defeat you only to the degree that you don't allow God's truth to come into your situation to liberate you. Listen closely to what Jesus said: "If you abide in My word, you are My disciples indeed. And you shall know the truth, and the truth shall make you free" (John 8:31–32). What this means is that whatever stronghold you are trapped in today, truth from Jesus will set you free!

Strongholds are wrong thoughts and lies that have been perpetuated in your mind over weeks, months, or even years. These entrenched wrong beliefs cause you to live in bondage to addictions and in a state of fear, guilt, anxiety, or chronic depression.

God's Word tells us in no uncertain terms that the warfare takes place in our minds and is won by us "pulling down strongholds, casting down arguments and every high thing that exalts itself against the knowledge of God, bringing every thought into captivity to the obedience of Christ" (2 Cor. 10:4–5). There is a battle for your mind, and the place where the enemy launches his attacks against you is in your thoughts and imagination. I believe that once you are aware that there is a war for your mind, and that it is between wrong beliefs and right beliefs, you have already won half the battle!

> *There is a battle for your mind, and the place where the enemy launches his attacks against you is in your thoughts and imagination.*

Anchor Your Identity in Christ

The Bible makes it clear that there is such a thing as spiritual warfare in our minds, and it is vital for you as a believer to understand this. Otherwise you will think every thought that crosses your mind comes only from you. You will then begin to believe those lies, not knowing that the enemy has planted those lies to confuse you.

Several years ago, I preached a message on how the devil sometimes uses the first-person pronoun to plant thoughts in our heads to deceive us. For example, he doesn't say, "You have an eating disorder," or "You have an addiction in this area." The devil uses the first-person pronoun to sow thoughts like these in your mind: "*I* have an eating disorder," or "*I* am addicted to pornography," or "*I* am a pervert." Notice how insidious and sly the crafty serpent is? He makes you think that you are thinking those thoughts of defeat. He wants you to believe that is who you are.

Upon hearing this message, a man who had been trapped in a destructive addiction for many years wrote a letter to me. Walter shared that this strategy of the devil using the first-person pronoun kept resounding on the inside of him after listening to my message. He went home after church, locked himself in his room, and for the first time declared out loud, "I am not an addict!" He just chose to reject this evil mind-set in the name of Jesus, and then he related this: "At that very moment, I felt something powerful happen inside me. I don't know how to describe this. It was as if life became spectacular because of the love of God, and I couldn't contain the feeling."

After making that confession out loud, Walter said, "My addiction stopped. I just lost all interest, and I don't feel even a little bit tempted. All the wrong desires are gone, and best of all, I know I love Jesus more than ever before and I can't live without Him. I am renewed. I am reborn. I know that everything is in His control, and I am blessed and forgiven."

Wow! What an amazing testimony of God's power and goodness in this brother's life. With just one declaration, he broke the mental stronghold that the devil had placed him under for many years. That is truly the power of right believing. If you can change what you believe, you can change your life, just like this brother did.

Are there lies about your identity that you believe in today?

Break the power of those lies by declaring your identity in Christ. Say out loud, "I am a child of God. I am healed, forgiven, righteous, and holy in Christ Jesus." Instead of believing the devil's lies when he uses the first-person pronoun strategy against you, speak your true identity in Jesus.

Bringing Every Thought into Captivity

Unfortunately, unbeknownst to many believers today, the enemy has launched malicious disinformation campaigns that have effectively enslaved them for years to low self-esteem, self-hatred, guilt, eating disorders, perversions, inordinate fears, and all kinds of crazy habits and addictions. And that is why I'm writing this book—to expose the enemy's lies and to help you see with pristine clarity the enemy's deceptive and manipulative tactics. These lies will collapse like a house of cards the second you see your true identity in Christ.

The weapons of this warfare are not natural and physical. Your weapons are found in the truth of God's Word, and they are mighty and have the power to overthrow and destroy every stronghold that has been built up through disinformation and wrong believing. And the way we can destroy these strongholds in our mind is by "bringing every thought into captivity to the obedience of Christ" (2 Cor. 10:5).

When I was a young believer, I was taught that it was my responsibility to bring my every thought into obedience *to* Christ. I tried and struggled with that for years and ended up with more mental oppression, stress, and guilt than I had started with. No one can bring every thought that crosses his or her mind to perfectly obey Christ.

One day God opened my eyes to see what He was really saying in that verse. He said to me, "Son, keep your focus and your thoughts always on the obedience *of* Christ, and that will be a powerful weapon to pull down the devil's strongholds in your mind." When He said that to me, it felt like the lights were suddenly switched on in my head.

If the way to destroy mental strongholds is dependent on your being able to perfectly capture every thought that crosses your mind and making it perfectly obedient to Christ, then that is a recipe for certain failure. Legalistic teachings always place the demand on man. Grace teachings always demonstrate how the supply comes from God. The law focuses on what man needs to do. Grace focuses on what Jesus has done and is still doing in our lives. You can apply this principle to test any teaching that you have received.

So what does it mean to capture every thought to the obedience *of* Christ? Let's look at what the Word of God says about the obedience of Christ and allow Scripture to interpret Scripture. The Word tells us that, "For as by one man's disobedience many were made sinners, so also by one Man's obedience many will be made righteous" (Rom. 5:19). What this means is that through one man's (Adam's) disobedience, we were all made sinners. But through Jesus Christ's (one Man's) obedience at the cross, we were all made forever righteous the moment we believed in Him. God wants you to focus on the obedience of Jesus and not on the disobedience of Adam. Adam's disobedience makes you sin- and judgment-conscious, whereas Jesus' obedience at the cross makes you forgiveness- and righteousness-conscious!

Does that mean that there is no obedience on our part? Absolutely not! The more you believe that your righteousness comes from Jesus' obedience and not by your own efforts, the more you will live a life of obedience unconsciously. People say that those who preach grace don't preach on obedience. What they don't realize is that under the old covenant of law, obedience was the root of all God's blessings. But under the new covenant of grace, God blesses us first, and obedience is the fruit.

> *The more you believe that your righteousness comes from Jesus' obedience and not by your own efforts, the more you will live a life of obedience unconsciously.*

Our obedience today under the new covenant begins with choosing to *believe* that we are made righteous by *Christ's obedience* at the cross. It is not this legalistic obedience to the law that many people are trying to bring back into the church. The apostle Paul describes our obedience as "obedience to the faith" (Rom. 16:26)—believing right about what Jesus has done to make us righteous. And when we believe right like this, we will find His grace motivating and empowering us to think and live right.

We've all heard many sermons on right living, but you know what? I hear pastors lamenting that there is still little right living in the pews. My personal belief is that it's not because believers want to be bad. They aren't living the way they should because their belief systems have not really changed. God's Word tells us, "The just [righteous] shall live by faith" (Rom. 1:17). You can say it like this: the righteous shall live by right believing. When you have right believing, you release the power of God to live right. When you believe the gospel, the true gospel that says you are righteous through Jesus' obedience (see Rom. 5:19), you will have right living. The right results will follow.

My friend, when it comes to obedience, there's certainly been a change because of the cross of Jesus. Under the old covenant of law, you had to obey before God blessed you. But under grace, God blesses you first, and then obedience is the fruit. The more you believe right that you have been made righteous and blessed through Christ's obedience, the more you will see the fruit of obedience in your life. Wow! Praise Jesus for His marvelous grace!

The Enemy Doesn't Play Fair

The enemy can only make inroads in your life when he successfully points you to your obedience or lack of it to determine your standing with God. He will use disinformation to make you feel rotten, dirty, and filthy, even though in Christ you are already completely righteous. Don't forget, the devil doesn't play fair.

Over the years, I've noticed that another one of the enemy's strategies involves him sowing a bad thought in your mind, then quickly turning around to condemn you for that very thought he planted. He'll say, "What kind of dirty, rotten person are you? How can you think that thought? You are disgusting!" He will accuse you, condemn you, and disparage you and keep pointing out areas where you have failed.

Even when you do right, it's never enough. If you read a chapter of the Bible, he will point you to someone else who read two chapters. He is a constant faultfinder. If you made a mistake, he will keep harping on your disobedience. If the devil can succeed in making you focus on your obedience or your lack of it instead of on Jesus' obedience, he'll succeed at all his mind games with you. That is why when you focus on *your* disobedience in your thought life, you will be discouraged, crushed, and oppressed.

So how should you respond when negative or even evil thoughts cross your mind? First of all, you need to know that those thoughts are not you; the real you is born again in Christ Jesus, a new creation believer! When bad thoughts come, focus on your true identity and who you really are in Christ by thinking about the cross of Jesus. Focus on His perfect obedience and how His obedience at Calvary makes you righteous, whole, favored, and complete. That is what it means to bring every thought into captivity to the obedience of Christ.

Focus on Jesus' Obedience

Scott, a brother from Florida, wrote to my team to share this very encouraging testimony:

I was born and raised in the church and have been a Christian all my life. However, I struggled to follow the law as that was what I had been taught, and I was always afraid to disappoint God.

The more I tried to be a "good Christian," the guiltier I felt! I struggled with pornography and would look at adult websites twice a day. Short of destroying my computer, I had tried everything under the sun to break this habit, but had always fought a losing battle. As a result, I withdrew from church altogether because I felt guilty, shameful, and worthless.

One day my aunt introduced me to Pastor Prince's teachings. His message was not on the law, but was filled with the missing ingredient—Jesus Christ! Everything that Pastor Prince taught resonated within me like a musical note in perfect tune. By grace, my relationship with Christ has been transformed, and I no longer carry that unimaginable burden of guilt and shame. Instead I feel joyful all the time! I also can't stop telling my friends about how this has transformed Christianity for me.

Miraculously, ever since my focus has been on Jesus, and not on my struggle, I have not looked at any pornographic material! Whenever I struggle with lust today, I keep my eyes on Jesus' unconditional forgiveness and feel joy instead of guilt. Jesus has cleansed me from my addiction, and I am amazed!

Thank you, Pastor Prince, for bringing new life and joy into my walk with the Lord. I feel transformed, joyful, blessed, and so much more! Praise God!

As I was reading this letter, I was especially moved when Scott shared how the missing ingredient is Jesus Christ! Once he began to believe right about Jesus, once he began to focus on Jesus' obedience and not on his own disobedience, he experienced his tremendous breakthrough!

My friend, there is a real battle for your mind. Many people succumb to it almost immediately when they have a sinful thought and then begin to feel guilty and condemned for having those sinful thoughts. Thoughts are triggers for your emotions. The enemy knows that if he can get you to believe those wrong thoughts of defeat, anxiety, greed, envy, and lust, then he can push your emotions toward feelings of guilt, fear, and condemnation. When you succumb to those self-destructive, toxic emotions, he can draw you in even further and tempt you to act out those sinful thoughts.

Thoughts are triggers for your emotions.

I pray that today you will be able to see that through the power of right believing, you can victoriously break out of this vicious cycle of defeat. The next time you have negative thoughts, catch yourself and look toward the obedience of Christ. See the cross. See Jesus. See Him washing your mind with His precious blood.

Beloved, your new righteous identity is found in Christ Jesus. And as He is, so are you in this world!

CHAPTER 11

VICTORY OVER THE ENEMY'S MIND GAMES

Several years before my television ministry began broadcasting in America, I received a letter from Max, a United States Navy personnel, who had passed through Singapore and had a life-transforming encounter with the gospel of grace. It contained a beautiful story best told in his own words:

> Pastor Prince, it has been my desire to write to you for some time now to share what God has done in my life through my experience in Singapore. I cannot tell you how thankful I am to God that I was miraculously led to your church.
>
> I attend the US Naval Academy and will be commissioned in four months as an officer in the US Marine Corps. I have been a Christian for about three years, but for well over a year, I was in heavy bondage. Like you, I was convinced that I had committed the unpardonable sin. To me, grace was a bad thing. I knew that I deserved to go to hell under the Old Testament, and because Jesus had come and I still sinned, I felt that I deserved hell all

the more. So in my heart, I wished that Jesus had never come. To make a long story short, I got desperate. I was willing to do anything to find peace with God.

Unfortunately, I did not realize that my focusing on doing more for God would only lead me farther away from the peace that I so desperately desired. Before long, I became very judgmental. I cut myself off from my Christian friends and even convinced a few that they were on the road to hell with me. I cannot tell you the hopelessness and misery I felt that year. In a journal entry on the night of April 18, 2001, I wrote, "What would I not pay for someone to show me the way to the Lord, not to a religion but to the living God." Little did I know at that time that God was preparing my heart, for fifteen pages later in the same journal, I would write words of hope and joy.

Well, the end of my junior year came around, and I received orders to catch a submarine out to Thailand. The day before I left, I was told that we would no longer be going to Thailand but rather to Singapore. The first four days after my arrival in Singapore were spent doing touristy things. One night I went out with all of the officers to a bar. The bar was especially distasteful, and I left early with a friend.

On my walk back to the hotel, I prayed to the Lord desperately for some fellowship. I said good-bye to my friend and continued walking down the busy street. Then, to my amazement, I heard a man ask me, "Are you looking for a church?" Of course I said yes to this man who turned out to be a member of your church. He gave me his home phone number and the directions to the church. He told me there was a Bible study service the following day. We only talked for about a minute before we both went our separate ways.

I am thankful that I managed to attend the Friday night Bible study service. I was still really judgmental so I was questioning everything, but the message that I heard was like nothing I had ever heard before. Then on Sunday, I attended the service at your church again and even ordered thirteen of your tapes. Like I said earlier, I was willing to try anything to find God, although I didn't really think these tapes were going to have an impact on me. I left that day on the submarine, and I listened to Winning the Battle of Your Mind *about eight times in a row.*

My life has never been the same. I listened to the other tapes and caught my first glimpse of God's grace. When I returned to the US after only three weeks on the sub, my mom could see a huge change in my attitude. Where there was once depression, there was joy. Where there was once a judgmental attitude, there was love. When I returned to the academy in August, I gave those tapes to the friends whom I had convinced were going to hell with me. The next time I saw them, they were full of joy!

My hope and desire is that this email encourages you. I pray that some day God can use me to take this message of His to the churches of America and the Marine Corps. I appreciate any prayers you could say for me.

I pray that some day I would be able to visit Singapore and your church again. I know Marines are supposed to be tough, but my desire to fellowship with you and your church is so great that it almost brings me to tears sometimes. I look forward to listening to new tapes some day. May God's grace and peace be with you and your family.

Max's story doesn't end here. Interestingly, two years after I received his email, one of the naval officers that he had given my tapes to actually wrote us to tell us how his own life had also been amazingly changed by the messages. As Robby told us his story, he mentioned Max—how two years after his trip to Singapore, he'd become a well-respected officer in jet pilot training and a man who stood out among his peers. The love and grace of God that had liberated him had also transformed him into someone that (in Robby's words) "had so much of God's love and joy in him that people just wanted to be around him."

What an awesome testimony of God's grace! I remember being so encouraged by what the Lord had done for Max when I first received his email some twelve years ago. Back then in 2002, God was beginning to show me how the gospel of grace needed to go beyond the four walls of our local church in Singapore. And about five years later, God opened the doors for us, and we began our first television broadcast in America in April 2007. Today we are broadcasting in more than two hundred countries across more than sixty television networks worldwide and are reaching millions with the gospel of grace. There is now a grace revolution sweeping across the globe!

Every day we are being contacted by precious people like Max, who write in to share how their lives have been utterly transformed as they began to believe right in the person of Jesus. Whenever Wendy and I read the emails and letters that we receive from the ministry team, we feel so deeply humbled and grateful to Jesus for everything that He has done and continues to do in these lives.

I believe with all my heart that you are next in line. Whatever you are in need of—a breakthrough, miracle, healing, restoration, or deliverance—is just around the corner. You may not even be conscious of it, but God has already begun a work in you and He will surely complete it in your life.

> *Whatever you are in need of—a breakthrough, miracle, healing, restoration, or deliverance—is just around the corner.*

There are so many powerful truths in *Winning the Battle of Your Mind,* the message that Max listened to eight times in a row when he was in the submarine. I would really like to bless you with this message. Books are powerful, but there is something special about listening to the preached Word. If you are interested, please log on to josephprince.com/power to download the free audio message. I believe that this resource will help you to receive a fresh impartation to win the battle for your mind.

The Enemy's Mind Games

The devil loves to play mind games. When I was a young, impressionable believer, I was taught erroneously that a Christian could commit what has become known as "the unpardonable sin" when he blasphemes against the Holy Spirit. Just the thought that I could commit this sin put me under severe oppression. That one thought opened up all kinds of terrible experiences in my life.

I was really worried that I had already committed the unpardonable sin and was on a one-way ticket to hell. The more I tried not to, the more I would have all kinds of blasphemous thoughts about the Holy Spirit when I prayed and even when I was earnestly worshiping God. It was a harrowing experience, with the devil relentlessly oppressing and attacking my mind with all kinds of evil thoughts.

So what is the "unpardonable sin"?

The unpardonable sin is simply the sin of an unbeliever continually rejecting Jesus as his or her Savior. By not accepting God's free gift of salvation, he or she is saying, "I don't need Jesus. I can very well save myself." This was what the self-righteous Pharisees were doing in Jesus' day, right in His presence. Despite all the amazing miracles of grace that He performed by the power of the Holy Spirit, they stubbornly refused to believe that He was the Messiah. They even had the audacity to say that His power and authority came from an evil spirit (see Matt. 12:24)!

My friend, it's therefore impossible for you as a believer to commit this sin because you have *already* received Jesus as your Savior. Furthermore, there is absolutely no sin that His blood has not already cleansed you of. Every sin of yours has been forgiven and pardoned through His finished work at the cross. It's an immaculate work. Jesus did not miss a single sin.

That's why the apostle Paul, who wrote two-thirds of the New Testament, never mentioned the "unpardonable sin" in any of his epistles to the churches. Don't you think that if Christians could commit this sin and lose their salvation, Paul would have at least mentioned it once?

Unfortunately, no one taught me about God's grace then, and I lived under this dark cloud of mental oppression for more than a year. Can you imagine that—just one thought kept me in bondage for such a long time! And it was through that traumatizing experience that I learned about the devil's mind games.

As I shared in the previous chapter, the devil knows how to use the personal pronoun to deceive you. Instead of blatantly telling me, "You have committed the unpardonable sin," I kept hearing in my mind, "*I* have committed the unpardonable sin." And because I believed wrongly that a believer could commit this sin, it reinforced the devil's lies in my head. I would constantly hear thoughts like, "*I* have blasphemed the Holy Spirit," and "*I* have committed the sin for which there is no forgiveness," and "*I* have failed and disappointed God." The enemy would always drop in the pronoun "I" even though all this while, it was he who was planting these wrong imaginations and sliding these blasphemous thoughts into my head.

I would be praying to God, and these wrong, sometimes vulgar, thoughts would come in, and my response then typically was, "Oh my goodness! What is wrong with me? I am a Christian— I shouldn't be thinking these kinds of thoughts!" At other times, the devil would knock me on the head with accusations like, "How can you think these thoughts?" or "What kind of sick person are you?" or "How can you think such nasty thoughts against that person and still call yourself a Christian?"

Have you experienced this before? The enemy is an expert at

throwing thoughts into your mind and then backing off and coming at you as a legalist to knock you on the head with the very thoughts that he first put in your head.

Winning the Battle

The key to winning the battle for your mind is to learn how to separate yourself from the evil thoughts planted by the enemy. Those thoughts are not yours! You are not responsible for those thoughts any more than you are responsible for any profanity spoken by someone who happens to be in your presence.

> *The key to winning the battle for your mind is to learn how to separate yourself from the evil thoughts planted by the enemy.*

In the same way, whenever the devil sows wrong thoughts in your mind, your part is to know that those evil or impure thoughts are not from you. Disregard them with a firm belief in your heart that the thoughts are not from you. Believe beyond a shadow of a doubt that you are the righteousness of God, and just ignore those thoughts like you would ignore a person who is spouting profanity in your presence. Don't give those thoughts any weight.

My mental oppression lasted for a year because I always felt that I had to do something about it. Have you been there before, where you felt like you just *had to* do something? Well, I felt responsible for those thoughts in my head, and the moment I believed those horrible thoughts were mine, the devil got me right where he wanted me—defeated, guilty, and feeling condemned. *Every major bondage begins in the mind.*

God's Word tells us, "Resist the devil and he will flee from you" (James 4:7). Do you know what the highest form of resistance is? It's to simply *ignore* the thoughts of the devil! Ladies understand this well. They know that the best way to resist a guy is to simply ignore him. Imagine a lady walking by a construction site where all the men start making catcalls at her. A cool lady will simply walk on by, ignoring their catcalls. She knows better than to respond to these guys by barking at them to stop.

As for me, when I was trapped in mental oppression, I would rebuke the devil every time a bad thought floated through my mind. As you can imagine, I ended up rebuking the devil *all the time*. At the end of the day, I was more focused on and conscious of the devil than of God! God doesn't want you devil-conscious; He wants you Jesus-conscious. You win the battle for your mind by simply ignoring the enemy. Don't feel that you need to do something about those thoughts. When the devil suggests things to your mind, just ignore him. Spiritual warfare doesn't have to be combative. It can be restful, peaceful, simple, and easy. It's all about seeing Jesus' finished work.

You win the battle for your mind by ignoring the enemy.

The Answer Is Simple

Many years after my experience with mental oppression—in fact, after I was already preaching the gospel of grace—I came across the autobiography of John Bunyan. As I read it, I discovered that he—this well-respected seventeenth-century English preacher who wrote the best-selling book *The Pilgrim's Progress*—had gone through a very similar experience with mental torment where he also found his mind constantly plagued by blasphemous thoughts against God.

In that autobiography, *Grace Abounding to the Chief of Sinners*, Bunyan shared how during that terrible season "all my comfort was taken from me; then darkness seized upon me; after which, whole floods of blasphemies, both against God, Christ, and the Scriptures, was poured upon my spirit, to my great confusion and astonishment...I often found my mind suddenly put upon it to curse and swear, or to speak some grievous thing against God, or Christ his Son, and of the Scriptures."[1]

When I read that, I was astounded but also greatly encouraged that someone like John Bunyan had gone through the same thing I did.

But even more significant for me was how freedom and victory finally came to him. One day while Bunyan was passing through a field, still having thoughts and fears that he wasn't right with God, "suddenly," he said, "this sentence fell upon my soul, Thy righteousness is in heaven." He went on to say, "I saw, with the eyes of my soul, Jesus Christ at God's right hand; there, I say, was my righteousness; so that wherever I was, or whatever I was doing, God could not say of me, He wants my righteousness, for that was just before him. I also saw, moreover, that it was not my good frame of heart that made my righteousness better, nor yet my bad frame that made my righteousness worse; for my righteousness was Jesus Christ himself, 'the same yesterday, and today, and forever.'"[2]

How do you win this battle for your mind? My friend, the answer is found in the person of Jesus. He is your righteousness. Your righteousness is a person. He is in heaven and He can never be removed, no matter what you have or have not done. Your righteousness is Jesus Christ Himself, and He is the same yesterday, today, and forever (see Heb. 13:8)!

So don't be deceived any longer. The apostle Paul says, "I fear, lest somehow, as the serpent deceived Eve by his craftiness, so your minds may be corrupted from the simplicity that is in Christ" (2 Cor. 11:3). The gospel is simple. It's all about Jesus. It's not about you. Christ is our righteousness. Christ is our obedience. Christ is our sanctification. Christ is our justification. Glory and boast in Christ and Christ alone. The enemy will try to make it all about you. Keep it simple. Unlike Eve, don't be deceived by his craftiness. Ignore him and simply focus on the simplicity that is in Christ.

Change Your Mind

The word "repentance" in the New Testament is the Greek word *metanoia*, which simply means "a change of mind."[3] *Meta* means "change" and *noia* refers to your mind. There are religious folks who have this idea that repentance means groveling in dirt and condemning themselves until they feel they have sufficiently earned God's forgiveness through their contrition.

My question is, how condemned and sorrowful do they need

to be before they have genuinely "repented"? And after they have "repented," should they fail again in the same area, does it mean that they did not really "repent" completely the first time round? I do not for one moment doubt the sincerity of people who believe in "repentance" this way. However, you can be sincere in your intent but still be sincerely wrong when repentance is not based on right believing that leads to inward heart transformation.

What I am saying is that you can beat your breast sorrowfully, put on sackcloth and ashes, cry your eyeballs out at the altar, and still go home unchanged. Sorrow doesn't equal transformation. It is right believing that brings about true repentance (change of mind) and hence genuine transformation. It is impossible to truly repent the Bible way—to experience Jesus, His love, His grace, and His power and to allow Him to change your mind and your belief system—and still remain the same.

> *It is right believing that brings about true repentance (change of mind) and hence genuine transformation.*

Can you see how man-centered teachings on contrition and repentance can sound so good, but in reality trap people in a permanent cycle of defeat and hypocrisy? Let me tell you this: if you are a born-again believer and you made a mistake or failed, nobody needs to teach you to be sorrowful. As a new creation in Christ, you already hate the sin and the wrongdoing. It vexes your soul, and there is a groaning for freedom. The truth is, you are looking for a way out of your bondage. The repentance you need—the change of mind you need—is to know that God has already forgiven you.

Stop condemning yourself and walk in His righteous identity to new levels of victory over sin.

Now that you understand what Bible repentance is, let's apply it to winning the battle for your mind. When wrong thoughts come into your head, the repentance or change of mind that you need is to know that those thoughts don't belong to you. Repentance in this situation is not about beating yourself up over those thoughts. I used to do that and it only left me more oppressed and defeated. No, give them no room to flourish by ignoring them while you continue to be established and secure in your identity in Christ. Fill your mind with His thoughts, His living Word, His peace, His joy, and His love.

And that is why every time you hear preaching or read books that are Jesus-centered and not man-centered, repentance is happening. Anointed Jesus-filled messages and resources set you free from wrong thinking and calibrate your believing and thinking so that your beliefs and thoughts can be in line with God's Word. And by now, you should know that right believing and right thinking always produce right results in your life.

> *Right believing and right thinking always produce right results in your life.*

How God Assesses Your Thoughts

We have talked about the breastplate of the high priest and how the Lord depicts us as precious gems close to His heart in chapter 6.

Here, I want to unveil to you the significance of another item the high priest wears—the gold plate that is around his forehead.

The high priest wears a gold plate bearing the words "Holiness to the Lord" on his forehead.

You can read about this gold plate in Exodus 28:36, 38: "You shall also make a plate of pure gold and engrave on it, like the engraving of a signet: HOLINESS TO THE LORD...So it shall be on Aaron's forehead, that Aaron may bear the iniquity of the holy things...and it shall always be on his forehead, that they may be accepted before the LORD."

In the Old Testament, Aaron was the first high priest of Israel. The high priest of Israel is a picture of our Lord Jesus Christ, who is our permanent High Priest today. God instructed that this golden plate of the miter (headdress), which has the Hebrew words *Kadosh Le Yahweh* engraved on it, should always be on the forehead of the high priest. The engraving means "Holiness to the Lord," and the high priest had to have it on his forehead always so that all Israel would be accepted before God. What this means is that even when Israel failed in their *thought life*, they were still accepted by God because He judged the nation of Israel based on their high priest. If the high priest was accepted, the entire nation was accepted.

Today we have a perfect High Priest in Christ. It's not your thoughts that qualify you to be accepted by God. Under the new covenant of grace, God is no longer judging you based on your thoughts. God judges you based on His Son. If He is righteous, God sees you as righteous. If He is blessed, God sees you as blessed. If He is under God's unclouded favor, God sees you as under His unclouded favor. If His thoughts are always perfect and filled with holiness unto God, God sees your thoughts as perfect in Christ!

You see, there are no insignificant details in the Bible. Now, don't think that Jesus is dressed like an Old Testament high priest in heaven today. The garments, breastplate, and miter are just visual aids that God describes in the Bible to show us what is intrinsically true about our Lord Jesus and our perfection in Him.

Today when the devil comes to torment your mind, point him to Jesus. Jesus' thoughts are always holy. Remember how the golden plate is always around the forehead of your High Priest and His thoughts are always filled with holiness to God. Look at Exodus 28:38 again: "It shall always be on his forehead, that they may be accepted before the LORD." Therefore, even when your thought life isn't always perfect, know that Jesus' thoughts are always perfect. And it's because of His perfection that you are *always* accepted in Him before God. God will never reject you because your thoughts are imperfect. He is looking at Jesus, and as long as His thoughts are holy, you are accepted!

> *When the devil comes to torment your mind,*
> *point him to Jesus.*

Beloved, what great assurance and security we have in Christ! Our thoughts can waver, but His thoughts are always perfect. Believe that you are always accepted and approved because of Jesus. That's what it means to bring every thought into captivity to the perfect obedience of Christ (see 2 Cor. 10:5), and in Christ you will always win the battle for your mind!

CHAPTER 12

BEWARE OF THE ROARING LION

One of the greatest battles people face in the battle for their minds is the wrong belief that God is angry with them. The devil knows that if he can cause you to believe that God is mad at you, he can keep you trapped in fear, defeat, and bondage.

I want to expose this lie from the devil and show you from God's Word that God is not mad *at you*. He is mad *about* you! God loves you passionately, and He wants you to be fully assured and confident of His love for you.

To be victorious in the battle for your mind, it's important that you believe with all your heart that God is for you and not against you. When you use the weapons of right believing to prevail against the wiles of the devil, the Bible calls this being strong in the Lord:

> *Finally, my brethren, be strong in the Lord and in the power of His might. Put on the whole armor of God, that you may be able to stand against the wiles of the devil. For we do not wrestle against flesh and blood, but*

> *against principalities, against powers, against the rulers*
> *of the darkness of this age, against spiritual hosts of wick-*
> *edness in the heavenly places.*
>
> —Ephesians 6:10–12

God wants you to be built up, established, and strong in His love and grace for you. Believe in His love and put on the whole armor of God so that you may be able to stand against the wiles of the enemy.

The Armor of God Is about Right Believing

When I was a young believer, whenever I heard about "putting on the full armor of God," I would imagine Bruce Wayne putting on the armor and gadgets of his Batsuit. Click. He secures his utility belt. Click. He fastens his cape. Click. He puts on his mask. Because of all the books I had read, I even used to mentally go through the motions of donning the "armor of God" every morning, imagining myself putting on my helmet, my breastplate, and all the other pieces of armor before leaving the house. If I didn't do so, I actually felt spiritually naked, and believe me, that's not a good feeling to have.

But that's not what the armor of God is.

The armor of God is all about right believing! The battle is for your mind, and it's right believing that keeps you protected and safe from the enemy's assault against your mind in the form of lies, negative thoughts, and evil imaginations.

How to Put on God's Armor

Let's go through the whole armor of God (see Eph. 6:10–20), and observe how right believing in all that Jesus has done will always lead us to victory.

Let's begin with the belt of truth. When the devil comes against you with his lies about you, gird your waist with the belt of truth. The devil cannot deceive you if you are established in what God's Word says about you. He can only make inroads into your mind when you don't know or are unsure about what God's Word says. That's why I encourage people to study God's Word for themselves and to listen to messages that are full of God's grace and truth. Fill your mind and heart with truth and you'll surely defeat the enemy.

> *The devil cannot deceive you if you are established in what God's Word says about you.*

Secondly, we already know that the devil will try to attack you with all kinds of accusations and condemning thoughts to make you feel guilty and lousy about yourself. That's why when you are established in the gift of righteousness, his attacks against you will not prevail. All the devil's fiery darts of accusations are ineffective against the breastplate of righteousness that guards your heart from all fear, guilt, and condemnation.

And when he comes against you with thoughts of fear, doubt, and confusion, stand strong and defend yourself with the shield of faith. In apostle Paul's time, a shield would refer to the kind of huge shield that was used by the Romans. So don't imagine a tiny little shield. This shield is as big as a door! See your faith as a mighty shield and picture this—as long as your shield of faith is up, you are untouchable. No matter how many fiery darts the devil may pitch at you, ALL of them shall be quenched. Too many Christians are taking up the shield of doubt and quenching the blessings of God instead. Don't let that be you—*face your future with boldness with the mighty shield of faith.*

Now, the enemy will also come in to try to steal the joy you have because of the gospel of peace, which is depicted as shoes here. But when he comes, the God of peace will surely crush Satan underneath your feet.

Another area the devil likes to attack in your mind is the area of your salvation. When you find yourself under attack, be sure to have on the helmet of salvation. The word "salvation" comes from a beautiful Greek word *soteria*. Now, don't make the mistake of understanding salvation as just the gift of eternal life. It definitely includes eternal life, but the word *soteria* actually means so much more. It is an all-encompassing word that means deliverance (from your enemies, diseases, depression, fears, and all evils), preservation, safety, and salvation.[1] So put on the helmet of salvation by meditating on Jesus, and be filled with God's wholeness, protection, healing, and soundness. Let His *soteria* insulate your mind against the enemy's lies.

Lastly, you have also been equipped with the sword of the Spirit, which is the Word of God. Wield the sword of the Spirit by praying in the Spirit and speaking out God's Word into your situation. Declare His promises and the truth of His grace over yourself and your circumstances to guard your heart against thoughts of hopelessness and fear.

My friend, in the same way the battle for your mind is not physical, the whole armor of God is also not a physical armor. Rather, it has everything to do with what you believe in Christ. When you believe right, there is nothing the devil can do with you. Every evil strategy he has against you will surely fail. So be strong in the Lord's love for you. Believe that God is for you and not against you. His truth, His righteousness, His faith, His gospel, His salvation, His Word, and His Spirit are all weapons of right believing to protect you against all the devil's attacks.

> *Be strong in the Lord's love for you. Believe that God is for you and not against you.*

Being "Undevourable" before the Roaring Lion

The devil doesn't want you to be strong in the Lord's love for you. Instead, he wants you to question God's love for you. To accomplish this, one of his key strategies is to try to make you think that God is mad at you.

God's Word tells us that the devil goes about as a roaring lion, seeking whom he *may* devour. I thank God that it says he is "seeking whom he may devour" (1 Pet. 5:8). This means that he cannot just devour anyone. He must look for those whom he *can* devour. Some of us are "*undevourable.*" There may not be such a word, but it certainly describes a great place to be when the enemy is on the prowl for his next victim.

I want to teach you how you can become "undevourable" to the devil. The secret is found in the preceding verse, 1 Peter 5:7—"casting all your care upon Him, for He cares for you." Can you see it? The secret to being "undevourable" is to be carefree and not be bogged down by anxieties and worries! It is to laugh a lot, enjoy your life, and to take no thought for tomorrow.

To the legalistic mind, this sounds terribly irresponsible. However, in God's mind, your greatest responsibility is to rejoice in the Lord always and not worry about your past failures, your present circumstances, and your future challenges! Why? It's because of what God's grace has already done for you. And it's because the One who has the power over death is caring for you and watching over you right this minute.

> *Your greatest responsibility is to rejoice in the Lord always and not worry about your past failures, your present circumstances, and your future challenges!*

If you want to see victory over the enemy's attacks, then learn to relax, to let go, and to release every oppressive thought, worry, and care into Jesus' loving hands. Believe with all your heart that He cares for you and that you are not alone in this journey. You have a constant companion in Jesus on this great adventure called life.

I think it's interesting to note how the Bible tells us that the devil goes about *as* a roaring lion (see 1 Pet. 5:8). In other words, he comes to you *like* a lion, which means that he is not a real lion;

he merely disguises himself as one. Why does he choose to imper-
sonate a "roaring lion"? It was a question that I had pondered in
my heart for a long time. Then, many years ago, just before I went
to Israel with a group of leaders in late 2002, God opened my eyes
using another Scripture. He showed me why the devil pretends to
be a roaring lion and helped me see the type of fear that the devil
tries to bring into our lives. I had never heard anyone preach on it,
so this was a fresh revelation I received from God.

The Devil Impersonates the King's Wrath

The Scripture that God used to answer my question was Proverbs
19:12: "The king's wrath is like the roaring of a lion, but his favor
is like dew on the grass." Now this is what I call letting the Bible
interpret the Bible. It says in 1 Peter 5:8 that the devil goes about
like a *roaring lion*, and Proverbs 19:12 is a parallel Scripture that
unveils why the devil chooses to do that.

When it comes to Bible interpretation, it's not so important to
know what this Bible teacher or that professor said, or even what
the author of this book says. The Bible is its own best commentary,
so let the Bible itself explain and unveil God's heart for you.

Now, who is "the king" in Proverbs 19:12? The king here is our
Lord Jesus. He is the true King of kings (see Rev. 17:14, 19:16).
Before I break this down further, let me establish first that you are
not the object of His wrath. When the king is angry, He is angry at
injustice, at the devil, and at what he is doing in your life.

When Jesus looks at a person filled with disease, He is angry at the disease but He loves the person. God loves the sinner, but He hates the sin. If there is someone you love who has cancer, you hate the cancer but you love the person. God hates divorce, but He loves divorcees. God hates drunkenness, but He loves drunken people. God hates sin, but He loves the sinner.

God hates sin because of what it is doing to the objects of His love. Sin destroys lives. It wrecks marriages, tears people apart, and it stops His children from living their lives to the fullest. Jesus loves people, and that is why He paid the ultimate price at the cross and once and for all redeemed us from the power of sin. In Christ, you don't have to live in the bondage of sin!

So let's be one-hundred-percent clear—God's wrath is directed against any evil thing that seeks to destroy us. His anger and wrath are not directed toward us, His children. His wrath toward all our sins has been completely exhausted on the cross.

But the devil comes to you all dressed up as a lion, impersonating the King. He wants to give you the impression that God is angry with you, even though He isn't.

Let's be clear on another thing: there is only one true lion and that is the Lion of Judah, Jesus Christ (see Rev. 5:5), the King of kings. The devil is going about *as* a roaring lion because he is pretending to be Jesus and trying to intimidate you through the impression that God is angry with you. The devil is an imposter! He wants to make you feel alienated and cut off from Jesus. He wants you to think that Jesus is saying, "I am not pleased with you. I am really disappointed in you. How could you make such a mistake?" My friend, when you find yourself thinking these thoughts, you must know that's not Jesus. Jesus doesn't talk like that.

Fear and Love Cannot Coexist

Unfortunately, many sincere and well-meaning believers fall into the devil's trap, and they end up with the wrong belief that God is disappointed and mad at them. Because of this, they start feeling like hypocrites. They stop attending church, stop reading the Bible, stop listening to sermons, and stop talking to God in prayer—not because they are bad people, but because they are really sincere, responsible people who believe that God is really mad at them.

They love the Lord, but because of this wrong belief that He is angry with them, they start taking premeditated steps to avoid God. When this happens, do you know who has succeeded? The devil, who goes about like a roaring lion.

There are also some believers who may not even know they have been roared at by the devil. They really believe they have fallen short of God's expectations and have angered Him. They live in a constant state of trying to appease and please this angry God. Instead of enjoying a sweet, intimate relationship with Jesus, they feel like they are always treading on eggshells when it comes to their walk with the Lord.

If you have experienced such thoughts about God before, I would like to share this very important principle with you. Highlight it here or write it down somewhere:

> *Fear and love cannot coexist in a healthy relationship.*
> *Insecurity and love cannot coexist in a truly intimate relationship.*

Take for example our relationship with our children. In your dealings with your children, there will definitely be correction and guidance, but you never want your children to fear you or be insecure about your love for and acceptance of them. Fear and insecurity will only lead to hatred. If your children fear you, they will grow up hating you. Now, that is certainly not the kind of relationship that God wants with you and me, His children.

What, in our relationship with Him, does our loving heavenly Father want us to be conscious of then? Look at the rest of Proverbs 19:12: "but his [the king's] favor is like dew on the grass." God wants you, His beloved child, to live with a strong consciousness of His favor, His acceptance, and His love blanketing you like dew on grass. Because Jesus has borne the judgment for all your sins, you can live life every day not judgment-conscious, but favor-conscious.

> *God wants you, His beloved child, to live with a strong consciousness of His favor, His acceptance, and His love.*

The Right Fear of the Lord

I can hear you asking, "But what about the fear of the Lord then? What about Ananias and Sapphira in the Bible?"

These are great questions, my friend.

I've answered the first question in my book *Unmerited Favor.*[2] I also talk about this in chapter 15. Suffice it to say here that the "fear of the Lord" in the new covenant of grace is about honoring, worshiping, and reverencing God as God in our lives. "Fear" here does not refer to being terrified or afraid of and feeling threatened by God. Just ask yourself, which understanding of God resonates in your spirit? A loving Jesus who gave up everything for you, or an angry God looking for every opportunity to judge, condemn, and punish you? The Holy Spirit in you will point you to a God of love, while the devil will pretend to manifest the King's wrath and find every opportunity to roar at you.

As for Ananias and Sapphira, rest assured that they were *not* believers. They were con artists who came into the early church to try to deceive God's people financially. Like a good shepherd, the Lord protects His sheep from wolves that come to molest and fleece His sheep. The story of Ananias and Sapphira should not make you fearful of God, but rather give you confidence that He is watching over you and protecting you from those who want to inflict harm. It's a story of God's protection, not God's anger at His people.[3] If you believe that God will punish you or strike you dead like Ananias and Sapphira, then you have been roared at by the devil.

For decades upon decades, God has been portrayed as an angry God by the devil, and unfortunately, many Bible teachers have unwittingly helped him by painting a picture of a God who is full of wrath. This depiction of God is an error. We are now under the new covenant, and you will not be able to find a single New Testament Scripture that says God is angry with believers because of their sins. You would have to go into the Old Testament to look for verses that speak of God's anger at the sins of His people.

Does God not being angry with you mean that there is no place for God's correction in our lives? Is there correction and wise guidance that come by the Word of God in the new covenant of grace? Absolutely. But as for His anger toward you and your sins, all that has been settled at the cross. I guarantee you, when you come into Jesus' sweet presence with all your challenges, failings, and struggles, He is not going to roar at you. He is going to love you into wholeness and set you on a trajectory of freedom from all your fears, guilt, and addictions. Jesus is the end of all your struggles!

> *Jesus is the end of all your struggles!*

Why God Isn't Angry with You

Because God's perfect love is the answer to overcoming the struggles in your life, the devil is doing everything he can to alienate and cut you off from this love. He knows that you will avoid God if you think that God is mad at you, just like you would avoid someone to whom you owe a debt. As long as the debt is on your conscience, you'll never feel relaxed and at ease when your debtor is around.

The beautiful thing about Jesus is that He not only paid the sin debt of your entire life, but He also *overpaid* it. Unlike the high priests of the Old Testament, He didn't offer the blood of bulls and goats to pay for your sins. This High Priest paid for your sins with His own perfect and sinless blood. God didn't go soft on sin under grace! No way. He offered His only begotten Son, Jesus, who is an absolute overpayment for your sins.

It's as if you owed a debt of a million dollars, but Jesus paid a billion dollars to settle that debt. The truth is, if you knew who Jesus is and the value of the Son of God, you would know that His payment at the cross was worth more than a billion dollars. It's a payment that has wiped out your entire life's sins—past, present, and future, once and for all! No longer is there a chasm of sin separating you and God. It has been bridged by the bloodstained cross.

> *No longer is there a chasm of sin separating you and God. It has been bridged by the bloodstained cross.*

Believe God's Not Mad at You

Isaiah chapter 53 in the Old Testament is all about what Jesus accomplished at Calvary—His work at the cross was so efficacious that God says in the next chapter:

> *"For as I have sworn that the waters of Noah would no longer cover the earth, so have I sworn that I would not be angry with you, nor rebuke you. For the mountains shall depart and the hills be removed, but My kindness shall not depart from you, nor shall My covenant of peace be removed," says the* Lord, *who has mercy on you.*
> —Isaiah 54:9–10

Beloved, it's time for you to stop listening to the roaring of the lion and to start seeing God as your heavenly Father who loves you with an unconditional love and who will never leave you nor forsake you, no matter what.

I received this letter from Lorraine who lives in Louisiana. I'll let it speak for itself as you soak in how a person can be completely changed by believing the right things about our heavenly Father. All I can say is, *Hallelujah*!

> *I have been a born-again Christian for twenty-two years since I gave my life to Jesus in college. Today, at forty-four years old, I have a wonderful husband and beautiful one-and-a-half-year-old daughter. I love my life!*
>
> *As far back as I can remember, I have always loved Jesus. But I had lived my entire life feeling guilty as I believed that God was always mad at me. I had always felt that I could not do enough "right" or "good" things. After I gave my life to Christ, that feeling of not being good enough actually got worse because I felt a greater responsibility to live up to a higher standard to be right with God. I was always repenting, always feeling that I'd done wrong and that my best was never enough.*
>
> *I am in the process of reading* Destined To Reign *and am only at chapter 9. I have to read this book very, very, slowly so that I can digest its contents. I cannot tell you how my life has changed since I began reading your book.*
>
> *It was not until I began reading it that I felt relieved of the weight of not being good enough. It has shaken the very foundation of my world and dissolved the insecurity I've had about Jesus and His love for me.*

Forty-four years of my previously painful existence and mind-set are GONE. I am CHANGED forever. I am forgiven. I can't get through the rest of this book without stopping to thank the Lord for you and for giving you the message of grace to spread worldwide.

Don't you just love it that when right believing comes in, years of a painful existence and mind-set are obliterated, and permanent, liberating change happens!

That's what it is all about, my friend. Winning the battle for your mind is all about your freedom and liberty in Christ Jesus, your Lord and Savior. Be strong in His love for you. Put on the full armor of God, and don't allow any wrong believing to rob you of a life of great joy and great peace. Remember, God is not mad at you, He is mad about you.

God is not mad at you, He is mad about you.

PART FIVE

BE FREE FROM SELF-OCCUPATION

CHAPTER 13

BE FREE FROM SELF-OCCUPATION

As we press deeper into the power of right believing, I want to show you practical ways in which you can be transformed by the renewing of your mind. Right believing is all about renewing your mind and uprooting the wrong beliefs that shape your thinking and behavior. That's why the Word of God says, "Do not be conformed to this world, but be transformed by the renewing of your mind, that you may prove what is that good and acceptable and perfect will of God" (Rom. 12:2). I like how the New Living Translation says it: "Don't copy the behavior and customs of this world, but let God transform you into a new person by changing the way you think."

> "Let God transform you into a new person by changing the way you think." (NLT)

It's clear that if we desire to enjoy liberty instead of bondage, joy instead of fear, and peace instead of anxiety, then we need to allow God to transform us by changing the way we think so that our minds are renewed through the power of right believing.

This is not about behavior modification, which is just outward. We are talking about being transformed by the Lord from the inside out. Behavior modification is sustained by your own discipline, self-efforts, and willpower. It works only as long as you keep on working. We are talking about change that comes from an inward heart transformation sustained by the power and love of our Lord and Savior, Jesus Christ. His power and grace work best when we stop striving and depend wholeheartedly on Him.

Renew Your Mind—Be Christ-Occupied

God wants to change the way we think by shifting our thoughts from self-occupation to Christ-occupation. Our human tendency is to be focused on ourselves. In other words, we are prone to excessive self-introspection and are easily susceptible to becoming preoccupied with ourselves rather than with Jesus.

Very often, we are not even conscious that we are self-occupied. This could be happening to you right now. You don't believe that you tend to be occupied with yourself? All right, whenever you look at a photograph with a bunch of people including yourself in it, who do you look for first? Your mother-in-law? Of course not. You look for yourself.

Like it or not, to some degree, we are all self-occupied. Of course, looking for yourself first in a group photograph is not a serious issue—most of us do that. The problem occurs when our thoughts are centered on and preoccupied with "I," "I," "I," and more of "I," while Christ is noticeably absent from our thoughts.

Have I done enough?

What is wrong with me?

I have so many weaknesses and shortcomings!

I believe that many of our greatest pains, struggles, and miseries stem from us being "I" centered. Self-occupation is the reason for many of our failures and defeats. When people become overly occupied with self, they become obsessed, oppressed, and inevitably depressed. The only way that we can be delivered from occupation with self is to be occupied with Christ. We need to be occupied with the One who is greater than us and worthy of all our praise, worship, and adoration.

> *The only way that we can be delivered from occupation with self is to be occupied with Christ.*

That is why God gave us the Bible. It's not a rule book of dos and don'ts. It was given to reveal the beauties of the glorified Man, Jesus Christ, so that when our hearts are utterly absorbed and engrossed with Him, we will find peace, freedom, and rest for our weary souls.

Jesus says, "Come to Me, all you who labor and are heavy laden, and I will give you rest" (Matt. 11:28). Notice that He doesn't say, "Come to Me after you have examined your heart." All He says is, "Come to Me...and I will give you rest." You don't have to be perfect to come to Jesus. He wants you to come to Him just as you are—with all your bondages, addictions, and failures, and He will give you rest from all your mess.

Jesus will give you rest from all your mess.

When you become occupied with Christ, you will become increasingly untouched by the things that hold the world captive. It doesn't really matter anymore what this person says about you or what that person thinks about you. You are no longer a slave to their approval and good opinion of you when you are established and secure in the approval and good opinion of Almighty God, the Creator of the universe.

The Problem with Self-Occupation

Is your mind filled constantly with thoughts of how you have failed, how you have missed it, and how unworthy you are? That is symptomatic of someone who is clearly self-occupied. Thoughts like that cause a person to develop an inferiority complex. They start feeling like they are not as good as the brother over here or that sister over there. They are constantly berating themselves, thinking, "Why am I such a failure? I can't even control my own thoughts. What's wrong with me? Why do I always feel so down and depressed all the time?"

People who suffer from this are ever ready to condemn themselves. Their minds are clouded with negativity and pessimism. For example, when they see some of their friends talking and laughing, they think to themselves, "They must be gossiping and mocking me for the mistake I made last week." In reality, their friends were only talking about a funny movie they had caught over the week-end. However, because these people generally harbor thoughts of inferiority, they project their thoughts of inferiority and insecurity into every situation they are in. This in turn adversely affects their friendships and relationships with the people around them.

Self-occupation doesn't just rear its ugly head in the form of an inferiority complex. It can also manifest at the other end of the pendulum's swing as a superiority complex. There are people who think they are always better than everyone else. They are painfully arrogant, and they think their perspectives and opinions are always right. Do you know someone like that? Well, that's self-occupation too. Whether you are feeling superior or inferior, your focus is still on yourself, and in the end that causes you great pain, misery, and heartache.

As long as our minds are not occupied with Christ, all of us can at times feel inferior and at other times feel proud, arrogant, and superior. Only in Christ will you experience true transformation and walk neither in pride nor in false humility. Both extremes are the product of our human flesh. When we are self-occupied, our flesh is strengthened and it is ugly. It's no wonder the apostle Paul says, "In me (that is, in my flesh) nothing good dwells" (Rom. 7:18).

The good news is when you are Christ-occupied, the flesh in you becomes inconsequential and you begin manifesting all the lovely, wholesome, and beautiful attributes of Jesus unconsciously. The fruit of the Spirit, such as love, joy, peace, and kindness, flow through you effortlessly when your mind is renewed and occupied with the person of Jesus.

There are some religious people who get very uncomfortable when I use the word "effortless." "What do you mean there is no effort?" they argue. My reply is simple—a healthy tree bears good fruit without any strain, effort, or stress. When you are planted in the fertile soil of God's Word and His grace, fruits of righteousness will manifest effortlessly out of your relationship with Him. It's an inevitability! You cannot touch His grace and not become holy any more than you can touch water and not get wet.

> *When you are planted in the fertile soil of God's Word and His grace, fruits of righteousness will manifest effortlessly out of your relationship with Him.*

Supernatural Transformation

When our minds are occupied with Jesus, we don't have to try to be humble. In the presence of the Servant-King, our hearts become supernaturally transformed, and we will carry His servant heart. In other words, when you hang out with Jesus, all that He is will rub off on you. Your thoughts and your words will be full of the fragrance of His sweet presence and grace. All your inferiority and insecurities will melt away in His marvelous love for you. It takes people who are truly secure in Christ to be able to bow down and serve others with genuine humility.

Similarly, when you are courageous and bold *in Christ* and in His love for you, it doesn't manifest as fleshly pride and arrogance, but rather as complete dependence on Almighty God. Think of how young David charged down the Valley of Elah and challenged the giant Goliath, while the rest of the well-trained and full-grown men of the army of Israel cowered in fear. Was that simply a display of youthful bravado or a genuine dependence on God?

To the untrained eye, David could have appeared like an impudent little brat. Especially since the loser of this one-on-one battle would enslave his entire nation to the enemy. The fate of the entire nation of Israel was at stake. But we know where this steely chutzpah comes from when these bold words of a mere teenager resonated throughout the valley: "You come to me with a sword, with a spear, and with a javelin. But I come to you in the name of the LORD of hosts, the God of the armies of Israel, whom you have defied" (1 Sam. 17:45). From his words, we can tell that young David was clearly occupied with the Lord of hosts and not with himself or his abilities.

When your thoughts are occupied with the Lord, you become a giant slayer! Are there giants in your life today that need to be slain? Like young David, occupy your mind with the Lord, and God will fill you with the courage and audacity to overcome all your adversities. Listen to the words of David in Psalm 18:29: "For by You I can run against a troop, by my God I can leap over a wall." Let these words of faith and boldness be established in your heart. With God on your side, nothing is impossible!

> *When your thoughts are occupied with the Lord, you become a giant slayer!*

Keep Your Eyes on Jesus

Christ-occupation makes you bold but not superior, humble but not inferior. Doesn't that sound so much like our Lord Jesus Christ? Here, then, is the key to being occupied with Christ:

> *But we all, with unveiled face, beholding as in a mirror the glory of the Lord, are being transformed into the same image from glory to glory, just as by the Spirit of the Lord.*
>
> —2 Corinthians 3:18

The more you keep your mind, your thoughts, and the eyes of your heart on Jesus, the more you are transformed into His image from glory to glory.

> *Christ-occupation makes you bold but not superior, humble but not inferior.*

Stop looking at yourself! Stop dwelling on negative thoughts about yourself and feeling lousy. Turn your eyes away from you, and look at Jesus. Your freedom from every fear, anxiety attack, bondage, and addiction is found in the person of Jesus.

In the preceding chapters, we dealt with how to win the battle for your mind. While spiritual warfare is real and there is a devil that is out to accuse and condemn you in your mind, I also want you to know that not every bad thought you have comes from the devil. Charismatic Christians are notorious for this—they blame the devil for everything. They stub their toe on the bedpost when they get up in the morning and think it's spiritual warfare. Come on!

There *is* spiritual warfare, but do exercise some godly discernment and don't think that every bad thought in your mind comes from the devil. He is a defeated foe, and he doesn't wield that much power and influence over our lives. My point is this: While it is necessary to understand that there is a battle for your mind and not be ignorant of the devil's mind games, the devil should never be our primary focus.

Our primary and central focus is Jesus and Jesus alone. God doesn't want us to be occupied with the devil or occupied with ourselves and our flesh. He wants us to occupy our minds with Jesus. Jesus is the answer to all our pain, misery, and struggles.

Understanding the Flesh

The flesh in us can produce a whole gamut of emotions and thoughts, from defeat, jealousy, greed, and lust to anger, inferiority, condemnation, and arrogance. As long as we are in this physical body, the flesh is active in us.

But we can rejoice because when Jesus died on the cross, the Word of God tells us that He "condemned sin in the flesh." All the negative thoughts and toxic emotions from the flesh have already been judged and punished at the cross. Today we can experience victory over the flesh through the power of the cross.

You can read all about the apostle Paul's struggle with the flesh in Romans 7:18–19: "For *I* know that in *me* (that is, in *my* flesh) nothing good dwells; for to will is present with *me*, but how to perform what is good *I* do not find. For the good that *I* will to do, *I* do not do; but the evil *I* will not to do, that *I* practice" (emphasis mine).

Did you notice how many times the words "I," "me," and "my" are mentioned in just the two verses above? I'm sure many of you can identify with the apostle Paul here in his struggle with the flesh. It's the struggle we all face when we are occupied with ourselves and warring with the flesh within us. It's a life of vexation, angst, defeat, and despair.

This is not where God wants you to live, my friend. A believer doesn't live in Romans chapter 7. Through Christ Jesus, we should be living in Romans chapter 8. Let's read on and discover how Paul broke free from this bondage of self.

Just a few verses later, Paul cries out, "O wretched man that I am! Who will deliver me from this body of death?" (Rom. 7:24). The answer, my friend, is found in a *person*, and Paul tells us this person is Jesus: "I thank God—through Jesus Christ our Lord!" (Rom. 7:25).

Only our beautiful Savior, Jesus Christ, can deliver us from the flesh. And in Christ we can step into the first verse of Romans chapter 8, which proclaims, "Therefore there is now no condemnation for those who are in Christ Jesus" (NASB). This is where we as new covenant believers ought to live. Not in the domain of constant struggle and despair, but in the domain of no condemnation and victory.

Every time a bad thought, an evil imagination, or a temptation comes into your mind, see yourself in Christ, in whom there is absolutely no condemnation. I love Romans chapter 8, for it begins with no condemnation in Christ and ends with no separation from the love of Christ:

> *Who shall separate us from the love of Christ? Shall trib-ulation, or distress, or persecution, or famine, or naked-ness, or peril, or sword? . . . Yet in all these things we are more than conquerors through Him who loved us. For I am persuaded that neither death nor life, nor angels nor principalities nor powers, nor things present nor things to come, nor height nor depth, nor any other created thing, shall be able to separate us from the love of God which is in Christ Jesus our Lord.*
>
> —Romans 8:35, 37–39

Nothing will be able to separate you from the love of Christ. That is why God doesn't want you to live under a cloud of guilt and condemnation. He has already made you more than a con-queror in Christ. The victory has already been won at the cross. Self-occupation as demonstrated in Romans chapter 7 will prevent you from enjoying the life that God has given you. It will make you perpetually conscious about how you have fallen short and where you have missed the mark.

Nothing will be able to separate you from the love of Christ.

Freedom from Condemnation

Have you met people who are always oppressed and depressed? They can be in Hawaii and be surrounded by swaying palm trees, rolling waves, and the most beautiful sunset and still be lost in their own depressive thoughts.

If that is you, I want you to know that God wants to set you free from this painful existence. When your heart and mind are full of Jesus, the flesh has no power over you. Bad thoughts, desires, and emotions can try to harass you, but when your heart and mind are occupied with Jesus, these fleshly thoughts and emotions have no hold over you, and they slide off you like water off a duck's back.

You won't even feel guilty and condemned for thinking those thoughts and feeling those emotions because you know that in Christ, the flesh is not you. Jesus is your new identity, not the flesh. Let me give you Scripture to back that up. The Word of God proclaims, "Those who are Christ's have crucified the flesh with its passions and desires" (Gal. 5:24).

The flesh is not you because it has been crucified with Christ at the cross. You are a new creation in Jesus—the old is gone and the new has come (see 2 Cor. 5:17). Whenever the old desires and thoughts try to creep back into your consciousness, don't entertain them. Look to Jesus and see all these things crucified at the cross. Receive afresh the gift of no condemnation.

Behold the Lamb of God

I encourage you to start every new day with this thought: "God loves me and gave His only Son for me. Jesus is all for me today. I am saved, healed, favored, and accepted in Christ the Beloved."

Start your day by occupying your mind with Jesus. For a season in my life, before I even got out of bed, I would repeat to myself over and over again, "I am the righteousness of God in Christ." Some mornings I would say it more than fifty times. I didn't want it to just be words in my head. I wanted it to be a revelation pulsating in my heart. I wanted to have an unshakable belief that God is *for* me and *with* me even before I got out of bed. I can tell you from firsthand experience that when you occupy your mind with Jesus, every struggle, fear, and bondage that you are entangled with will lose its evil grasp on you!

> *Start your day by occupying your mind with Jesus.*

There is a beautiful picture of Jesus hidden in the Old Testament. God knew that under the old covenant of the law, it was impossible for the children of Israel to be perfected by the law. So He provided a way out. God told them that if they sinned, they should bring a sheep that is without blemish, wrinkle, or spot to the priest. Now, when a person who has sinned brings a sheep to the priest, the priest does not examine the person to see if he is perfect (without sin)—the priest already knows that this person is there because he has sinned. So the priest examines the sheep.

If the sheep is indeed perfect, the person who has sinned lays his hands on the sheep in an act of transferring his sins to the innocent sheep. At the same time, the innocence and perfection of the sheep are transferred to the person. The sheep is then killed, and the person leaves with his conscience cleared and his sin debt forgiven. He walks away under an open heaven of God's favor and blessing.

Can you see Jesus in this Old Testament practice that God instituted under the law?

The sheep without blemish, spot, or wrinkle is a picture of the perfect Lamb of God, Jesus Christ Himself, who takes away the sins of the world. The priest is a picture of God. He doesn't examine you for your sins. Instead, He examines Jesus, and because Jesus is gloriously perfect, you can live today with your conscience cleared and your sin debt forgiven. You can walk under an open heaven and expect God's favor and blessings in your life. What a beautiful picture of God's abundant and lavish grace.

Now, if God is not examining you today, why are you still struggling in self-occupation and relentlessly examining your own thoughts, emotions, failures, and shortcomings? Trust me, the longer you examine yourself, the more you will find imperfections, blemishes, spots, and wrinkles. Turn your eyes away from yourself and stop the self-introspection! Look to Jesus, the Lamb of God, and see His perfection as your perfection. See His innocence as your innocence, His righteousness as your righteousness. Be occupied with Him, and be transformed from the inside out.

CHAPTER 14

JESUS, BE THE CENTER OF IT ALL

As the two disciples began their seven-mile journey from Jerusalem to a village called Emmaus, they spoke with heavy hearts about the events that had transpired during the last three days. Grieved and shell-shocked, they talked about how Jesus, whom they greatly esteemed, had been taken by the religious leaders, condemned to death, and crucified.

As they were discussing these events, the risen Jesus joined them on their trek to Emmaus, but He kept them from recognizing who He was. Seeing their faces clouded with sadness and apprehension, He asked them, "What are you discussing so intently with each other as you walk along? And why are you so sad?"

Cleopas, one of the disciples, was incredulous that this stranger was asking such an uninformed question and snapped, "Have you been living in a cave? You must be the only person in Jerusalem who is ignorant of the terrible things that have just happened."

Cleopas then went on to recount the events that eventually led to Jesus' crucifixion. With disillusionment in his voice, Cleopas expressed how they had hoped that Jesus would be the one who would redeem Israel. He also related the curious story he had heard from the women who went to the tomb early in the morning only to find it empty. He even repeated their outrageous claims that they had seen a vision of angels proclaiming to them that Jesus was alive.

Jesus, hearing Cleopas's unbelief, gently corrected him and the other disciple: "O foolish ones, and slow of heart to believe in all that the prophets have spoken!" (Luke 24:25). Seeing their reaction of surprise, He went on to say, "Wasn't it clearly predicted that the Messiah would have to suffer all these things before entering his glory?" (Luke 24:26 NLT). Jesus was referring to the many Bible prophesies and pictures in the Scriptures that foretold the cross—how the Messiah would suffer and pay a hefty price for man's sins and transgressions.

Witnessing the two disciples' wrong believing firsthand, Jesus, "beginning at Moses and all the Prophets...expounded to them in all the Scriptures the things concerning Himself" (Luke 24:27) as they journeyed seven miles together to Emmaus.

Extraordinary Encounter

I love how the Holy Spirit intricately records for us this meeting that Jesus had with the two disciples on the road to Emmaus. Meeting them must have been extremely important to Him, as their encounter took place on the very first day of His resurrection. This was also the first record of Him teaching from the Scriptures after He had conquered the grave.

It was thus no ordinary meeting, and God has hidden so many

precious gems in this story for us. The Bible tells us, "It is the glory of God to conceal a matter, but the glory of kings is to search out a matter" (Prov. 25:2). So let's dive into this account of the Emmaus journey and hear the early words of the resurrected Christ.

Occupy Your Thoughts with Jesus

We have already established how painful self-occupation can be and how we can only be delivered from self when we become Christ-occupied. Through this story, I want to show you how to practically occupy your thoughts with your loving Savior by seeing Him in God's Word.

First, notice that the two disciples were caught up with their own understanding of the events that had transpired and with their thoughts about the redemption of Israel. As a result, they were downcast, disappointed, and depressed. This is what happens when the truth about Jesus is absent from our minds.

The disciples had hoped that Jesus would be the one who would redeem Israel. To them, Jesus was simply a means to an end. They were more consumed with Israel's redemption than with the Redeemer Himself. No wonder they were depressed! Jesus can never simply be a means to an end, no matter how noble that end may be. We need to be occupied with Him and allow everything to revolve around Him as He takes center place in our lives.

If you are feeling fearful, anxious, or depressed today, do a quick check. What's on your mind? What's your heart occupied with? Are your thoughts filled with faith in Jesus, the Shepherd of your life, or are they filled with apprehensions about the future, fears about your current situation, and excessive self-introspection?

> *Are your thoughts filled with faith in Jesus, the Shepherd of your life, or are they filled with apprehensions, fears, and excessive self-introspection?*

The disciples were downcast because they didn't believe in what God's Word had prophesied about Jesus' suffering and resurrection. If they had believed and understood that the events in the last three days were all orchestrated by God and that the cross was His grand redemption plan to save all men, they would be rejoicing with faith, love, and hope. They would be greatly anticipating their reunion with the resurrected Christ instead of being so inward-looking and discouraged. But because of their wrong beliefs, they had become disillusioned and were mentally defeated.

It's no wonder that Jesus said to them, "O foolish ones, and slow of heart to believe in all that the prophets have spoken!" (Luke 24:25). Before I continue, let me point out that the word "foolish" here is the Greek word *anoetos*, which means "not understanding and unwise."[1] In contrast, when Jesus rebuked the Pharisees as being foolish in Matthew 23:17, the Greek word used here is *moros*, which means "dull or stupid."[2] This is a much harsher term He reserved for the religious Pharisees. Jesus didn't use such harsh terms to describe His disciples or those who were down-and-out.

So He was gently correcting the disciples and saying, "You *not understanding* and *unwise* ones, who are *slow of heart to believe...*" I believe it's important for us to understand that Jesus spoke these words in a loving tone because He is also speaking the same words to us today. He is gently reminding us that we (His disciples) have a proclivity toward the same two challenges—not understanding His Word and being slow to believe it.

Beware of Zeal without Knowledge

There are believers today who don't know or understand what God's Word really says. And even in instances where they do know what His Word says, they are slow of heart to believe.

My friend, Jesus doesn't want us to be ignorant about His Word and be defeated by our lack of knowledge. The reason we study God's Word is not to merely accumulate Bible knowledge and historical facts. It is to have a constant revelation of Jesus. And how do we do this? We can start by asking the Holy Spirit. Many times when studying the Word, I would pray this simple prayer: "Holy Spirit, open my eyes to see Jesus in the Word today." That is what it's all about—*seeing Jesus.*

> *The reason we study God's Word is not to merely accumulate Bible knowledge and historical facts. It is to have a constant revelation of Jesus.*

There are people who read the Word and, instead of seeing Jesus, everything becomes a law to them and they become hard, legalistic, and pharisaical. Paul describes this phenomenon in the book of Romans: "They have a zeal for God, but not according to knowledge"

(Rom. 10:2). What knowledge is the apostle referring to? Read the very next verses: "For they being ignorant of God's righteousness, and seeking to establish their own righteousness, have not submitted to the righteousness of God. For Christ is the end of the law for righteousness to everyone who believes" (Rom. 10:3–4).

In other words, they read the Word without seeing Jesus in it and they become zealous for the law. They end up unknowingly seeking to make themselves righteous by the law. Legalism is very subtle and insidious. Many legalists are unaware that they are trapped in legalism. They would never admit they are legalists and may even preach strongly against legalism.

There are also people who attack the gospel of grace because they are blinded by their zeal for the law and how man needs to make himself better through right doing. I truly believe that many of them are genuine and sincere; nevertheless, they are sincerely wrong.

Grow in the Knowledge of God's Grace

You need to know beyond any doubt that the law can never make you righteous. Jesus is the end of the law. You are made righteous when you believe right in the person of Jesus and His righteousness. That's what I mean by the power of right believing.

The apostle Paul is the best person to write about this because he was the Pharisee of Pharisees, the legalist of legalists. There was a time in his life when he didn't know that he was bound up in legalism. Don't forget that when Paul was still known as Saul, he wasn't zealous for sin; he was zealous for God's law. In fact, it was his passion for God's law that made him persecute the early church, drag many into prison, and consent to the slaughter of Christians. He only stopped doing all this when the risen Jesus Himself began to open his eyes to the truth on the road to Damascus (see Acts 9:1–8). Take a moment to look at the dramatic encounter that Saul had with Jesus:

> *"Saul, Saul, why are you persecuting Me?"*
> *Saul replied, "Who are You, Lord?"*
> *"I am Jesus, whom you are persecuting. It is hard for you to*
>   *kick against the goads."*

My friend, when others come against you for what you believe about God's grace, don't feel like you have to argue with them and try to convince them. Love them and pray that God will open their eyes to see Jesus. The law is a veil, and it blinds them. However, once the veil is removed, like when Paul's eyes were opened to the truth about Jesus, there is no turning back. Just look at what happened to Paul—he became the apostle of God's grace and his zeal was no longer without knowledge.

Therefore, don't take their attacks personally. People of grace carry a spirit of graciousness. Those who persecute you for believing God's grace will have to encounter Jesus when He asks them, "Why are you persecuting Me?" Grace is, after all, not a teaching; it is a Person. If they choose to attack grace, they are attacking the person of Jesus. That is why I highly recommend that you love and keep them in prayer. Remember, and this bears repeating, people of grace carry a spirit of graciousness.

Be Quick to Believe

In many places there are believers who still think that God is mad at them whenever they fail. They simply don't have a revelation of the gospel of grace and what God's unconditional love means. Like the two disciples on the road to Emmaus, such believers are undiscerning and unwise.

Then there are believers who know about the gospel of grace and who even know that God loves them unconditionally. However, this knowing is only in their heads. When they fail, even though they have the knowledge of grace, they are nevertheless still afraid to come with boldness to God's throne of grace to receive mercy, favor, healing, and restoration.

What's the problem in this instance? That's right, they are slow of heart to believe God's promise of abundant grace and gift of righteousness to reign in this life. Knowing God's truths and the gospel of grace intellectually is not enough. You have to be quick to believe everything that Jesus has accomplished on the cross for you, especially when you are struggling with failure, guilt, and fear. God doesn't want you defeated because of a lack of knowledge of His grace. At the same time, He wants you to be quick in believing in His promises for you.

> *God doesn't want you defeated because of a lack of knowledge of His grace. He wants you to be quick in believing in His promises for you.*

You have already learned many things about God's love for you in this book. If you want to see the power of right believing operating in every dimension of your life, I challenge you to believe in His grace, His love, His righteousness, His forgiveness, and His finished work. I promise you that you will be transformed beyond your wildest imagination if you dare to lean hard on His love for you. His love never fails!

Ignite Your Heart

I want to show you another interesting aspect of the Emmaus story. The word "Emmaus" means "warm baths,"[3] and I have taken this walk to Emmaus with some of my pastors. Of course, we didn't do the full seven-mile hike. We got off the tour bus about a mile away from Emmaus because I am merciful to my pastors. After all, they are not as "strong" and "young" as I am. I'm just kidding.

On a more serious note, when you think about it, seven miles is a long distance. In fact, if you read the entire story, the two disciples didn't just walk seven miles. On the same day, they walked back to Jerusalem from Emmaus, making it a total of 14 miles or 22.5 kilometers. When was the last time you walked 14 miles in the same day?

How was it that the disciples were not tired or exhausted, especially given their initial frame of mind as they set out on their journey? Something must have happened to the disciples' bodies as they walked with Jesus. Their physical bodies were quickened, strengthened, and invigorated. Their youth was most certainly renewed as God's Word promises that "those who wait on the LORD shall renew their strength; they shall mount up with wings like eagles, they shall run and not be weary, they shall walk and not faint" (Isa. 40:31).

What happened on the road? What caused the disciples' bodies to experience such a burst of energy and life? Listen to how the disciples described to each other what they had felt as they walked with Jesus: "Did not our heart burn within us while He talked with us on the road, and while He opened the Scriptures to us?" (Luke 24:32).

Therein lies the key! When the Scriptures are opened to you and things concerning Jesus are unveiled, your heart will be set aflame and burn within you like it did for these two disciples! Don't forget what Jesus did when He heard their wrong believing and conversation of defeat: "Beginning at Moses and all the Prophets, He expounded to them in all the Scriptures *the things concerning Himself*" (Luke 24:27, emphasis mine).

In other words, beginning with the first five books of Moses (Genesis, Exodus, Leviticus, Numbers, and Deuteronomy, collectively known as the Torah), Jesus expounded all the things concerning Himself. Then He continued to reveal Himself in the books of the prophets, books such as Samuel, Kings, Isaiah, and Jeremiah.

Wow! What a journey it must have been! No wonder the disciples' hearts were ignited and burned within them. Like the name of the village that they were traveling to, their hearts were bathed continually in a warm bath as Jesus opened their eyes to see Him in all the Scriptures.

What Are You Looking At?

On the first day of His resurrection, Jesus set a precedent for us on how we ought to read and study the Bible today. He doesn't want us to approach the Word to find out what we need to do and go away with a bunch of laws. Absolutely not! Jesus wants us to open the Scriptures to see HIM. See Him in everything from Genesis to Revelation. The more you see Him, the more you will be free from all forms of self-occupation and be transformed from glory to glory.

> *Jesus wants us to open the Scriptures to see HIM. The more you see Him, the more you will be free from all forms of self-occupation.*

When you look at yourself—your weaknesses, failures, mistakes, and even strengths and righteous deeds, there is no lasting hope, joy, or peace. The apostle Paul considered all his accomplishments as "dung" (Phil. 3:8 KJV), while the prophet Isaiah states that "all our righteousnesses are like filthy rags" (Isa. 64:6).

Jesus shows us that the way to become completely occupied and consumed with Him is to turn away from our own dark thoughts and depressing conversations and to open up the Scriptures to see Him. Be occupied with Jesus, fill your thoughts with His goodness, and saturate your heart with His love.

Open up the Bible and see Jesus in the types and shadows in the Old Testament. Every sacrifice, every feast, and even the tabernacle and priests point to Jesus. In the New Testament, see Jesus loving and forgiving those whom the world despised, like the woman caught in adultery. See Him healing the blind, lame, and all who were oppressed with sicknesses and diseases. See Jesus multiplying provision for those who lacked. I promise you that your heart will burn, your body will be renewed, and your mind will be filled with His shalom-peace, joy, and soundness. I promise you that sin, addictions, bad habits, fear, guilt, anxiety, depression, and condemnation will drop off from your life when you are absorbed and occupied with the person of Jesus. They simply cannot coexist in your life when you are occupied with Christ and not yourself.

> *Addictions, fear, and guilt cannot exist in your life when you are occupied with Christ and not yourself.*

Open Up the Scriptures to See Christ

Many years ago when I was studying the Emmaus story, I asked the Lord why He chose to restrain the eyes of the two disciples such that they couldn't recognize Him. I asked Him, "Wouldn't it have been better for them to see You with Your nail-pierced hands?" I reasoned to myself that those nails must have been huge and one could possibly see light shining through those wounds. Wouldn't it have been better if Jesus had walked down the busiest streets of Jerusalem, lifted up His hands, and hollered, "Yo! Everyone, check this out!"

But Jesus didn't do that. He knew doing that would not produce true faith. He revealed to me that it was more important for the disciples to see Him in the Word than to see Him in person. Wow, those words brought so much hope and encouragement to my heart. If the faith of the disciples was based on them seeing Jesus physically in the flesh, then what hope do we have today? Jesus purposefully restrained their eyes so that they would see Him first in the Scriptures. That places you and me on *equal ground* and with *equal opportunity* as the two disciples. Jesus wants us all to see Him in the Word.

God's Word tells us that "faith comes from hearing, and hearing by the word of Christ" (Rom. 10:17 NASB). This means that the more you hear Jesus unveiled, expounded upon, and pointed to in the Scriptures, the more faith will be imparted to your heart to believe everything God's Word says about you. Could it be that the reason many believers are still living in defeat today is that Jesus has not been unveiled in the Scriptures to them?

There seems to be a spiritual famine in the world today, a dearth of teaching and preaching that unveils the person of Jesus in a way that causes people's hearts to burn as if they were in a warm bath. Instead what we often hear is teaching on right doing and more right doing. My question is, is that the gospel? Is Jesus being unveiled?

The gospel is all about Jesus. It's not about right doing. It's all about right believing about Jesus that makes a difference in people's lives. The apostle Paul says, "For I am not ashamed of the gospel of Christ, for it is the power of God to salvation for everyone who believes, for the Jew first and also for the Greek. For in it the righteousness of God is revealed from faith to faith; as it is written, 'The just shall live by faith'" (Rom. 1:16–17).

The gospel is the gospel of Christ, and everything is about Jesus. It's not the gospel of morality and character, and it definitely isn't the gospel of money and prosperity. But do you know what the gospel does? It produces all of those things. The true gospel of Jesus Christ always produces godliness, holiness, morality, character, provision, health, wisdom, love, peace, joy, and much more. They all flow from the gospel of Jesus Christ.

> *The true gospel of Jesus Christ always produces godliness, holiness, morality, character, provision, health, wisdom, love, peace, joy, and much more.*

That's the gospel that I am not ashamed of. That's why what I do every Sunday, and in every place where I speak, is preach messages that unveil Jesus. I know that when He is central in people's lives, their fears, guilt, and addictions will no longer be central. When the righteousness of God (not their own righteousness) is revealed, they will live from faith to faith. They will live from one level of right believing to the next level of right believing, and from one level of breakthroughs to the next level of breakthroughs.

Romans 1:17 says that the righteous shall live *by faith*. It doesn't say that the righteous shall live by their own works. The essence of the Christian faith is founded upon this verse. It was this verse that launched the Reformation. Martin Luther received the revelation that a believer is righteous by faith and not by the works of the law.

In other words, the righteous shall live by believing right in everything that Jesus has accomplished for them at Calvary and not by their own accomplishments. In fact, faith is all about believing that you are righteous through the finished work of Jesus! The centrality of the gospel is based on right believing, not right doing. The truth is that when you believe right, you will end up living right. Right believing always leads to right living.

When you believe right that your righteousness comes from Jesus, God's Word says, "The path of the [uncompromisingly] just and righteous is like the light of dawn, that shines more and more (brighter and clearer) until [it reaches its full strength and glory in] the perfect day [to be prepared]" (Prov. 4:18 AMP).

We know that only Jesus is uncompromisingly just and righteous. What hope do you and I have if the brightness of our paths is based on our own righteousness? But because we have been made righteous through His finished work, God guarantees that our paths will shine brighter and brighter as we are transformed from glory to glory.

In Christ, your future is blessed. It's full of His favor and full of all the right open doors, opportunities, and promotions. In Him, you can expect good, victory, favor, and success. Take comfort today knowing that your best breakthroughs are not behind you, but ahead of you. Jesus is taking you to a place so good that it's beyond what you can even ask, think, or imagine.

> *In Christ, your future is blessed. It's full of His favor and full of all the right open doors, opportunities, and promotions.*

How to See Jesus in the Word

The Bible from Genesis to Revelation points to the person of Jesus. As Jesus walked with the two disciples, I'm sure that He would have camped at Genesis chapter 22. This is where God told Abraham to offer up his son, his only son, the son whom he loved.

Think about this story for a moment. It's a story of a son carrying wood up Mount Moriah on his way to be sacrificed. Many people don't understand this story. Why would God ask for Abraham's son to be sacrificed? The entire passage in Genesis chapter 22 is really the gospel story. God Himself would send His Son, His only Son, the Son whom He loved. His Son would carry a heavy wooden cross up the same mountain range. But He would go all the way to the highest peak, known as Mount Calvary, and sacrifice Himself as payment for the sins of all humanity.

It's a beautiful picture of Jesus! Can you see it?

Now imagine being in Abraham's position: You are going up the mountain with your son, Isaac. When you arrive at the place of the sacrifice, your boy turns to you with his big, beautiful eyes and innocently asks, "Papa, I see the fire and I see the wood, but where is the lamb?"

I am sure that question must have rent Abraham's heart. Holding back his emotions, he looked the boy in the eyes and said, "My son, God will provide Himself a lamb." Abraham spoke those words by faith, and it was a prophetic word of what God would do.

Now just as Abraham was about to slay his son, God said,

"Withhold your hand and look." Abraham looked behind him, and he saw a ram caught in a thicket by its horns (see Gen. 22:12–13). I believe that when Abraham turned around and looked, not only did he see the ram caught in a thicket, but he also saw a prophetic vision of the true Lamb of God, Jesus Christ, with a crown of thorns (not unlike the thicket the ram's horns were caught in) surrounding His brow. He saw the Lamb fastened with coarse nails to the cross.

How do I know that? Because Jesus told the Pharisees, "Abraham rejoiced to see My day." And they mocked Him, saying, "You are not even fifty years old, and You claim to have seen Abraham?" He replied emphatically, "Before Abraham was, I AM" (see John 8:56–58).

What did Abraham rejoice at? That day on Mount Moriah, Abraham saw a prophetic picture of Jesus on the cross, and he rejoiced to see His day! He saw that God would indeed provide Himself as the sacrificial Lamb, and so he called the place *Yehovah Yireh* (*Jehovah Jireh*), which means "Jehovah will see (to it)"[4] or "The-Lord-Will-Provide" (Gen. 22:14). My friend, God saw our desperate need for an offering, and He provided His own beloved Son as *the* sacrifice for all men.

God told Abraham, "Now I know that you love Me because you have not withheld your son, your only son, the son whom you love, from Me" (see Gen. 22:12). Do you know why He said that? It's so that today we can believe and say with assurance in our hearts, "Dear God, now I know that You love me because You have not withheld Your Son, Your only Son, the Son whom You love so dearly, but gave Him up at the cross for me."

Immerse Yourself in His Love and Grace

My friend, you will never know how much God loves you unless you understand how much God loved Jesus and yet gave Him up to rescue you. God didn't have to send His Son to suffer the cross, but He chose to do it because of His infinite love for you.

> *You will never know how much God loves you unless you understand how much God loved Jesus and yet gave Him up to rescue you.*

Don't forget that in Abraham's case, God stopped him from sacrificing Isaac. In Jesus' case, no one stopped the sacrifice. No one spared God's heart. No one assuaged the Father's grief. It was a heavy sacrifice made with a heart of love.

The entire story of Abraham offering Isaac is about the immensity of God's love for us. The story reveals to us the anguish, pain, and heartache that God Himself would go through. As the Father, He offered His own precious and beloved Son, Jesus Christ, to redeem us from our sins. God doesn't treat sin lightly. The only way to save us was to allow the punishment for sin to fall completely upon His own Son. Jesus is the "ram" that allowed Himself to be caught in a "thicket" as the payment for all our transgressions.

When you see Jesus unveiled in the Scriptures, when you see His love, suffering, and sacrifice revealed in the Scriptures like this, your heart will burn with the warmth of His love, as did the hearts of the two disciples who heard Him expound from the Scriptures all the things concerning Himself. Unconsciously discouragement, worries, and all your apprehensions will melt away as His unconditional love ignites hope and faith in your heart.

God wants you to be occupied with Jesus, to be free from self-occupation, through seeing His Son in the Word. Fill your mind with His love and power, and your heart will find rest in His lavish love for you. I pray that you will experience your own Emmaus Road journey as you open up the Scriptures and allow His Word to bathe your heart in the warmth of His loving grace and tender mercies. It's truly all about Jesus!

CHAPTER 15

WORSHIP WITH THE WORDS OF DAVID

As we continue learning how we can be set free from self-occupation, let me share with you the journey taken by a lady, Barbara, from Texas, who found that Jesus was the answer to her struggles.

Dear Pastor Prince,

I was saved as a young child, but because of sins—committed by me and to me—I never felt worthy. Anxiety attacks, migraines, and other physical symptoms continued to plague me for years, becoming worse over time. I recently hit rock bottom when the lies of the accuser made me go from fearing every time I left my house, to having full-blown anxiety attacks even in my own home. I would wake from sleep having these attacks. I knew something needed to change, but didn't know where to start.

I fought against taking medication that the doctor prescribed. I would pray and had my mother pray, but something was missing. I was determined to get well, so I bought self-help books, including a "Christian" book. I believed that God was willing to heal me and that Jesus died for my healing, but I had to "do my part" if my healing was going to manifest. I read the "Christian" book to be set free, to get spiritual, mental, and physical healing, but it only caused me to relive and recount my entire past and put me in greater mental torment.

The accuser began to attack me even more. I felt worse than ever as he tormented me with things that had happened twenty years ago and beyond. I actually thought that I had a taste of what hell might be like, being tormented day and night. I even thought that this was what I had to go through to get my healing. By my own failing efforts, I worked hard for redemption, trying to be good and to do right for the last several years. But my efforts only worked for small periods of time before the anxiety and fear would return with a vengeance.

But praise God I have a praying mother and I got hold of your books and teachings and received the revelation of grace and of the gift of righteousness. The earlier resources required my self-efforts, which only made things worse, but thankfully, they brought me to the end of myself.

Through the truth of your messages and books on grace and the person of Jesus, I am whole. I have stopped looking at myself and started looking unto Him. Each day, I draw from the living waters of Jesus. Day by day, I become more like Him because "as He is, so am I in this world."

I thank God for the revelations that I have had and continue to receive through your ministry. For the first time, I realize what it really means to be the righteousness

> *of God through Christ Jesus and understand the real, true*
> *power of Jesus' blood and His finished work on the cross.*
>
> *I'm excited about having a real relationship with my*
> *heavenly Daddy. I look forward to living the rest of my*
> *life enjoying the blessings of God through His unearned,*
> *unmerited favor. I asked for healing, but He has given*
> *me so much more!*

All praise and glory to Jesus! Isn't it amazing to see what happens when people simply turn their eyes away from themselves and occupy themselves with Jesus?

I love how Barbara describes the way she practices the presence of Jesus daily in her life: "I have stopped looking at myself and started looking unto Him. Each day, I draw from the living waters of Jesus. Day by day, I become more like Him because 'as He is, so am I in this world.'"

All she did was look away from herself and look to Jesus. And as she drew daily from His living waters, she found herself becoming more and more like Him—whole, stable, and sound in mind and body.

The One-Week Challenge

Can I encourage you to start doing what Barbara did? Every time you feel defeated, practice being conscious of Jesus in your life. Despite what you're feeling, see Him loving you, being with you, holding your hand, and guiding you out of your fear, pain, doubt, and adversity. Don't be slow of heart to believe; be quick to believe that Jesus is with you.

> *Be quick to believe that Jesus is with you.*

Before you give up and decide that things are never going to change in your life, I have an assignment for you. Would you try practicing the presence of Jesus for just one week? That's all I am asking—one week of your time. Throughout this week, the moment you think thoughts of failure, guilt, fear, anxiety, and defeat, *immediately* occupy your mind with positive thoughts of your Savior, Jesus Christ! The key word here is *immediately*. This is about being quick to believe, so it needs to happen fast! Immediately, see Jesus in your situation. Immediately, occupy your mind with thoughts of His love, His peace, His loving hand over your life, and His finished work.

At the end of this one week, write to me at praise@josephprince .com and share with me what you have experienced. I sincerely hope that you will take on this challenge, and I look forward to hearing from you.

How to Be Occupied with Jesus

Have you noticed that when you are experiencing pain in your body, it's extremely difficult to think about anything else? For example, if you have a bad toothache, you won't be thinking about the starving children in the world and their needs. No, you'll be consumed with the pain in your own mouth and nothing else really matters. The pain is all you feel, and it's all you can think about.

In the same way, when we are going through a difficult time or dealing with a heavy burden of stress, anxiety, fear, or condemnation, it's extremely challenging to make the shift from self-occupation to Christ-occupation because we are preoccupied with our own troubles. Like the bad toothache, our problems are all that we can think about. Self-occupation is like that. It is painful, and it keeps your attention on self.

So how do we make the paradigm shift from being occupied with our own problems and ourselves to being occupied with Jesus?

To answer that question, let me show you how David encouraged himself in the Lord whenever he was fearful, anxious, or depressed. Let's learn from someone whom God describes as "a man after My own heart" (Acts 13:22). God's Word reveals to us that whenever David was in trouble, he worshiped the Lord with beautiful psalms, hymns, and praises. Instead of wallowing in his own defeat and groping in darkness, David would turn his eyes to the heavens and lift up his voice to the King of kings.

In his closing years, when Absalom, his own son, tried to usurp the throne, David could have chosen to retaliate by sending out his loyal troops against Absalom. However, he didn't have the heart to fight against his own son. So instead of battling with Absalom, whom he loved immensely, David fled from Absalom with tears in his eyes and a broken heart. Just imagine how crushed David must have been, betrayed by his own flesh and blood.

But rather than be overwhelmed by the excruciatingly painful circumstances surrounding him, David looked to the Lord and worshiped Him with these eternal words as he ascended the Mount of Olives: "But You, O LORD, are a shield for me, my glory and the

One who lifts up my head. I cried to the LORD with my voice, and He heard me from His holy hill" (Ps. 3:3–4).

Isn't it wonderful to know that when we cry out to God in worship, He hears us? As David worshiped the Lord, God turned his circumstances around for his good. God allowed a person in Absalom's camp to give him unsound advice, and as a result Absalom's coup d'état failed.

Worship Jesus in Your Valley of Trouble

I am telling you that no matter what your trouble is today, learn to worship Jesus in your valley of trouble and praise His lovely name. See Him as your shield. See Him as the glory and lifter of your head. Be consumed with Jesus, and He will turn your circumstances around for your good. Let your heart find rest and peace in the security of His love.

> *Learn to worship Jesus in your valley of trouble.*

Some people think that when they worship God, they are *giving* something to Him. On the contrary, I believe that as we worship Him and praise Him, *He is giving to us*, imparting His life, wisdom, and power into our lives. Our minds are being renewed, and I believe that our youth and physical bodies are being renewed as well in His sweet presence.

Think about it for a moment. God doesn't need us to worship and praise Him. He has an entire army of angels who can sing to

Him and praise Him twenty-four hours a day, seven days a week. And unlike you and me, these angels don't grow weary and they never sing out of tune! God isn't a megalomaniac, demanding worship and praise from us. Absolutely not! Whether you worship and praise Him or not, He is still God.

Worship then is a response on our part to His love for us. We don't have to, but when we experience His love and grace in our lives, we want to. It's a response birthed out of a revelation in our hearts of just how great, how awesome, how majestic, and how altogether lovely our Lord and Savior truly is. As we worship Him and become utterly lost in His magnificent love for us, something happens to us. We are forever changed and transformed in His presence. All fears, worries, and anxieties depart when Jesus is exalted in our worship.

> *As we worship Him and become utterly lost in His magnificent love for us, we are forever changed and transformed in His presence.*

The Power of Worship

Our ministry team received this letter from Emma in Germany, and I believe it will help you see just what worship can do for you:

> *I am sixty-two years old. Whenever the devil tries to attack me with symptoms of a disease, I would listen to*

your worship albums and worship Jesus, my Lord, my Savior, and my Redeemer. I would also often partake of the Holy Communion while listening to the worship songs. After a few minutes, all the symptoms would disappear!

After experiencing these miracles, I began to take the worship songs to the home for the aged that I work in. At this home, there were a few elderly folks who would cry through-out the night. No medicine could help them, and one would hear them crying from 8 p.m. to 6 a.m. I work the night shift, and one night I put the CD player in the corridor of their rooms and played your worship CD A Touch of His Presence. That night, none of those elderly folks cried. They were all quiet and slept peacefully through the night.

There was also a lady at the home who was suffering from schizophrenia. One night she was very restless and kept speaking loudly to herself. Her neighbor, a lady with dementia, was singing shrilly. I took my iPod and played the songs from A Touch of His Presence to them. After three minutes, both women fell into a deep sleep.

My two colleagues who were with me were astonished by what they had witnessed, and they asked to have a CD player in the women's room so that the other ladies could listen to the worship songs. Up till today, these elderly patients no longer cry themselves to sleep at night.

As for me, I have been listening to the worship songs on my iPod during my break at work, and every time the glory of God would come to this home for the aged and bless the old people. All praises to Jesus!

I love this testimony. It really showcases how powerful worship can be!

The CD that Emma mentioned comes from a worship collection, *A Touch of His Presence (Volumes 1 and 2)*. This is not a regular recording of songs. The songs were compiled from live services and are all spontaneous worship songs that flowed from my spirit during intimate times of worship when we simply occupied ourselves with the person of Jesus. I would sing out what God was putting in my heart, and He would manifest His loving presence. That's when the gifts of the Spirit would operate and healings would break out among the people in the congregation.

On the popular digital music website iTunes, which features this collection, one person shared how playing the songs in *A Touch of His Presence* as he worshiped the Lord or while he was lying in bed just ushered in the sweet presence of the Lord. These times have been so instrumental in anchoring and steadying him that he has made it part of his daily routine.

Another brother described how this worship music freed him from much fear and chronic sleep problems. Every night for a few years, a paralyzing, irrational fear would awaken him from sleep every thirty minutes or so and leave him in the throes of even greater terror. Despite praying for peace, this poor man found that he could not go to sleep with the lights off.

One day as he played the songs in his room, all of a sudden he felt the tangible presence of the Lord's calm and peace. And as he listened to the music, for the first time in a very long time, he slept like a baby. He was so happy that all he could do was thank the

Lord and cry! He listens to the album every night now and even has it downloaded to his iPod in his car.

I wanted to share these testimonies with you because I believe that some of you want to worship God, but you may not know where to begin when you are alone at home. If that sounds like you, then start by getting ahold of anointed Christian music that can fill your room with the presence of the Lord. Allow the music to simply wash over you like rivers of living waters. Let His presence flush out every fear and every anxiety. Let His love take away the cares that burden you. Let Jesus be magnified and glorified, and watch Him turn all things around for your good!

Learn from the Sweet Psalmist

Long before the enemy can steal your victory, he steals your song. Long before he can steal your joy, he steals your praise. Before you know it, you start becoming critical, pessimistic, moody, and depressed. Don't allow him to do that. Let praises be continually on your lips and always be conscious of the Lord's presence, His favor, His goodness, and His blessings in your life.

Don't know what to sing? There is no one better for us to learn from than the sweet psalmist of Israel, David. There was a king after David named Hezekiah, who did just that. Take a look at how the Bible describes this king in 2 Kings 18:5, 7: "He trusted in the LORD God of Israel, so that after him was none like him among all the kings of Judah, nor who were before him…The LORD was with him; he prospered wherever he went."

King Hezekiah brought revival to his people and restored praise and worship to the house of God. He also brought back sovereignty to his nation after his father, King Ahaz, plunged the kingdom into pagan worship and brought the nation under the curse (see 2 Kings 16, 18–19).

In 2 Chronicles 29:25–26, 30, it records that Hezekiah "stationed the Levites in the house of the LORD with cymbals, with stringed instruments, and with harps, according to the commandment of David... The Levites stood with the instruments of David... Moreover King Hezekiah and the leaders commanded the Levites to sing praise to the LORD with the words of David..."

Aren't you glad that God gave us the book of Psalms in the Bible so that like King Hezekiah, we can worship the Lord with the words of David? David wrote a large number of the psalms, and God is unveiled in a special way when we sing with the words of David. He gave David a special gift to write songs that unveil His love and heart.

We certainly can't improve on the words that David wrote, so let's join David in exalting the name of the Lord and allow Him to become our rock and fortress when we feel besieged by the issues of life. Let's magnify the Lord and watch Him deliver us. Let's follow after Him and let Him be our shepherd. Let Him bring us to rest in green pastures and lead us beside still waters.

How Jesus Defined the Fear of God

Something happens when you sing with the words of David. Your fears will begin to melt away. You cannot psych yourself out of fear. Maybe even as you are reading this right now, your mind is besieged with fear about your future, or a fear of lack or of losing your youth. Perhaps you are afraid of some disease or of losing your loved ones to some sickness. Maybe you are tormented daily by the fear of rejection. My friend, the only fear God wants you to have is a wholesome fear of the Lord, which Jesus Himself defines as the *worship* of God.

When the devil tempted Jesus in the wilderness, he said, "All these things [all the kingdoms of the world and their glory] I will give You if You will fall down and worship me." Jesus, quoting from the book of Deuteronomy, replied, "Away with you, Satan! For it is written, 'You shall worship the LORD your God, and Him only you shall serve'" (Matt. 4:9–10).

Now, if you do a quick check on what Jesus quoted in the book of Deuteronomy, it actually says, "You shall fear the LORD your God…" (Deut. 6:13). So Jesus defined the "fear" of God as the "worship" of God. In other words, the only "fear" that you should have in your life is the *worship* of God. Worship Him and all your fears will fade away in the light of His glory and grace.

> *Worship Him and all your fears will fade away in the light of His glory and grace.*

The Shepherd's Psalm

The most quoted psalm in the Bible, Psalm 23, was written by David. You might be familiar with these words that God has preserved in His Word for us to learn about His love and goodness toward us: "The LORD is my shepherd; I shall not want" (v. 1). Psalm 23 is an amazing psalm for you to memorize and meditate on every time you face a challenge.

A brother in Maryland wrote me to share how he was healed of chronic pain in his shoulder simply by meditating on Psalm 23. John had read one of my daily devotionals on meditating on God's Word, where I demonstrated how to do this with Psalm 23. On his way home from work that very day, John began to meditate on "The Lord is my shepherd, I shall not want." He focused on how kind the Lord is to want to be our shepherd and how He has truly provided for all our needs. John saw the Lord protecting him on the road, healing him of his pain, and giving him favor at work. By the time he reached home, he discovered that the pain, which had plagued him for two years and restricted his movements, had completely left!

My friend, I want you to know that the power to heal you right where you are is found in God's Word. There is healing power in the psalms! They are not just songs written to fill up pages in your Bible. Something happens to your physical body and external circumstances when you memorize, meditate on, and worship with the words of David.

Psalm 34—Choose to Bless the Lord

Another beautiful psalm is Psalm 34, which was written by David in the cave of Adullam. I find it really interesting that David wrote one of the most powerful psalms during one of the most challenging seasons in his life. The introduction to the psalm in some Bible translations, such as the New King James Version, describes Psalm 34 as "A Psalm of David when he pretended madness before Abimelech, who drove him away, and he departed."

It's by no stretch of the imagination for us to see that this was one of the lowest points in David's life. David was on the run from King Saul and sought refuge with the king of Gath (referred to as "Abimelech" in the introduction to the psalm). Remember Gath? Goliath, the giant who had terrorized the children of Israel, was from Gath. And now David was in such a state of disarray that he was seeking asylum from Goliath's king! Oh, how the mighty had fallen!

When David was in Gath, the servants of the king of Gath recognized him and said, "Is this not David the king of the land?" They probably recognized him as the one who slew their champion Goliath and severed his head. It was, after all, a major defeat that would not be easily erased from their minds. So they reminded their king, "Did they not sing of him... 'Saul has slain his thousands, and David his ten thousands'?" (1 Sam. 21:11).

When David heard their words, fear seized his heart and he became very afraid of what the king of Gath might do to him. The Bible tells us that "he changed his behavior before them, pretended madness in their hands, scratched on the doors of the gate, and let his saliva fall down on his beard" (1 Sam. 21:13). Can you imagine the mental state that David was in? The champion of Israel was now groveling on the floor with saliva all over his beard!

Incensed that his servants had brought a "madman" before him, the king of Gath threw David out. Then, in the very next verse, the Bible records for us that "David therefore departed from there and escaped to the cave of Adullam" (1 Sam. 22:1).

Now that you understand the context, you can appreciate the words that were penned from the depths of that cave. After such a demeaning episode, David could have hidden in the cave and indulged in self-pity and condemnation, but instead he sang these words:

> *I will bless the* LORD *at all times; His praise shall continually be in my mouth. My soul shall make its boast in the* LORD; *the humble shall hear of it and be glad. Oh, magnify the* LORD *with me, and let us exalt His name together. I sought the* LORD, *and He heard me, and delivered me from all my fears.*
>
> —Psalm 34:1–4

In his darkest hour, David chose not to be defeated by his circumstances. Instead he chose to bless the Lord and let the praises of the Lord be continually in his mouth. Was he fearful? Absolutely! That is why he was hiding in a cave. However, despite his fear that King Saul would capture him or that the king of Gath would slay him to avenge Goliath, he sought the Lord in worship, and God in His faithfulness delivered him from all his fears.

From 3D Army to Fearless Warriors

My friend, I want you to see that David entered the cave in despair, but something happened as David worshiped the Lord. And it didn't just transform him, but it also transformed all the men who were gathered with him. The Bible tells us that when David was in the cave, "everyone who was in distress, everyone who was in debt, and everyone who was discontented gathered to him. So he became captain over them. And there were about four hundred men with him" (1 Sam. 22:2).

I call this the 3D army since everyone who was distressed, in debt, or discontented gathered to David. And in the psalm, David encouraged all of these four hundred men to sing out loud in the cave and "magnify the Lord" with him (Ps. 34:3). As they did, their faces became "radiant" and they "were not ashamed" (Ps. 34:5).

So these men didn't remain as the 3D army. They were transformed from glory to glory and became known as David's mighty men. You can read all about their great exploits in 2 Samuel 23:8–39. They became fearless warriors, giant slayers in their own right, and faithful men who served David all the days of their lives.

In the same way today, when you choose to worship the Lord in the midst of your trials, you can't help but be transformed. You may start out being distressed, in debt, or discontented. But your story doesn't end there. As you keep your eyes on the King of kings, *He* will exalt you and cause you to become mighty!

> *Keep your eyes on the King of kings. He will exalt you and
> cause you to become mighty!*

From Fear to Faith

Let's take a closer look at what happened to David. In Psalm 34, he wrote, "This poor man cried out" (obviously referring to himself), and continued, "and the LORD heard him, and saved him out of all his troubles" (v. 6). David was hiding from his enemies, but as he worshiped, we see a change in his frame of mind.

He started out terrified, but we see how he kept shifting his thoughts away from himself and his own fears. We see how he kept practicing the power of right believing by declaring in his psalm how the Lord had heard him and delivered him. In the end, he stopped seeing himself as alone and besieged. Instead he declared with boldness that "the angel of the LORD encamps all around those who fear Him, and delivers them" (v. 7).

In other words, as David worshiped the Lord, he was no longer afraid of his enemies. The angel of the Lord became more real to him than King Saul or the king of Gath. And David, who had just escaped by feigning madness and debasing himself before the people of Gath, could now boast in the Lord and proclaim this with confidence: the angel of the Lord encamps around and encircles those who worship Him, and He will surely deliver them.

Do you believe that today? It doesn't matter if you are feeling fearful, if you are in distress, in debt, or discontented. Believe right.

Believe that when you seek the Lord in worship as David and his men did, the Lord will indeed hear you and deliver you from all your troubles. Worship is one of the easiest, yet most powerful ways of being free from self-occupation. Look away from the painful symptoms or the fearful circumstances that are bothering you, and worship Jesus. Be occupied with Him and everything will work together for your good.

> *Worship is one of the easiest, yet most powerful ways of being free from self-occupation.*

Would you do me a favor? I would like you to visit josephprince .com/power, where I have included a worship video of me leading my church in singing the words of David in Psalm 34. This is not something I can accomplish in a book, but I want to demonstrate to you through the video how worship is one of the quickest ways for you to focus on Jesus and overcome your feelings of defeat.

I am believing that as we worship the Lord, you will be completely free from any trouble or area of defeat that you are struggling with today. Let's agree together that your body will be healed, that all your fears will disappear, and that all your addictions will be gone in the mighty name of Jesus.

Come magnify the Lord with me, come worship Jesus with the words of David, and experience His goodness and deliverance!

PART SIX

HAVE A CONFIDENT EXPECTATION OF GOOD

CHAPTER 16

THE BATTLE BELONGS TO THE LORD

As the marauding armies of Moab, Ammon, and Mount Seir descended upon Jerusalem, Jehoshaphat, the king of Judah, called for a state of emergency and gathered all of Judah to seek help from the Lord. All the men of Judah, with their wives and their little ones, stood before the house of the Lord with grim faces, waiting anxiously to hear from their king. They knew their enemies outnumbered them many times over, and the fear of losing everything they had now crushed their spirits. Some of the women cried uncontrollably, fearing for the lives of their husbands in the ensuing battle. The children in their midst, who had never witnessed their parents and relatives so fearful and downcast, just waited with uncharacteristic quietness for the king to speak.

Have you been in a situation like this, where your circumstances appear to be completely hopeless? Where you felt immobilized and overwhelmed by the challenges surrounding you, with no way out or even a temporary respite in sight?

That is exactly what happened to the small tribe of Judah when they were besieged on all fronts by three powerful and bloodthirsty armies rapidly advancing toward them (see 2 Chron. 20:1–4). With their enemies mercilessly bent on annihilating them and all the inhabitants of Jerusalem, it was a forlorn and hopeless situation, and it looked like they were bound for a tragic end.

Hope for Hopeless Times

There may be seasons in our lives where it seems as if our challenges are coming at us simultaneously from every direction, and we are completely inundated by problem after problem. Perhaps the strain of a financial challenge led to cracks in your marriage as well as the development of a medical condition *and* a heavy mental oppression. Under the accumulated weight of it all coming against you at once, you feel as if your entire life is spiraling out of control and falling apart. Day by day, your circumstances appear to be fast deteriorating despite your best efforts to salvage things.

In such desperate times, what do you do when you honestly don't know what to do?

I believe that the answer can be found in the Bible's account of the battle of Jehoshaphat. There are many precious and practical gems of wisdom there that you and I can benefit from, especially when it comes to facing great pressure and feeling paralyzed by the sheer scale of the adversities surrounding us.

Overcoming Fear

I just want to draw your attention to the fact that when Jehoshaphat was informed that a great multitude was coming against him, he feared. That's right, Jehoshaphat's first reaction was fear! I don't know about you, but this gives me hope! I'm so glad that the Word of God doesn't censor unglamorous details. It gives us an authentic portrait of who Jehoshaphat was. He wasn't a valiant warrior king who was always full of faith and endowed with a disproportionate dose of fiery courage, always ready to take down his enemies. No, he was a regular guy. He was just like us. When he heard the bad report about his enemies, he did what you and I would have done—he panicked.

But what set Jehoshaphat apart was that even when he was fearful, the very first thing he did was to "set himself to seek the LORD" (2 Chron. 20:3). That is something you and I need to learn to do as well whenever we are fearful. Instead of spiraling deeper into the abyss of self-defeat, know that when you are feeling overwhelmed by your circumstances, that is the time you need to set yourself to seek the Lord. It's certainly not the time to run away from God or get bitter, angry, frustrated, and disappointed with Him. Hey, God is not the author of your troubles. He is the author and finisher of your faith, victory, and success.

God is not the author of your troubles. He is the author and finisher of your faith, victory, and success.

Jehoshaphat shows us that it's quite all right to be fearful. We all experience bouts of fear from time to time. God doesn't condemn you when you are afraid. But when you receive a negative medical report or some bad news about your family or business, set yourself to seek the Lord. Jesus is your answer! His perfect love for you will cast out all fear.

Having True Bible Hope

After Jehoshaphat had gathered all Judah to him, he stood before the people in the house of the Lord and prayed, "O LORD God of our fathers, are You not God in heaven, and do You not rule over all the kingdoms of the nations, and in Your hand is there not power and might, so that no one is able to withstand You?" (2 Chron. 20:6).

What do you see in the words of Jehoshaphat's prayer? Instead of rehashing his fears to the Lord and lamenting about how overpowered by their enemies their small tribe was, Jehoshaphat centered his prayer and thoughts on just how big and powerful his God truly is. He proclaimed boldly that "no one is able to withstand" the Lord. No one, not even the mighty warriors of Moab, Ammon, and Mount Seir! In a hopeless situation, Jehoshaphat *hoped* in the Lord.

I call that Bible hope! Hope is a beautiful word in the Bible. Hope in the New Testament is the Greek word *elpis*, which is defined as a "favorable and confident expectation" or "the happy anticipation of good."[1] This means that when you hope in the Lord, there is a joy in your countenance (simply put, a smile on your face). There is a confident assurance in your heart that, bleak as the circumstances appear to be, it's not over yet.

Say it out loud right now: "It's not over!"

> *Hope in the Lord is a confident assurance in your heart that, bleak as the circumstances appear to be, it's not over yet.*

God is working behind the scenes on your behalf, and He is turning the situation around for your good (see Rom. 8:28). He is preparing a table before you in the presence of your enemies (see Ps. 23:5). All His abundant heavenly resources, His power, His healing, His restoration, His deliverance, His provision, His favor, His help, His comfort, and His love are with you and on your side, waiting to be unleashed upon you. The Lord your God will open up the windows of heaven over your life and pour out for you such a blessing that there won't be room enough to receive it! When our entire hope and trust is in Him, we can count on His promises toward us. He will rebuke the devourer for our sakes and not allow the enemy to take what rightfully belongs to us.

Unfortunately, the word "hope" as used in our modern vernacular is completely different and sometimes even antithetical to the way the Bible defines it. When we use the word "hope" today, we say things like, "I hope that I will get the job" and "I hope that it will not rain tomorrow." Our use of the word connotes uncertainty, doubt, and ambivalence. Many times we even use the word "hope" in a negative sense, as if expecting the worst. For instance, we might say, "I hope that the medical report is not going to be bad," in tones full of fear, apprehension, and insecurity. This is not Bible hope.

Hope That Doesn't Disappoint

The Word of God declares that "this hope will not lead to disappointment. For we know how dearly God loves us" (Rom. 5:5 NLT). In the English Standard Version, it says that "hope does not put us to shame, because God's love has been poured into our hearts through the Holy Spirit who has been given to us." We can have true hope—a certain, joyful, confident expectation of good—when we rightly believe how dearly God loves us! There is a direct and proportionate correlation between hope and rightly believing in God's love for you. Hope springs in your heart when you believe that God loves you. You can have a confident expectation of good because you have a good God who will never leave you in the lurch!

> *You can have a confident expectation of good because you have a good God who will never leave you in the lurch!*

No matter how adverse your circumstances may seem today, put your trust in the Lord. Man may disappoint and fail us, but God never fails. Psalm 118:8–9 spells this out for us when it says, "It is better to trust in the LORD than to put confidence in man. It is better to trust in the LORD than to put confidence in princes." Just look at the results when we do so—despite being attacked on all fronts, the psalmist is able to boldly declare, "All nations surrounded me, but in the name of the LORD I will destroy them" (Ps. 118:10).

Do you want to know why the psalmist could put his trust in

the Lord instead of man? The secret is revealed in how this psalm begins and ends. The very first verse begins with an emphatic, "Oh, give thanks to the LORD, for He is good! For His mercy endures forever," and the psalm ends with the identical refrain, "Oh, give thanks to the LORD, for He is good! For His mercy endures forever" (v. 29).

My friend, hope in the Lord for *He is* good, and His love for you endures forever! No matter how difficult, impossible, or dire your current situation may be, you can have a positive, optimistic, and confident expectation of good. And it's because you know and believe that your God is good and that His love for you endures for all eternity. You are the apple of His eye! This hope never disappoints, which means that your greatest victories are ahead of you.

> *Hope in the Lord for He is good, and His love for you endures forever!*

Stand Still

After Jehoshaphat set himself to seek the Lord and prayed before all the assembly of Judah, the spirit of the Lord came upon Jahaziel and he spoke the words of the Lord:

> *"Listen, all you of Judah and you inhabitants of Jerusa-
> lem, and you, King Jehoshaphat! Thus says the LORD to
> you: 'Do not be afraid nor dismayed because of this great*

multitude, for the battle is not yours, but God's... You will
not need to fight in this battle. Position yourselves, stand
still and see the salvation of the LORD, who is with you,
O Judah and Jerusalem!' Do not fear or be dismayed;
tomorrow go out against them, for the LORD is with you."

—2 Chronicles 20:15, 17

On hearing these words of hope, all Judah humbled themselves before the Lord, bowing before Him and worshiping Him.

Today the Lord is saying the same words to you in your situation. Hope in Him for He loves you! You don't have to live in fear and discouragement when you know that the battle is not yours, but the Lord's. Stand still and see the salvation of the Lord. The battle is His, and you will not need to fight in it.

What do you do when you don't know what do? The best thing you can do is to *stand still.*

Stand still and see the salvation of the Lord in your situation.

But Pastor Prince, if I stand still, nothing will happen!

My friend, standing still is not inactivity or doing nothing. It's a posture of hope, and it involves keeping your hope anchored on the person of Jesus and having a sure and confident expectation of good. When the marauding armies of Pharaoh were charging toward the children of Israel, hell-bent on annihilating them, Moses simply declared to the terrified Israelites, "Do not be afraid. Stand still, and see the salvation of the LORD" (Exod. 14:13). The Hebrew word for salvation is *yeshua,* which is actually the name of Jesus. So salvation is the person of Jesus, and He is with you.

When you are caught in a hopeless situation, learn to position yourself—stand still and see the saving power of Jesus work on your behalf. He will never leave you nor forsake you (see Heb. 13:5). And as you center yourself, your thoughts, your beliefs, and your hopes on Him, He will lead you concerning what to do, just as He led Jehoshaphat to a triumphant victory over his enemies.

> *When you are caught in a hopeless situation, learn to position yourself—stand still and see the saving power of Jesus work on your behalf.*

Believe in the Lord

We are about to come to the climax of the story. Are you ready to read about Jehoshaphat's battle?

The Bible tells us that "they rose early in the morning and went out into the Wilderness of Tekoa; and as they went out, Jehoshaphat stood and said, 'Hear me, O Judah and you inhabitants of Jerusalem: Believe in the LORD your God, and you shall be established; believe His prophets, and you shall prosper'" (2 Chron. 20:20).

I want to encourage you to commit this simple and powerful Scripture to memory. I call this the 20/20 vision because this verse is found in chapter 20, verse 20. To have 20/20 vision is to have what eye doctors consider healthy visual acuity. This means that you are not suffering from myopia or shortsightedness and are able to see with clarity when you stand 20 feet away from the eye chart.

If you desire to have spiritual visual acuity and a 20/20 vision of the good that God has for you in your future, then believe in the Lord and the words of His prophets (the pastors and preachers whom God has placed in your life)! That is the power of right believing. Don't be myopic and be caught up with your current challenges, running around like a headless chicken, trying to solve your problems in your own strength. God doesn't want you to live in a perpetual state of uncertainty, anxiety, stress, and fear.

Believe in the Lord your God, and you will be established.

Believe His prophets, and you shall prosper.

Believe that the battles you are facing belong to the Lord.

> *Believe that the battles you are facing belong to the Lord.*

When you believe right, you will experience true Bible hope and start living with a certain, joyful, confident expectation of good regardless of your current circumstances.

Many are struggling because they don't believe in the Lord. They don't believe in His Word, and they don't believe in His prophets. Their crisis is a crisis of belief! That's why it's so essential to understand the power of right believing. Right believing will always produce right living. If you can change what you believe, you can most definitely change your life and begin living with hope, joy, and confidence.

Jehoshaphat's Unusual Military Strategy

Just before the army of Judah marched out to the battlefield, Jehoshaphat consulted with the people. Then he did a very unusual thing. He appointed worshipers who would sing praises to the Lord to go before the army! This was a very peculiar military strategy, to say the least. Ask any warfare expert. No one would advise you to send your musicians to the battlefield, much less position them right in front—unless you had a death wish for them.

From the little that I know about military warfare, you need to send in your elite forces first, such as your commandos or Navy Seals, to gather intelligence or strike at key targets. And they are supposed to operate in stealth mode to gain tactical advantage against your enemy. A band of worshipers praising God at the top of their voices and giving away their very position to the enemy sounds more like a suicide mission than a good military strategy.

But remember, this was no ordinary battle. The battle belonged to the Lord, and the Word records for us that the moment "they began to sing and to praise, the LORD set ambushes against the people of Ammon, Moab, and Mount Seir, who had come against Judah; and they were defeated" (2 Chron. 20:22).

God caused confusion among the enemies' camps and instead of coming against Judah, the soldiers of Ammon and Moab formed an alliance to "utterly kill and destroy" the inhabitants of Mount Seir. Then, when they had completely annihilated them, they turned against each other and began destroying one another until everyone was killed (see 2 Chron. 20:23).

All this while, as their enemies were destroying one another, the worshipers of Judah were praising God, oblivious to what was going on among their enemies. So when they arrived at the place that overlooked the battlefield, they braced themselves for an all-out attack by the combined forces of three different enemies.

Imagine their faces when the sight of the dead bodies of their would-be executioners sprawled across the valley greeted them instead. The destruction of their enemies was so complete that the Bible records, "No one had escaped" (2 Chron. 20:24).

Praise the Lord for He Is Good

Judah did not draw a single sword that day, but the battle was won. In fact, it was won before Judah's troops even arrived at the scene.

Did you notice *when* the Lord began to set ambushes against their enemies? It was when they *began* to sing praises to God. When I hear this story being taught over the pulpit, the emphasis is usually on how praise defeats our enemies. That's a great teaching. But today I want to take you one step deeper. I want to show you that the words of praise used are just as important, if not even more important. You can praise the Lord for different things, but in seasons when pressures, challenges, and problems come at you on all fronts, what do you do when you don't know what to do? In times of great adversity, how do you maintain a confident expectation of good and continue to hope in the Lord?

You should know by now that one of my favorite phrases is, "There are no insignificant details in the Bible." God deliberately records for us the words that the people of Judah praised Him with as they marched into battle. And that is why we know that they were singing, "Praise the LORD, for His mercy endures forever" (2 Chron 20:21). Sounds familiar? We talked about this earlier in this chapter when we were studying how Psalm 118 begins and ends with this same refrain. But this phrase doesn't only appear in the book of Psalms. In fact, this refrain is so close to God's heart that it features very prominently in many key moments in Israel's history.

For instance, the Bible chronicles that on the very day that David finally brought the ark of the covenant back to Jerusalem, he delivered a psalm into the hand of Asaph that contained this refrain: "Oh, give thanks to the LORD, for He is good! For His mercy endures forever" (see 1 Chron. 16:7, 34). Then on the day of the dedication of the temple that David's son, Solomon, built for God, the Bible also notes that all the children of Israel worshiped and praised the Lord, saying, "For He is good, for His mercy endures forever" (2 Chron. 7:3). Again, we hear this powerful refrain.

My friend, I think it's obvious that there is something very special about these two simple lines of praise. I believe God wants us to meditate upon and praise Him with these simple words even when we are feeling down, overwhelmed, or fearful. In such times, we can still praise Him because He is good and His mercy endures forevermore. Do you believe that today? Praise Him with these words until you believe it in your heart, and I promise you that hope will spring forth from within you.

Many are struggling today because they don't believe that God is good and that His mercy endures forever. The word for "mercy" here is the very potent Hebrew word *hesed*, which speaks of God's grace, love, tender mercies, and loving-kindness.[2] No matter how many times you have failed and fallen short, and even if the troubles that surround you are a consequence of your own actions, would you turn to the Lord today and praise Him for His goodness and His *hesed* (His grace)?

I have experienced His goodness and His *hesed* (His grace) in this way myself. Some years ago when I was going through a challenging time in my life, God gave me a heavenly tune and these words just flowed out of my spirit: "Praise the Lord for He is so good, and His love endures forever. Praise the Lord for He is so good, and His mercy endures forevermore." It was a very simple, pure, and uncomplicated tune, and I just sang it over and over again until all my fears, anxieties, and worries disappeared and I felt completely free.

Praise the Lord for He is good, for His *hesed* (grace, love, tender mercies, and loving-kindness) in your life endures forever. Worship Him with these words, and as you praise Him, He will ambush all your enemies, troubles, fears, challenges, and addictions. By the time you reach your battlefield, I believe your enemies will all have fallen. Not a single one of your adversaries will escape because the Lord Himself fights your battles.

> *Praise the Lord for He is good, for His hesed (grace, love, tender mercies, and loving-kindness) in your life endures forever.*

The Valley of Blessing

Do you know how the story of the battle of Jehoshaphat ends? Jehoshaphat and his men spent three full days gathering the spoils of war that they had found among the dead bodies of their enemies. They recovered "an abundance of valuables...and precious jewelry" (2 Chron. 20:25). On the fourth day, they gathered with all their spoils in the Valley of Berachah, and they worshiped and gave thanks to the Lord there (2 Chron. 20:26). How apt it is then that they named the valley "Berachah," which means "blessing."[3]

After this, the Bible tells us that "they returned, every man of Judah and Jerusalem, with Jehoshaphat in front of them, to go back to Jerusalem with joy, for the LORD had made them rejoice over their enemies" (2 Chron. 20:27). God had turned their fear into rejoicing, their sorrow into joy, and their troubles into blessings.

That is what happens when we hope in the Lord. Praise Him for He is good and His *hesed* (His grace) endures forever. You can have a confident expectation of good because your God is a good God. Like the people of Judah, which means "praise" in Hebrew (see Gen. 29:35), you will not need to fight, for the battle belongs to the Lord. Hallelujah!

CHAPTER 17

GOD LOVES IT WHEN YOU ASK BIG

I want to begin this chapter by giving you this challenge: Ask God for big things! What do you desire to see in your life—in your family, health, finances, and career? Ask God for them! Jesus said the enemy comes only to steal, kill, and destroy, but He came so that you might have life and have it more abundantly (see John 10:10). Jesus came so that you might live a life that is marked not by lack, but by abundance; not by despair, but by the fullness of His love, joy, and peace.

Do you desire to see yourself living free from fear, guilt, and addictions? Then ask the God of abundant grace and life.

Do you desire to see your body strong and healthy and your youth renewed like the eagle's (see Ps. 103:5)? Ask the God who is good.

Do you desire to see your marriage, children, and loved ones blessed in every way? Ask the God whose love for you endures forever.

Do you desire a career or business that you can be passionate about and in which you can exercise all the gifts that God has placed in your life? Ask the God who is more than enough.

Take a moment and don't rush through this. What would you ask God for if you knew beyond the shadow of a doubt that He is good and that His love for you endures forever?

> *What would you ask God for if you knew beyond the shadow of a doubt that He is good and that His love for you endures forever?*

What Would You Ask For?

I would like you to do something right now. Would you put this book down for a moment and grab your journal?

I would like you to write down what you would ask God for if you knew that He hears your prayers. What are your dreams, hopes, and aspirations? What would you like to see come to pass in your life? What are you battling with today? Which area of your life would you like to see God's power work in? Write it down. Write it all down. Write what you want to see happen with Bible hope in your heart that He hears you and will supply. Write with a certain, joyful, positive, and confident expectation of good.

Don't just ask God for small things. Ask Him for big things! For instance, don't ask Him for just a job. Ask Him for a position of influence. Don't just ask Him to restore your health. Ask Him for a long and healthy life filled with many good days. Enlarge your faith to believe in God's goodness. He is pleased when our faith is big. He is not offended when we ask Him for big things.

> *God is not offended when we ask Him for big things.*

Would you do that right now? Just take a few moments and pen down your requests to God—God, who is almighty and more powerful than we can ever imagine. God, who hung the planets in their places and spoke order into the world. God, who led His people in a pillar of cloud by day and a pillar of fire by night. God, who rained manna from heaven and brought forth water from dry rock. God, who helped Judah to overcome her enemies without even the drawing of a single sword. God, who turned bland water into the finest wine. God, who made the lame walk, the blind see, and the deaf hear. God, who multiplied five loaves of bread and two small fish to feed five thousand men. God, who rebuked the wind and turned a raging storm into a great calm. God, who raised the dead and conquered the grave.

Ask what you need of God, who loves YOU with an everlasting love!

God Loves It When You Ask of Him

There was a man in the Bible by the name of Jabez. His name was rather unfortunate. It means "sorrow"[1] because his mother "bore him in pain" (1 Chron. 4:9). What a name to have! But Jabez cried out to God, "Oh, that You would bless me indeed, and enlarge my territory, that Your hand would be with me, and that You would keep me from evil, that I may not cause pain!" (1 Chron. 4:10).

I have come across some preachers who claimed that believers should not pray "selfish" prayers for themselves to be blessed. Jabez's prayer would probably fall under their definition of a "selfish prayer" as it was all about him asking God to bless him, enlarge his territory, be with him, and protect him. But did you know that God didn't reprimand Jabez for asking Him for these blessings? Without any fanfare, the Bible in the very same verse simply records that "God granted him what he requested." In fact, the Bible also says that "Jabez was more honorable than his brothers" (1 Chron. 4:9) because he asked God for what he needed as opposed to fighting for it.

That was all. No drama, no long list of what Jabez had to do or not do. It's really that simple. God heard his prayer and granted his request! No rebuke, no instructions, no "Jabez, if you want Me to bless you, you must first do this." No, God honored the man's faith and turned his sorrow into *joy* and his pain into *blessings*—all because he had an unshakable confidence in how good God is and asked big!

My friend, have a good opinion of God. He is not out to get you. He loves you and desires to unleash His favor into every area of your life. He loves it when you call upon Him. And He promised that He would answer when you do. Just see Him declaring to you

Jeremiah 33:3: "Call to Me, and I will answer you, and show you great and mighty things, which you do not know."

> *Have a good opinion of God. He is not out to get you.*
> *He loves you and desires to unleash His favor into every area*
> *of your life.*

Could it be that we are not seeing many breakthroughs because we have made asking God for big things a taboo with our religious and legalistic rhetoric? Could it be that we are just not seeing many blessings because we have not been asking God and seeking Him with a confident expectation of good?

Let me show you what Jesus had to say about asking from God:

> *"Ask, and it will be given to you; seek, and you will find; knock, and it will be opened to you. For everyone who asks receives, and he who seeks finds, and to him who knocks it will be opened. Or what man is there among you who, if his son asks for bread, will give him a stone? Or if he asks for a fish, will he give him a serpent? If you then, being evil, know how to give good gifts to your children, how much more will your Father who is in heaven give good things to those who ask Him!"*
>
> —Matthew 7:7–11

My friend, it gives your heavenly Father great joy when you ask Him. It's His good pleasure to bless you as well as your family (see Luke 12:32). Stop being held back by erroneous beliefs about God, and start asking Him for whatever is on your heart today!

> *Stop being held back by erroneous beliefs about God, and start asking Him for whatever is on your heart today!*

God Honors Our Faith

Joshua, Moses' successor who led the children of Israel into the promised land, was someone who dared to ask big. When Joshua was caught in the thick of battle with his enemies and the sun was about to set, he cried out, "Sun, stand still over Gibeon; and Moon, in the Valley of Aijalon" (Josh. 10:12). The Bible goes on to record, "So the sun stood still, and the moon stopped, till the people had revenge upon their enemies…For the LORD fought for Israel" (Josh. 10:13–14).

I love this story. When my leaders and I were in the plains where this battle took place, we could see the sun over Gibeon on one side and the moon over the Valley of Aijalon on the other side. Both the sun and moon could be seen at the same time from that location. Standing there, I could just imagine Joshua in the midst of the battle, raising his voice and pointing to the sun on one side to stand still and then turning to the moon to issue the same command. Joshua was asking God for more daylight because the momentum of the battle was to their advantage. He wanted to completely rout his enemies and not give them time to regroup.

When you think about what Joshua asked, it was both an audacious and inaccurate request! If you had been attentive during your science classes in school, you would know that the earth orbits around the sun, not the sun around the earth! So technically, when Joshua called for the sun and moon to stand still, God made the *earth* stand still instead. Joshua's request was scientifically inaccurate, but nevertheless, God honored Joshua's chutzpah faith! He understood that what Joshua needed was more daylight, and He made it happen.

Isn't it encouraging to know that God didn't correct Joshua and give him CliffsNotes on how the solar system that He built actually functions? It gives me great encouragement to know that even when our faith confessions may not always be perfect, God still honors our hope and faith in Him. He loves it when we ask Him for big things. My friend, you can ask of Him, knowing that the battle truly belongs to the Lord, and that He will fight for you the way He fought for Israel because you are His covenant child.

A Story of God's Goodness

We have looked at God's Word and seen how He honored those who had a positive and confident expectation of good and who dared to ask Him for big things in their lives. Jabez cried out to the Lord to bless him, and God did. In the heat of battle, Joshua asked for the sun to stand still, and even though he got it scientifically wrong, God answered his prayer. Are you ready to hope in the Lord, to have a good opinion of Him, and to have a confident expectation of good for your life and future?

Let me encourage you further with the extraordinary story of a lady who is recognized today as one of the most outstanding entrepreneurs in the world. This lady had a rough start in life. Unlike most babies, who are greeted by the smiles and embraces of their loving parents as they welcome their bundle of joy into the world, her biological parents abandoned her at birth.

Fortunately, an illiterate widow whom she affectionately refers to as her "grandmother" adopted her. Together with four other orphans, she was raised in a tiny makeshift hut with a leaky zinc roof with neither running water nor electricity in a little village in Perak, Malaysia.

At only nine years of age, she started working to help make ends meet. While other children were laughing and playing after school, she was squatting in a dusty factory, pulling rigid strips of rattan to weave them into bags. Her tender fingers were often left raw and bleeding from this arduous work, but she had no choice, as she would only be paid for bags that were tightly and properly woven.

The fifteen Malaysian cents (a little less than an American nickel) that she was paid for each bag may have been a paltry sum, but it meant that her family did not have to go without food. And that was just one of many odd jobs that she took on in order to eke out a living. She still remembers the joy that she felt when she held a five-dollar note for the first time. Before handing that hard-earned note over to her grandmother for household expenses, she had ironed it till it was perfectly crisp and kept it in her textbook so that she could look at it all day while she was in school.

When Things Seem Hopeless

Having been abandoned at birth and given the meager means of her adoptive grandmother, it seemed by all human reasoning that she was destined to be trapped in a cycle of poverty. So how did God turn her situation around in the face of such hopeless circumstances?

By sharing her testimony, I want to encourage you to see that it's not how or what you begin with. You may have been born under severely challenging circumstances, or perhaps your parents are separated, or you may even have suffered abuse as you were growing up. My friend, I am here to tell you that with God in your life, it's *not* the end of the road! You can have hope and expect good even when things in your life seem hopeless.

Although it was very challenging to make ends meet, this lady shared with me that even as a child, she always felt there was a God somewhere, a God who was watching over her, protecting her, and blessing her. She related that as a little girl, she used to "talk" to this God and even wrote to Him in a little diary that she kept. She also remembered praying a simple, innocent prayer to this unknown God, saying, "If You are the true God, please come and look for me so that I may come to know You."

Today as she looks back, she is filled with gratefulness toward the Lord, whom she declares had known her even when she was in her mother's womb. She knows that it is God who had brought the right people across her path and protected her from danger in so many instances even before she had gotten to know Him.

When I heard her sharing this, I was reminded of the promise in the Bible that says God is a Father to the fatherless (see Ps. 68:5). Her own biological parents may have abandoned her at birth, but her Father in heaven had an amazing plan for her life. In the same way, He has an amazing plan for your life. Hold on to His promise recorded in His Word for you:

> *"For I know the plans I have for you," says the* LORD.
> *"They are plans for good and not for disaster, to give you*
> *a future and a hope."*
>
> —Jeremiah 29:11 NLT

She ended up doing so well in school that her vice principal encouraged her to continue her studies in Singapore instead as the opportunities in her hometown were comparatively limited. With her grandmother's blessing and only ten Malaysian dollars in her pocket, she headed to Singapore.

Despite having to take on various jobs to support herself as well as her grandmother, she continued to thrive in her academic pursuits, went on to a top-tier local university, and graduated with honors in chemistry. She then landed a well-paying job at a multinational company. But after three and a half years, she decided to venture out to build her own business in 1989.

In the year 2000, God honored the prayer that she had prayed as a young child when a friend invited her to New Creation Church in Singapore. Having heard different things about God over the years, she remembers the freedom that she experienced when she learned for the first time through my preaching on grace that God loved her so much more than she could ever love Him.

She stopped seeing God as someone far away and instead had a personal encounter with the God whom she knew had been watching over her all these years. She shared with me that when she encountered the love of Jesus, she began to faithfully come for service every Sunday despite the long queues that she had to wait in to get into our auditorium.

Some time later, she felt the Lord leading her to take her business public to remain competitive. She approached a bank for its assistance to underwrite her company's attempt to undertake an initial public offering (IPO). The bank manager to whom she had presented her business plan turned her down and explained that it was not the right time to attempt an IPO as market sentiments were dismal and the Dow Jones had been on a massive downward slide. As his parting shot, the bank manager said, "If the Dow Jones starts going up today, you can come back tomorrow and we can talk again."

She shared with me that when she walked out of the bank, she remembered a message that I had preached on being bold and asking God for big things. She said, "You told us not to insult God by asking only for small things. You said, 'Ask God for big things, compliment Him, and have a positive, confident expectation of good.'" So she went home and before going to bed, she decided to step out in faith and ask God to do a big thing for her. She believed that He could move the market in her favor and simply prayed, "God, You are Almighty. Surely You can influence the US market and make the Dow Jones go up in Jesus' name."

Now, Singapore is twelve hours ahead of New York, so the market opens when it is night in Singapore. At about 4 a.m., this lady felt a prompting to get out of bed to check on how the Dow Jones was doing…and found that it had bucked the downward trend and was beginning to climb upward! In the space of just four hours, the Dow Jones had risen by an astonishing 18 percent because of an unexpected announcement by the then Chairman of the Federal Reserve, Alan Greenspan.

The Power of Having a Confident Expectation of Good

Pastor Prince, can God do things like this?

Of course He can. God did it for this lady, didn't He? That's the power of right believing!

Anything is possible for those who believe God and have a confident expectation of good. She had the boldness to ask God to bless her and turn things around for her, just like Jabez did, and God answered her request. Ask God for big things in your life and expect good. He is a good God.

> *Anything is possible for those who believe God and have a confident expectation of good.*

This lady had a good opinion of God. In fact, she shared that one of the Bible verses that sustained her time and again was John 10:10, which says, "I have come that they may have life, and that they may have it more abundantly."

Even when her business was faced with challenges, she would declare that her abundant God would supply. She would stand on

His promise that she was the righteousness of God in Christ and whatsoever she did would be abundantly blessed. When times were hard and the economy was going through a difficult period of recession, she would maintain a confident expectation of good and look to the God who is good and who came to bring us abundant life.

What I want you to see is that not everything in this life will become smooth sailing the moment you start to hope in God. Jesus said, "In the world you will have tribulation; but be of good cheer, I have overcome the world" (John 16:33). There will be trouble, challenges, and issues to deal with in this world. But you can rest in Jesus, be encouraged in Him, continue to hope in Him, and know beyond the shadow of a doubt that He will see you through all your adversities. He has already overcome the world! On your part, determine to be of good cheer, rejoice in the Lord always, and keep on having a confident expectation of good.

The very next day, she marched into the bank manager's office and showed him the incredible lift the Dow Jones recorded in just one day! The bank manager reasoned that this could simply be a temporary spike and listed further conditions that she had to fulfill. Undaunted and knowing that her God would surely bless her, she quickly called her former classmates and professors to canvass for support and was able to present to the bank manager a long list of committed investors that very day.

The manager was eventually won over, impressed that she could garner such tremendous support and interest in a single afternoon. Of course, he didn't understand that this was the favor of the Lord in action! The bank proceeded to make a firm commitment to underwrite the IPO and to help her take her company public.

At the very time that she launched the company's IPO, the Singapore government launched an initiative to highlight the importance of recycling wastewater into drinkable water and released news of a big tender to build the nation's first wastewater recycling and treatment facility.

The news media was thus abuzz with the value and strategic importance of water for the nation of Singapore. Nobody could have orchestrated this. She had no idea that water—her very industry—would be the talking point the very year she took her business public when she followed the prompting from the Lord to do so. She knew absolutely nothing about this project and was just keeping her eyes on Jesus. But God was working behind the scenes. Nevertheless, people began speculating that she must have known all along about this big government tender, and interest surrounding her company's IPO kept on mounting.

With all the media hype, publicity, and excitement over water, her company's IPO became a sensational hit and was oversubscribed seven times. Her company, Hyflux, became the first water treatment company to be listed on the Singapore Exchange.

She shared with me so many other amazing testimonies of how the Lord continued to open doors of favor and blessings for her in China, India, and the Middle East after the public listing of her company. When she submitted tenders for multimillion-dollar infrastructural projects to build wastewater plants or some of the largest membrane-based seawater distillation facilities in the world, she would be the little David among the Goliaths in the industry. Yet she came up tops, and many times was awarded the projects. That, my friend, is called the *favor* of God. His favor is undeniable in her life, and she continues to be conscious of the good God who is watching over her, no matter how tough, adverse, and challenging the business climate might be.

In 2011, Olivia Lum, in a competitive field with close to fifty top-notch entrepreneurs from around the world, was accorded the prestigious Ernst & Young World Entrepreneur of the Year award in Monte Carlo. In her acceptance speech, she thanked her Lord Jesus Christ. Unbeknownst to her at that time, she was the first woman to be recognized with this honor in the prestigious award's eleven-year history.

How does a young girl who was abandoned at birth go from weaving rattan bags for a nickel to building a billion-dollar, public-listed company? My friend, that is the power of right believing. Olivia's story is an amazing one, which tells of the goodness, favor, grace, and power of our God.

I pray that you will be encouraged to see that nothing is impossible when you believe right in the person of Jesus and in His love and goodness. Ask God for big things. He loves you, and He has a track record of doing exceedingly and abundantly above all that we can ask, think, or even imagine (see Eph. 3:20).

> *God loves you, and He has a track record of doing exceedingly and abundantly above all that we can ask, think, or even imagine.*

CHAPTER 18

FINDING HOPE WHEN ALL SEEMS HOPELESS

She had heard so many wonderful stories of the carpenter from the little town of Nazareth. How He walked all over Galilee teaching about a God whom He affectionately referred to as His "Father." How He taught about the love of this Father-God. How miracles were performed by His hands. How He healed all who came to Him.

The blind left His presence seeing. The lame, leaping. The lepers, whole. Those held captive by demons, completely freed.

Eyewitness accounts of meetings with this Man were told and retold in vivid detail: how His eyes and voice carried such warmth, tenderness, and humility that even the despised tax collectors, unclean lepers, disdained criminals, and scorned prostitutes—in fact, all who usually hid in the shadows—would venture out to follow Him wherever He went.

Like them, she knew what it was like to be an outcast. She knew what it was like to receive harsh rebuke and condemnation whenever she was out in public—particularly from those who taught legalistically about God and His laws. But the other outcasts seemed to all agree that this carpenter-teacher was different. She observed how their faces would glow whenever they spoke about this Man.

She remembered how one of them had exclaimed, "He talks about a God who cares even for the birds and flowers, a God who loves us so intensely that He even tracks the number of hairs on our heads!" She watched their eyes gleam as they shared excitedly about how He made them feel human again. And she listened with a strange warmth in her heart as they told of how the dignity, affirmation, and grace He afforded them had transformed their beliefs about God and changed their lives forever.

Who was this Man, whom they called a friend of sinners?

She devoured story after story since she was an outcast just like them. For twelve long years, she had been suffering from a hemorrhage that had ravaged her body, bankrupted her finances, and banished her from pretty much any social interaction with her own community. And even though she had spent all her money seeing every doctor from Jerusalem to Galilee, her condition continued to deteriorate.

But everything she heard about this Man refreshed her and filled her with something that had previously been foreign to her—hope. For the first time in many years, she felt confident about her future. She knew that at last, things were going to turn around for good.

When she heard that this Man, Jesus, would be passing her street en route to Jairus's house to pray for his daughter, her heart leaped. After more than a decade of being driven away each time she tried to appear in public, she had grown genuinely afraid of crowds. But she said to herself, "If only I may touch His clothes, I shall be made well" (Mark 5:28).

This thought fortified every step she took searching for Jesus until finally she saw Him in the midst of a crowd that was thronging Him. She pressed in from behind, refusing to be daunted by the jostling mass of people. She stretched her arm toward Him, felt her fingers graze the hem of His garments.

And a miracle happened. The moment her fingertips made contact with the microfibers of His linen prayer cloth, power immediately infused her body. The incessant bleeding that had been her constant companion instantaneously ceased, and she was completely healed.

What Are You Hearing about Jesus?

Perhaps like this woman (whose story you can read about in Mark 5:25–34), you are facing an impossibly hopeless situation in your life. Maybe you are struggling with a debilitating sickness, marital situation, financial crisis, or prolonged challenge. In the natural, the future looks dismal and there appears to be no reason to hope. If that is you, I want to encourage you to believe that you too can experience the kind of breakthrough this woman experienced.

Imagine: for twelve long years, she had watched helplessly as her condition went from bad to worse no matter what she tried. Most of us would have thrown in the towel and given up on hope.

How did this woman find hope in the midst of her hopeless circumstances?

What was the turning point for her? What gave her the courage to hope again?

I believe that the secret to her faith can be found in the first five words of this verse: "She had heard about Jesus, so she came up behind him through the crowd and touched his robe" (Mark 5:27 NLT).

All the Word of God records for us is that "she had heard about Jesus."

What do you think she heard about Jesus?

This is an important question because whatever she had heard about this Jesus imparted an audacious sense of Bible hope and confidence in her. And this imbued her with a boldness and tenacity to risk everything just to touch the hem of His garment. She knew well the religious laws concerning unclean persons such as herself and had fought against the thought that if she were recognized or found out, she would be subjected to public humiliation and, very possibly, violence.

So for her to have ventured out and pushed through the crowd to get to Jesus, clearly she must have had no doubt in her heart that she would be completely healed the moment she touched the hem of His garment.

Now remember, she was not hoping to be healed from a common cold or passing headache. She was believing to be completely healed from a condition that had plagued her for twelve years, a sickness that every physician she had seen had pronounced incurable.

The Bible doesn't go into detail about *what* she heard about Jesus, but I submit to you that she must have heard story after story of how Jesus healed the sick everywhere He went, how He didn't despise even the unclean lepers who came to Him, and how good and gracious He was to those who were down-and-out. What she heard about Jesus produced hope. It produced in her a positive, confident expectation of good, which we can see in what she declared: "If only I may touch His clothes, I shall be made well." This hope then resulted in a faith that was effortless.

Faith as defined in God's Word is "the confidence that what we hope for will actually happen" (Heb. 11:1 NLT). In other words, the hope that she had in the goodness of Jesus became faith, and this faith gave her the boldness to press through the crowd and receive her healing from Jesus.

Hearing Right Produces Right Believing

Hearing plays a huge part in right believing. You cannot believe right unless you are hearing right. Man, that was good! I don't want you to miss that. *You cannot believe right unless you are hearing right.* I believe the woman with the issue of blood began to believe right when she began to hear right. God's Word tells us that "faith comes from hearing, that is, hearing the Good News about Christ" (Rom. 10:17 NLT).

> *You cannot believe right unless you are hearing right.*

What you hear is vital. If you are believing God for a breakthrough in your life, pay attention to what you are listening to.

Are you hearing messages that are full of the good news of Jesus? After you listen to these messages (or read these resources), are you filled with the heavy sense of what *you need to do*? Or are you filled with the empowering sense of who Jesus is in your life and everything *He has done for you* at the cross?

> *What you hear about God is vital.*

This woman certainly didn't hear about the law. The law would have drained her of all her hope and faith. The law would have exposed her and pointed out just how unclean, unworthy, and disqualified she was. If she heard that Jesus was no different from the religious Pharisees of her day, there was no way she would have had a positive expectation of good, much less have the gumption to push through the crowd to touch Jesus. Based on the law, an unclean person would be entertaining a death wish by just mingling with the rest of society, much less touching the garment of a clean person.

Under the law, when the unclean touches the clean, the clean becomes unclean. Under grace, when the unclean touches the clean (Jesus), the unclean becomes clean! This woman didn't defile Jesus with her uncleanness when she reached out and touched His garments. Neither did the leper, whom Jesus touched after He had preached the Sermon on the Mount (see Matt. 8:3). On the contrary, both of them were infected with Jesus' health and wholeness. Both of them were made completely whole. Oh, the beauty and the depths of God's amazing grace!

What have you been hearing about Jesus? Are you hearing about a hard, legalistic, and religious Jesus that is demanding, harsh, and unforgiving? Or are you hearing the true good news of His love, grace, and tender mercies toward you?

> *Are you hearing about a hard, legalistic, and religious Jesus? Or are you hearing the true good news of His love, grace, and tender mercies toward you?*

The true gospel of grace always imparts hope and faith to you to believe in Jesus. Because when you hear right about who Jesus really is, you'll know that He doesn't look at you to embarrass you and to point out all your uncleanness, addictions, and sins. No, He sees you as someone precious, as someone He loves personally, intimately, and infinitely. He sees you as someone He suffered and died for at the cross. When you believe this and see His love, grace, and goodness toward you, it will build hope in your heart. So keep hearing and hearing the good news of Jesus!

No matter how long you have been struggling or how long it has been since you saw any results, I want to encourage you to fill your ears, eyes, and mind with the good news of Jesus. Trust me, when you incline your ear to messages that are all about His grace, you will inevitably begin to have a positive, confident expectation of good. When your heart is filled with hope through hearing all the amazing stories about Jesus, like the woman, you'll reach out in faith. Beloved, reach out and receive your miracle and freedom from your loving Savior!

The Power of Hearing Right about Jesus

Not too long ago, I received an email from George, who lives in California. He shared that he had been diagnosed with Evans syndrome, a rare autoimmune disease where a person's antibodies attack his or her own red blood cells and platelets. At one point, this brother had to be rushed to the emergency room because he was at risk of spontaneous bleeding. His blood platelet count had dropped dramatically to just 4,000/mcL. The normal range for a healthy person is between 150,000 and 400,000/mcL.[1] This is what he wrote:

> *The doctors administered infusions of blood products and had me on super-high doses of steroids. The steroids, which I reacted terribly to, made me so depressed that at one point I even had to tell my wife to hide the guns in our home because I couldn't get the terrible thought of using them on myself out of my mind.*
>
> *Due to taking the steroids, I couldn't think or even have normal conversations. I cried constantly. Our three kids didn't know what to think of what was happening to their daddy. It was very hard on our family. I actually started telling people that God was punishing me for things I had done.*
>
> *Every time I received an infusion and the doctors upped my steroid dosage, my platelets went up to a normal range, but it would never last for very long. My immune system continued attacking and destroying my*

platelets no matter what treatment I was getting. I was constantly getting my blood drawn, constantly checking to see what my count was, constantly aware of all the symptoms Evans was causing and the side effects of the steroids.

Then, somewhere in the middle of all of this, the Holy Spirit led me to your television ministry. By the grace of God, I ended up on a channel I had never turned to before and saw the Grace Capsule. The lady on the phone told me that it would take one to three weeks for it to arrive, but guess what? It came in two days! It arrived right before my wife and I had to go on another trip to the hospital, which was a three-hour drive away.

And let me tell you, your Grace Capsule was a gift from God. Through your teachings, Daddy God showed me His love. I went from feeling condemned, like God was punishing me, to beholding the finished work of Jesus on the cross. He miraculously took all the bondages in my life away—the cigarettes, the pornography, the marijuana, everything that had been a struggle.

I had back pain and acid reflux for years, but by listening over and over again to your sermons and hearing and hearing them constantly—at home or in the hospital, all through the night—the pain and acid reflux went away. It is now four months later, and PRAISE BE TO JESUS, I still have no acid reflux or back pain!

Three months ago, my spleen was removed with the hope that the Evans syndrome would go away, or at least be lessened. But even after the surgery, my count dropped again. The only two options for treatment were more severe in our minds—one of them being chemotherapy. By this time, I'd been listening to the Grace Capsule for about a month, and finally I decided to give the Evans syndrome to God. I stopped doing blood counts, stopped giving weight to all of my symptoms, and started thanking the Lord for my complete healing.

Now Jesus has restored everything to me better than it was before. He has given me more strength, more energy, and a lot more love. I thought I understood love before, but now I know what true love is because of my Father's love and Jesus' love for me. I haven't had a count done in months. My wife and I take the Lord's Supper every day. We thank Jesus every day for healing us with the stripes He bore for us.

The Lord is using both my wife and me to reach others, and the Holy Spirit is doing amazing things through your materials and the drastic transformation they see in me without a single effort from me because Jesus has done it all for me. All praises be to Him!

Wow, all glory to Jesus! I can't express how excited I was when I read about George's amazing journey. No matter how bleak and hopeless your situation is, I want to encourage you to listen your way out of all your troubles like this brother did. You can't worry your problems away, but I believe that you can certainly listen your problems away.

George listened radically. He kept on listening and listening to messages that were all about Jesus until he got better. Faith indeed comes by hearing and hearing the good news of Christ!

The Fight to Hear

You may be wondering what the Grace Capsule is. It's an MP3 player preloaded with more than seventy hours of messages that I had personally selected from my message library. Each message is full of the person of Jesus and His grace. I believe that innovations in technology, be they MP3 players, smartphones, digital downloads, or podcasting, are all tools that we can use to get into the habit of hearing about Jesus and God's amazing grace. Today there is so much we can do on our mobile devices. But while it's great to play games, listen to music, or read the news on these cool gadgets, I want to encourage you to make listening to the good news of Jesus a daily priority.

Make listening to the good news of Jesus a daily priority.

Listen, I know there is a fight involved with so many things clamoring for our attention the moment we open our eyes. There is always a phone call that we need to make, an email that we need to reply to, somewhere that we need to be, and something else that we need to do. Before we know it, the day is over and we have heard nothing about Jesus. The Bible remains on the shelf, the Bible apps in our phones remain unopened, and we wonder why at the end of the day we feel empty, stressed out, worried, fearful, and depressed.

My friend, Jesus is the bread of life and the living water. No matter how busy we get, it is prudent not to neglect feeding on His person. I know that in the natural, this can sound simplistic. You may be asking yourself, "How can simply listening about Jesus change things in my life and circumstances?" The truth is, the things of God are really not complicated. Just think about the woman who suffered from hemorrhaging for twelve years. Simply hearing about Jesus and His grace infused her with so much hope, so much faith, and so much courage that she was able to receive the healing she had started to believe for. Don't underestimate the power of hearing about Jesus just because it sounds simple.

> *Don't underestimate the power of hearing about Jesus just because it sounds simple.*

Redeem All Lost Time

There is a beautiful verse in the psalms that says, "Teach us to number our days, that we may gain a heart of wisdom" (Ps. 90:12). Do you want to know the secret of numbering your days and not allowing a single day of your life to be put to waste? The key is found two verses down where it says, "Oh, satisfy us early with Your mercy" (Ps. 90:14). The word "mercy" here is the Hebrew word *hesed*, which means God's grace.[2] God is telling us to be satisfied every day with His grace.

This means that before you do anything—read the papers, check your emails, get started on your to-do list, or even drink your morning coffee—start the day with Jesus and be satisfied with His grace. You can read a devotional about God's grace, feed on the Father's love, meditate on His grace, listen to a message that is all about Jesus, and open up His love letter—His Word—to you. Start your day being satisfied by His grace.

> *Before you do anything, start the day with Jesus and be*
> *satisfied with His grace.*

But Pastor Prince, how long do I spend doing this? You don't know how crazy things get in the morning! How much must I read, listen, or pray?

My friend, the key is not to be legalistic about it. If morning doesn't work for you, then find a time that best suits your schedule. It could be during your lunch break or just before you go to bed. The key principle here is to be satisfied daily with His grace. Feed on Him until your heart is full and satisfied with His grace. Some days it could be longer and other days shorter. It's really not about the duration, but your level of satisfaction.

There are days when my heart is troubled, and just being in the Lord's presence and thinking about His love for me fills my heart with inexplicable peace and joy. At such times, it takes only a few seconds for my heart to be satisfied with His grace. On other days, I feel like the Lord wants to show me something in His Word, and I end up studying it for a long time until I feel a release. This means that you and I can't be legalistic about our relationship with God. God doesn't want us to have rigid rituals with Him. In the new covenant, He is more interested in having a relationship with us.

So enjoy His presence daily—that's how you redeem the time you have lost and never waste another day in bondage, fear, guilt, or addiction.

The psalmist says, "For a day in Your courts is better than a thousand. I would rather be a doorkeeper in the house of my God than dwell in the tents of wickedness" (Ps. 84:10). In other words, a day spent in God's presence satisfied by His grace is better than a thousand spent elsewhere.

Think about this for a moment. There are 365 days in a year, so a thousand days is almost three years of your life. What this means is no matter how much time you think you have lost to being in bondage to fear or being trapped in an addiction, God can redeem those days for you by His grace. One day in God's grace is equivalent to a thousand days of striving by your own efforts. Begin every day therefore satisfied in His grace, and God will restore to you all the years the locusts have eaten and stolen from you (see Joel 2:25).

> *One day in God's grace is equivalent to a thousand days of striving by your own efforts.*

Have a joyful, positive, and confident expectation of good because there are many good days ahead of you—days of blessings, days of favor, and days of great grace. Overcome every wrong believing by plugging in and hearing about the good news of Jesus. Hope will come flooding in even when everything around you seems hopeless. When you hear right, you will start to believe right!

PART SEVEN

FIND REST IN
THE FATHER'S LOVE

CHAPTER 19

RECEIVE THE FATHER'S LOVE FOR YOU

He sat at the front porch every day, scanning the horizon for any sign of movement. He did this faithfully, even as the days rolled painfully into weeks and then months. When his friends came by to persuade him to give up and move on, he would simply smile and wave them on and persist unflinchingly. Keeping his gaze on the surrounding hills, he waited unwaveringly and patiently for the return of his son. As he waited, he rehearsed in his mind over and over again what he would do the moment he saw his son. And every day, as he looked earnestly across the fields, he wondered if that day would be the day.

One evening the familiar silhouette of a lone figure appeared in the distance. Recognizing his son, he enacted without hesitation what he had done a thousand times before in his mind: he pulled up his robes, cast aside all dignity, and ran toward his son with all his might. He could feel his heart pumping wildly and his lungs expanding and contracting as his feet tried to outdo each other across the field. Tears streamed down his face as his son grew larger in his sight with each pace. And before any words could be traded, he had leaped forward, embraced the young man, and rained kisses on him.

This unexpected, joyous reception from the father overwhelmed the young man. He had expected to be disowned and even had a rehearsed speech to tell his father to make him one of his hired servants. How could he have known that his father had a rehearsed plan of his own? Without waiting to hear the son's rehearsed speech, his father commanded the servants to bring out the best robe for him, to place a ring on his finger and sandals on his feet. The young man thought he had lost the right to be called a son because of the bad choices he had made that resulted in shame and loss to the family. But his father made it clear that wasn't so and even called for a party to celebrate the homecoming of his beloved son.

Unveiling the Heart of the Father

What an amazing and moving story. Jesus shared this parable, and I think it's one of the most beautiful parables in the Bible. It's a parable that Jesus used to skillfully unveil to us the true heart of our gracious and loving heavenly Father.

Bible commentators call this the parable of the prodigal son, but the real hero of this story isn't the son, but the father. This is a story about the father and his love for his two sons. You may already have heard this parable shared a hundred times, but I want you to look at it again to see how this parable exposes the wrong beliefs that many believers today still have toward their Father in heaven.

Consider this for a moment: What is your opinion of God, especially when you've made a mistake? Do you see Him as an all-powerful, distant, and unfeeling judge who is angry whenever you fail and who constantly has to be appeased? Or do you know Him as your Daddy, your Abba Father whom you can run to anytime, even when you have fallen short?

As I was studying the Word, the Lord revealed to me that many believers have come to a place where they have forgotten their heavenly Father. They have forgotten about His love, His grace, and His loving-kindness. They relate to God in a judicial and transactional fashion.

Today many believers come before Him with apprehension and trepidation, presenting their failings to Him and quickly leaving before they get the punishment and condemnation *they think* they rightly deserve from Him. They perceive Him *exclusively* as a God of holiness, judgment, and justice—His face steely and stern, His mighty arms folded in dissatisfaction and disapproval. They see a God who is easily displeased, quick to anger, perpetually disappointed with them, and waiting impatiently to be placated.

This wrong belief of who God really is has driven many into fear, guilt, depression, and insecurity. And that is why it's so vital we see the heart of the Father as unveiled by Jesus in this timeless parable.

A wrong belief of who God really is has driven many into fear, guilt, depression, and insecurity.

Not too long ago, Lydia, a sister from South Africa, wrote to me. I believe that many of you would be able to identify with what she shared about her struggles in relating to God as her Father:

> *Dear Pastor Prince,*
>
> *I grew up with very low self-esteem, having been labeled the difficult child in my family. I was an unplanned baby, and my parents already had one child—a girl, so they really wanted a boy. They were disappointed when I turned out to be a girl and even considered giving me to a paternal family member who did not have children.*
>
> *My dad comes from a very cold, strict family, and he has a very bad temper, so I grew up naturally fearful of him and always felt like I was walking on eggshells around him. My mom also grew up in a household where she had not received love. Both my parents are extreme perfectionists and very organized. On top of that, they raised us with military discipline and no compassion. It was your own fault if you got hurt—you brought it on yourself.*
>
> *Thus, I could never relate to God as a Father. God was unapproachable and sitting with a lightning bolt ready to strike me whenever I wasn't good enough, didn't pray enough, or wasn't obedient enough. I was under the impression that God was only pleased with me when I obeyed the law. Being a perfectionist myself, I felt that I never met His expectations and I was always under condemnation.*
>
> *Since encountering your teaching resources, the veil in my life has been torn. For the first time, I am free. I no*

*longer walk under the heavy burden of condemnation. I
learned that God loved us first and I can now have a love
relationship with my heavenly Father and Jesus.*

*I have experienced victory over fear and sin that kept
me captive for years—not by trying to be obedient, but
by just learning that my sins have already been forgiven
on the cross. And no, I am not sinning more now. I am
actually overcoming more and sinning less, and I have a
grateful heart for what Christ has done on the cross.*

Do you feel the same way Lydia did about God?

Do you feel as though you are never good enough, can never do
enough and be obedient enough for God to love and accept you?

Do you feel like you are always living under perpetual condemnation?

Perhaps you can't relate to God as a loving Father because you've
never experienced the love of your earthly father or because your
own father has hurt you terribly.

My friend, I pray that as we study the Word of God together, you
will supernaturally experience the intimate love of your heavenly
Father in a deep and personal way like never before. I pray that this
experience will heal, renew, restore, and transform you in a spectacular way because His love for you is nothing less than spectacular.

See the Father's Perfect Love

There is a vacuum in our hearts that can only be filled by the
Father's love. So stop trying to find love and approval in all the

wrong places and getting entangled with all kinds of fears, insecurities, and addictions. I believe that if you would allow the Father to come into your heart today and fill you up with His perfect love, you will find the joy, confidence, fulfillment, and freedom that you have been looking for in life.

> *Allow the Father to come into your heart today and fill you up with His perfect love.*

God's precious Word declares, "There is no fear in love; but perfect love casts out fear, because fear involves torment. But he who fears has not been made perfect in love. We love Him because He first loved us" (1 John 4:18–19).

Today, under the new covenant of His amazing grace, our Father in heaven isn't looking to judge you for your failings because He has already judged your every failing, mistake, and sin in the body of His own Son, Jesus Christ. The name that Jesus came to reveal in the new covenant of grace is "Father." Today God wants to reach out to you as a caring and loving Father.

Do you know His heart of love toward you?

Do you know that it was His idea to send Jesus to be punished at the cross for you?

Read the most famous passage in the Bible and personalize it so that you can see God's heart for *you*: "For God so loved *you* that He gave His only begotten Son, that *you* who believe in Him should not perish but have everlasting life. For God did not send His Son into the world to condemn *you*, but that *you* through Him might be saved" (John 3:16–17). Know beyond the shadow of a doubt today that your Father loves *you* and sent His own Son to save *you*.

Understand that we are not belittling the work of Jesus at the cross when we talk about the Father and His love for you. The truth is Jesus came to reveal the love of the Father to you. God so loved you that He sent His one and only beloved Son to pay the heavy price at the cross to cleanse you of all your sins.

Do you know that God loves Jesus dearly? Jesus is God's darling Son, the apple of His eye. Now, if your Father in heaven didn't withhold His precious Son, Jesus Christ, and sacrificed Him for you, how much do you think He loves you? You cannot begin to comprehend the intensity and sheer magnitude of your Father's love for you until you realize how much the Father loves Jesus—because He gave up Jesus to ransom you.

I hope you are beginning to experience and see for yourself just how loved you are by the Father and how precious you are to Him! Don't fear Him—see the heart of your Father's love unveiled through Calvary's cross.

> *God wants to reach out to you as a caring and loving Father.*
> *See His heart of love unveiled through Calvary's cross.*

No Matter What You Have Done

But Pastor Prince, you don't understand my past and all the mistakes I've made.

You are absolutely right. I don't.

But your Father in heaven sure does, and He who knows you perfectly, loves you perfectly.

At the very beginning of the parable of the prodigal son, the younger son came to his father and demanded his share of his inheritance. In the Jewish culture, this was tantamount to the young man telling his father to "drop dead." He was effectively saying, "Give me my share of the inheritance right now. I can't wait for you to die." It was a stinging slap on the face of his father. The young man completely humiliated and dishonored his father by making such an insolent request.

We need to understand this because if we are unable to grasp the extent to which this young man utterly rejected his father and chose his own way, we cannot appreciate the extent of his father's love and grace in receiving him back home as his son. In the same way today, if we don't realize how much we have rejected the Father through our sins, we cannot fully grasp, appreciate, and respond to the immense grace that He extends toward us in forgiving us totally. Those who think they have sinned little and are thus forgiven little, love little. But those who know they are forgiven much, love much (see Luke 7:47). Remember *who* told this parable—our redeemer Jesus, and He has firsthand knowledge of the Father's heart of love.

Coming back to the story, upon his younger son's demand, the father divided to his two sons what was due them. We know that the younger son then spent all his inheritance on riotous living and, when a severe famine arose in the land, he became penniless and was reduced to feeding swine on a farm.

It's recorded for us that he was so famished that even the pods he was feeding the swine looked delectable to him. Let's listen in on what he says at his lowest point: "How many of my father's hired servants have bread enough and to spare, and I perish with hunger! I will arise and go to my father, and will say to him, 'Father, I have sinned against heaven and before you, and I am no longer worthy to be called your son. Make me like one of your hired servants'" (Luke 15:17–19).

Despite Your Hidden Agenda

Let me ask you a question. Based on what you have just read, was it the son's love for his father that made him journey home?

Do you think for one moment that he was truly contrite? Or that he even cared that he had broken his father's heart?

I think not! He was clearly motivated by his stomach. He wanted to go home because he remembered that even the hired servants in his father's house had more food than he did! The words that he planned to say to his father—"I have sinned against heaven and before you"—was what he thought would be the right dramatic, religious rhetoric to ensure that he would be allowed *some benefits* for returning home. You and I know that he wasn't genuinely remorseful. What we are hearing is his stomach talking, not his heart. So it wasn't repentance that drove him home. It was his stomach and perhaps even his sense of pride that he deserved at least what his father's servants were getting.

When I was growing up, I would hear people teach about how

the son repented and decided to go home to his father. The truth is there was no repentance here. The young man began the trek home because he was starving. He was even prepared to go through the motion of saying words like, "I am no longer worthy to be called your son. Make me like one of your hired servants," with the sole intention of getting his stomach filled since he had reasoned that the "hired servants have bread enough and to spare."

He never expressed any love for the father or said that he missed his father's presence and love. This is important for us to note because God wants us to know that even when our motivations are wrong, even when we have a hidden (usually self-centered) agenda and our intentions are not completely pure, He still runs to us in our time of need, just as the father ran to the young man and show-ered upon him his unmerited, undeserved, and unearned favor.

Oh, how unsearchable are the depths of His love and grace toward us! It will never be about our love for God. It will always be about His magnificent love for us. The Bible makes this clear: "Herein is love, not that we loved God, but that he loved us, and sent his Son to be the propitiation for our sins" (1 John 4:10 KJV). The hero in this parable is the father. It's about the father's perfect love for his imperfect son.

> *It will never be about our love for God. It will always be about His magnificent love for us.*

Some people think that fellowship with God can only be restored when you are perfectly contrite and have perfectly con-fessed all your sins. They think that you must apologize to God before He can be appeased. Please understand that I have nothing against saying "sorry" to God or confessing our sins. All I am saying is that we are not as important as we make ourselves out to be. The *father* was the initiator. Before the son even had thoughts of returning home, the father had already missed him, was already looking out for him, and had *already* forgiven him. Before the son could utter a single word of his rehearsed apology, the father had already run to him, embraced him, and welcomed him home.

It's All about His Love

We are not the heroes in this story. It will never be about our apologies to God, our repentance, our actions, our love, our confessions, or our obedience. In and of ourselves, our actions—even the best ones—are laced with imperfections and impure motives. For those who believe that one must apologize before fellowship with God can be restored, this parable will rock their theology.

Read the parable for yourself in Luke 15:11–32. Notice how the son never got to complete his rehearsed speech. He attempted to but was completely overwhelmed by his father's joyful response to his return. However impure his intentions or motivations were for coming home, the father lavished him with undeserved, unmerited, and unearned favor.

It's all about our Father's heart of grace, forgiveness, and love. Our Father God swallows up all our imperfections, and true repentance comes because of His goodness. Our Father is the hero—not us. Let's make it all about Him and not about us!

> *True repentance comes because of His goodness.*

Do I say "sorry" to God and confess my sins when I have fallen short and failed? Of course I do. But I do it not to be forgiven because I *know* that I am *already* forgiven through Jesus' finished work. The confession is out of the overflow of my heart because I have experienced His goodness and grace and because I know that as His son, I am forever righteous through Jesus' blood. It springs from being righteousness-conscious, not sin-conscious; from being forgiveness-conscious, not judgment-conscious. There is a massive difference.

You know, one can insist on the need to say "sorry" before we can be forgiven. But we all know that we can say "sorry" outwardly, yet deep in our hearts there is no true repentance. It's like the kid in school who, together with his buddy, has to see the principal for bad behavior. Told to sit down, he sits, but whispers to his friend, "Inside I am standing up!" It's like the account of Judas who betrayed Jesus. It's recorded for us that he "repented... saying, I have sinned in that I have betrayed the innocent blood... And he cast down the pieces of silver in the temple" (Matt. 27:3–5 KJV). But there was no true repentance as it was merely outward. We know this because the word "repented" here is the Greek word *metamelomai*, which expresses one's desire that what has been done might be undone, but it is not accompanied with an effective change of heart.[1]

That is why we are not interested in the outward. Let's go deep into the essence of our relationship with God and really experience His love when we have failed. If you understand this, you will begin experiencing new dimensions in your love walk with the Father. You will realize that your Daddy God is all about relationship and not religious protocol. He just loves being with you. Under grace, He doesn't demand perfection from you; He *supplies* perfection to you through the finished work of His Son, Jesus Christ. So no matter how many mistakes you have made, don't be afraid of Him. He loves you. Your Father is running toward you to embrace you!

> *God is all about relationship and not religious protocol.*

God Doesn't Want Hired Servants

The wrong belief of the younger son was that he wanted to come back and earn his own keep as a hired servant. He didn't want to receive his father's provision by grace or unmerited favor. In his own self-absorbed pride, he wanted to work as a hired servant and earn his own food in the father's house together with the rest of the servants. The father, of course, would have none of that.

You cannot merit by your own efforts the favor and blessings of God. They can only be received as gifts through His grace. He doesn't want you as His hired servant. Your identity is that of a child—God's child. He has a host of heavenly angels as His servants. What He desires of you is relationship. Instead of fearing Him and thinking that you must walk on eggshells in His presence, He wants you to come boldly into His presence.

> *Your identity is that of a child—God's child. What He desires*
> *of you is relationship.*

Your Father wants you to know that as His beloved child, washed by the blood of Jesus, you can "come boldly to the throne of grace" at any time to obtain mercy and find grace to help in your time of need (Heb. 4:16). For a child of God under the new covenant, it's not a throne of judgment; it's a throne of grace.

Do you believe in His grace?

Do you believe that the blood of Jesus has washed away all your sins?

Do you believe that your Father in heaven loves you?

Then come boldly into His presence whenever you fail. Come just as you are to receive mercy and find grace. He has promised in His Word that He will help you in your time of need. What is your need today? Talk to your Father about it. What struggles, fears, and addictions overwhelm you today? Lay it all before your heavenly Father and let Him help you.

My friend, you are no longer a slave to sin, you are a child of God. The Word says, "For you did not receive the spirit of bondage again to fear, but you received the Spirit of adoption by whom we cry out, 'Abba, Father'" (Rom. 8:15). The word "adoption" is more accurately translated as "sonship."[2] Through Jesus, you have received the Spirit of sonship by whom you cry out, "Abba, Father." Did you notice that the Holy Spirit refused to translate the word "Abba" into English? The original Aramaic word *Abba* is retained. Do you know why? It's because, to the Jews, *Abba* is the most intimate way in which you can address your father.

Cry "Abba, Father!"

I love it when I'm in Israel and I hear little children running around in playgrounds, calling out, "Abba! Abba!" and jumping into their daddy's embrace. It's a beautiful picture. In Abba's arms, a child is most secure, protected, and loved. No enemy can pull a child out of his or her Abba's strong arms. That's the image God wants us to have when we pray to Him and call Him "Abba." Of course, you can call Him "Daddy" or "Papa," or whatever term helps you to see God as a warm, loving, and caring Father.

Unless you can see Him as your Abba Father, you will continue to have a "spirit of bondage again to fear" (Rom. 8:15). This spirit of bondage refers to the Old Testament fear of God. It's a slavish fear of judgment and punishment that brings you into bondage and makes you afraid of God. But God doesn't want you to fear Him. He wants you to have a Spirit of sonship! Too many believers are living with an orphan, fatherless spirit. If you are entangled with all kinds of fears, guilt, and worries today, what you need is a good heavenly dose of the Father's love for you!

> *If you are entangled with all kinds of fears, guilt, and worries today, what you need is a good heavenly dose of the Father's love for you!*

Something amazing happens in your spirit when you see God as your Father. If my daughter Jessica has a nightmare, all she has to do is cry out, "Daddy!" and Daddy is there! And if there is a monster under her bed, that monster is about to be torn to pieces by Daddy! Jessica doesn't have to go, "O Father that liveth and inhabiteth the next room, I plead with thee to come to me at this time of peril, that thou mayest rescue me from this nightmare!" All she has to do is to cry out, "Daddy!" and I'm there.

Similarly, in your moments of weakness you don't have to approach God with perfect prayers. You just cry out, "Daddy!" and your heavenly Father runs to you! You are not coming before a judge. You are coming before your Father, your Daddy God, who embraces and loves you just the way you are.

Take time to come to your Abba Father today. Believe that He loves you unconditionally today. See Him welcoming you with a smile on His face and with outstretched arms. Run into His embrace, bask in His perfect love for you, and let it melt away every worry, fear, and insecurity. When you believe and receive your Father's love for you, it will put unshakable peace and strength in your heart!

> *When you believe and receive your Father's love for you, it will put unshakable peace and strength in your heart!*

CHAPTER 20

BE TRANSFORMED BY THE FATHER'S LOVE

When I preached a message series on the Father's love in my church, a young man, together with several others, came forward after one of the services to receive Jesus as His Lord and Savior. I couldn't help noticing that there were scars and scabs of dried blood on this man's face. I thought perhaps he was suffering from some sort of medical condition, so I told my youth pastor to follow up with him in the visitors' lounge after the service.

In the lounge the young man removed his jacket and revealed a body covered with tattoos. He shared that his face was cut up because he had been involved in many gang fights and had been in and out of prison numerous times. He then looked straight at the youth pastor and asked him somberly, "Can God forgive me for all the mistakes I've made?"

The youth pastor affirmed him, saying, "The moment you came forward to receive Jesus into your life, your Father in heaven forgave you of all your sins and made you His child. Right now, that's who you are—His beloved child."

Later that day the youth pastor received a text message from this young man expressing what he felt after he left the service: "I don't know how to explain this to you. I'm now experiencing a peace in my heart I've never felt before."

My friend, this is what happens when the burden of sin, guilt, and condemnation is lifted off your shoulders and placed upon Jesus. When you open your heart to the Father's unconditional love, you will experience a peace that surpasses all understanding.

Righteousness Is a Free Gift

No matter how many times you have failed, how many mistakes you have made, and how terrible you think your sins are, the cleansing power and blood of your Savior, Jesus Christ, is greater than them all. God made this promise to you in His Word: "Though your sins are like scarlet, I will make them as white as snow. Though they are red like crimson, I will make them as white as wool" (Isa. 1:18 NLT). That's the power of the cross in your life. The moment you believe in Christ, all your sins are washed away once and for all and you are made as white as snow. Have you seen how snow dazzles in the sunlight? That's how your Father in heaven sees you right now, clothed with the gleaming robe of righteousness.

But Pastor Prince, what have I done to deserve this robe of righteousness?

Well, you've heard the parable of the prodigal son. Let me ask you this: What did the son do to deserve the father's embrace? What did he do to deserve the best robe that the father commanded his hired servants to bring for him?

Absolutely nothing.

The "best robe" is a picture of the robe of righteousness that your heavenly Father clothed you with when you received Jesus. This robe of righteousness is a *free gift*. You cannot earn it, work for it, or merit it. That is why everything we hear about what the father did to welcome his son home is a picture of our heavenly Father's amazing and unconditional grace.

Our part is to just believe in His goodness and wholeheartedly receive the abundance of grace and the gift of righteousness from Him to reign victoriously over every area of defeat in our lives.

Receive and Reign

The truth is there is no other way to reign in life apart from believing and receiving. Since the Father's acceptance, grace, and gift of righteousness cannot be earned, the only way to get them is by humbling yourself before Him and saying, "Dear Daddy God, I know that I have done nothing to deserve Your love and blessings in my life. Thank You for giving me grace that is so unmerited. I humbly receive the abundance of Your grace and Your precious gift of righteousness."

> *There is no other way to reign in life apart from believing and receiving.*

Which do you think takes more humility—to work for and earn your own righteousness or to receive righteousness as a gift from

God? I submit to you that believers who try to *earn* God's approval, acceptance, and blessings through their service, prayers, and good works inadvertently fall into pride.

In the parable of the prodigal son, the younger son wanted to come home and say to his father, "Make me like one of your hired servants." Even though he was completely down-and-out, he still wanted to keep his pride and *earn* his own keep as a hired servant rather than humble himself before his father. Of course we know that even though he believed wrongly and was still entangled in self-occupation, the father heaped upon him the abundance of grace and the gift of righteousness and received him home with great celebration.

The Older Brother Mind-set

As for the older brother in the parable, he got massively angry when he heard that his shameless sinner of a brother returning home was the reason there was music and dancing in his father's house. His pride got the better of him, and he refused to go into the house because he felt that unlike him, his brother had not done anything to deserve such an honor.

The older brother said to his father, "Lo, these many years *I* have been *serving* you; *I* never transgressed your commandment at any time; and yet you never gave me a young goat, that I might make merry with my friends. But as soon as this son of yours came, who has devoured your livelihood with harlots, you killed the fatted calf for him" (Luke 15:29–30, emphasis mine).

Notice that the older brother was caught up with what *he* had done to "deserve" the fatted calf that was killed for his brother. His response also revealed what he believed about his father. He related to his father as if his father were a hard taskmaster. Instead of simply enjoying his position as a son, he was busy *serving* his father, busy trying to win his approval through his works.

The older brother believed he needed to earn the father's blessings, and in his mind he had performed much better than his disgraceful and rebellious younger brother. So he felt that he deserved more rewards from his father and was thus indignant because he thought his brother was being given more. In actual fact, the Bible records that the father had divided to *them* his wealth. According to Jewish custom, the older son always gets a double portion, so the older brother had already been given much more!

Clearly he missed the whole point of what it means to be a son. His eyes were not on his father's goodness, but on his own performance. There was no relationship with his father. He had a slavish mind-set and was persistently trying to please his father with his service and by the care he took not to transgress any of his father's commandments. He never understood the father's heart. Simply put, he never understood grace.

Love Relationship or Business Transaction?

Unfortunately, there are many believers today who are like the older brother. Rather than receive the Father's perfect love and acceptance by grace, they want to be able to say they have earned His blessings.

Do you think that brings joy and delight to the Father's heart?

Imagine if you wanted to give your child a special gift as an expression of your great love and your child tells you, "No, I want to work for it. I will earn it myself."

How would you feel if your child would rather earn your love and blessings by his own efforts than *receive* it? Certainly there are times when a child may "work" for something as a reward. He may get rewarded for doing well in school or keeping his room tidy. But I'm not talking about rewards. Something is very warped if your child cannot receive a gift from you without trying to earn it. It means that your relationship with him mirrors a business transaction.

Sadly, this is exactly how some believers behave today. They have an older brother mentality when they relate to God. They don't want to receive anything from Him by grace. Like the older brother in the parable, they want to work for it, and their relationship with God becomes businesslike and transactional. Instead of enjoying a love relationship between a Father and His child, they want to go back to the way it was under the old covenant of the law. Under the old covenant, if you did right, then God would bless you, and if you did wrong, you would be cursed.

It really is quite sad because they will inevitably end up becoming resentful and upset with God when they see their "undeserving" brothers being blessed by the Father's abundant grace. Like the older brother, they end up angry with God and saying to Him, "Lo, these many years *I* have been *serving* you; *I* never transgressed your commandment at any time; and yet you never gave me…"

Believers who still live under this veil of the law are like the older brother. They hear the music and the dancing, and they don't understand it. They hear about their Father's amazing grace, and they can't comprehend it. They read stories of lives transformed by grace, and they can't accept it. To them, God is all about keeping commandments, service, and obedience. Rewards should be meted out when right is done, whereas just punishment must be exacted on all who have transgressed.

If that is you, I pray this veil of the law will be removed and that you will experience the Father's grace in a deep and personal way.

All That Is God's Is Already Yours

Do you know what the father, who had left the party to seek out his older son, said in response to this son's complaint? "Son, you are always with me, and all that I have is yours" (Luke 15:31).

My friend, it's not about *your* love for God; it's about the Father's love for you. He is always the initiator. It has always been about *His* love for you. Don't live life mad, angry, guilty, and frustrated. Come into the Father's house and find rest for your soul. It's not about your own efforts. Your Father wants you to know that ALL He has is already yours—not because of your perfect performance, but because you are His child through Jesus' finished work.

> *Your Father wants you to know that ALL He has is already yours—not because of your perfect performance, but because you are His child through Jesus' finished work.*

Romans 8:32 declares, "He who did not spare His own Son, but delivered Him up for us all, how shall He not with Him also freely give us all things?" Daddy God has already *with Jesus* given you all things. Jesus is your acceptance. He is your righteousness, your holiness, your provision, and your wisdom. Whatever it is you need in your life, your Father has already given to you through Jesus.

So come home to His embrace. Come home to grace. Come and join in the music and dancing!

Transforming Power of the Father's Love

It's interesting to note that in the parable of the prodigal son, both brothers wanted to earn their own keep. I think that demonstrates to us that our fleshly propensity to want to merit blessings from God is far greater than our ability to receive from Him. We are generally more inclined to want to *merit* His love, acceptance, approval, and blessings than to *receive* them by His unmerited favor.

It truly takes a revelation of grace to see the Father's love and to receive from Him. And the Word tells us that it is only by receiving from our Father His grace and His righteousness that we can reign in this life (see Rom. 5:17). Perhaps that's the reason we don't see more believers reigning in life. The key lies in how they perceive their Father in heaven.

Is He a hard, heavy-handed taskmaster to you or a loving, generous Father? Will you allow Him to clothe you in His righteousness and by His loving grace put a ring on your finger and sandals on your feet? Or will you fight to earn your own righteousness, merit your own provision, and deserve your own possessions by your own works? The power to reign in life hinges on what you believe about God.

> *The power to reign in life hinges on what you believe about God.*

Pastor Prince, are you saying then that everything is just by grace and we can live any way we want with total disregard for God? Are you saying that we don't have to serve Him?

Well, ask yourself this: When someone genuinely encounters the Father's love, favor, and blessings in a way that is totally undeserving, how do you think he or she will live?

Take a moment to put yourself in the younger son's shoes: You've squandered away your father's wealth. You've run out of money and food, so you decide to go home because you know that even your father's servants have an abundance of food to eat. But when you reach home, instead of rebuke and condemnation from your father and having to beg him to make you one of his hired servants, he gives you a lavish reception filled with hugs and kisses.

Just a couple of days ago, you were starving and even eyeing the food meant for pigs. But now you are clothed with a fresh, clean robe. You are wearing the ring of your father, authorizing you to make payments in his name. And as if that is not enough, your father has invited all the neighbors, killed a choice calf, and they are having a homecoming barbecue party with music and dancing in your honor.

Imagine that all this has happened to you. You've just experienced your father's warm embrace and forgiveness. Now, does this make you want to rebel against your father again by leaving home and going back to the filthy pigpen, wallowing in the mud and feeding on things that will never satisfy you? Of course not!

There is a great misunderstanding that believers who struggle with and indulge in sin, and who are still in love with the world, do so because they don't love God enough. That's what we hear from a lot of preachers who tell believers to love God more, thinking that if people love God more, they would love sin and the world less.

But God opened my eyes one day to the real reason believers are still entangled with sin and the world. I've never heard anyone preach this before, so this is fresh from heaven. The apostle John tells us, "If anyone loves the world, the love of the Father is not in him" (1 John 2:15). Notice that it is the love *of* the Father, not the love *for* the Father. So people who love the world and are trapped by worldly pursuits are actually people who don't know or don't believe in their hearts the love of the Father for them.

Unfortunately, we hear a lot of messages that are all about our love *for* the Father—"You've got to love God more! You've got to love God more!" What we really need is more preaching that is all about the love *of* the Father. It will never be about our love for Him, but *His* love for us.

Beloved, when people come to truly know and believe the Father's love for them and have it burning in their hearts, they will no longer want to go out and live like the devil. There is just something powerfully transformative about grace. If you've tasted and savored grace from your heavenly Father, you never want to live in the wilderness of sin, away from the Father's embrace, ever again.

*If you've tasted and savored grace from your heavenly Father,
you never want to live in the wilderness of sin ever again.*

Living from Grace to Grace

Let's continue talking about the younger son. Does receiving forgiveness and grace from his father mean that he will never fail again? Of course not. But every time he fails, he knows now that he doesn't have to run away and hide in guilt and fear because he knows his father's heart. This is what it means to live from grace to grace—even if you stumble, it's an upward stumbling. You are conscious of the fact that there is fresh grace each day, in superabounding measure to swallow up all your failures. This is the goodness of God that leads you to repentance (Rom. 2:4).

Some people think that repentance must involve crying their eyeballs out. I've seen people do that, but they return home and their lives are not changed. Conversely, I've seen genuine repentance when people encounter God's grace by listening to a message or reading a book like this, and there are no dramatics involved. But when they go back to their families, you realize something in them has changed as days pass. Their thoughts and their beliefs have changed.

This in time brings about a complete shift in their lifestyles, behaviors, attitudes, and actions as they continue to grow in grace. Addictions start to lose their hold over their lives. Fears, doubts, and insecurities begin to dissolve. They begin to experience favor and succeed in their relationships, careers, and ministries. Instead of envying pigs' food, they now feast at the Father's table of abundance. Instead of living defeated in sin, they now live in the victory of their Father's love. That's what right believing in the Father's love brings.

I received an awesome testimony from twenty-five-year-old Nathan from New York, who shared about the breakthrough he experienced when he encountered the Father's love for him. He recounted how, since the age of fourteen, his life had revolved around drugs, pornography, sex, and gang violence. Growing up in such an environment, he never had a chance to see a different way of life. He never enjoyed a proper childhood and never experienced love and acceptance from his family members, who saw him as nothing more than a "war machine." With no father figure in his life except a man whom his mother married and who beat him regularly from the time he was three, Nathan struggled with his identity, his addictions, and his anger.

But his turning point came when he learned that his Daddy God loves him. He wrote:

> *I heard a sermon of yours about being God's beloved. I had never heard someone speak about Jesus as someone who died for my sins because He loved me so much. I thought there was no way anyone would die for me if they knew what I'd done. But the love I felt as I listened was something I'd never experienced before.*
>
> *I had to know more, so I bought your book* Destined To Reign, *and the Lord's words through your book changed my life…I've dropped every bad habit— everything—in my past and have given myself to the Lord Jesus Christ. Every day seems new to me, and I see*

> *life in a different light now. I know that I have a Father in*
> *heaven who loves and accepts me. I know that He hears*
> *my prayers and won't be slow to answer them.*

I am so glad Nathan had a revelation that despite his failings, his Daddy God has never stopped loving him. And simply by resting in his Daddy's love, he has been set free not just from his addictions, but also from the anger and self-doubt that had bound him for almost half his life.

In the same way, I pray you will have a revelation that you are right now loved by the Father and close to His heart. That He always hears your prayers and is more than able and willing to lift you out of every dark pit and set you in His love and light.

In the parable of the prodigal son, both sons were far away from their father, even the older son, who was technically at home with him.

Have you experienced your Father's love?

Right now, I want you to do something: close your eyes and just say, "Daddy."

That's a prayer right there. In fact, that's the deepest, most intimate prayer you can pray.

Call upon your Daddy God because He loves *you* and cares for *you*. You never did anything to make Him fall in love with you. And beloved, there is nothing you can do, nothing you could have done, that will ever take away His love for you.

> *Call upon your Daddy God because He loves* you *and cares*
> *for* you.

Already Beloved, Already Qualified

I want you to know today that as a child of God, you don't need to qualify for His love in any way. You are *already* His beloved. You may feel that you are far away from Him, but your Father sees you. He has been watching and waiting for you to come home, ready to sprint toward you to embrace you. He wants to lavish His love and kisses on you, over and over again.

You don't need to earn your Daddy's love. ALL that He has is already yours. He's not asking you to serve Him in order to earn His blessings. ALL that He has has already been freely and unconditionally given to you.

Jesus said, "Look at the birds of the air, for they neither sow nor reap nor gather into barns; yet your heavenly Father feeds them. Are you not of more value than they?" (Matt. 6:26). My friend, stop toiling. You are a child of God. You are of more value than many sparrows, and your Daddy even numbers the very hairs on your head (see Luke 12:7).

He gave up His only Son to die an agonizing death on the cross for the chance that you might one day accept His love.

So come. Come to the Father. Come with all your failings, with all your brokenness, with all your inadequacies.

Come as you are. As you realize that you are the object of His love, I pray that whatever is negative or destructive will be flushed out from your life and you will experience breakthrough after breakthrough like never before.

CHAPTER 21

FIND REST IN THE FATHER'S LOVE

In this last chapter of our journey in discovering the power of right believing, I want to leave you with one simple but critical truth.

Even if you forget everything else you've read in this book (of course, I pray that you don't!), memorize this truth I'm about to tell you. Feed on it. Let it take root in your spirit and become an anchor in your life. I promise that you will never be the same again.

Are you ready? Here it goes:

> *As a child of God, no matter what happens in your life, your Father in heaven loves you dearly and nothing you do can ever change that.*

Will you believe that today?

Whether you are going through good times or facing challenging times, you need to know that your Abba loves you. There is nothing that you can ever do to make Him love you more, and nothing that you can ever do to make Him love you less.

> *There is nothing that you can ever do to make Him love you more, and nothing that you can ever do to make Him love you less.*

Even—or perhaps *especially*—when you feel like you have failed, know that you will *always* be the apple of His eye. *Always.*

God loves you with an everlasting love (see Jer. 31:3). A love that is the same yesterday, today, forever. Feel your Daddy God enfolding you in His embrace right now. You are safe. You are utterly loved and completely accepted. He loved you before you ever knew Him. His love for you has *nothing* to do with anything that you have done for Him. And that is why you can be secure in the knowledge that *nothing* you do will ever affect His unwavering, unconditional love for you.

There is nothing for you to prove. You only need to rest. Rest and receive your Abba's love for you. Let your life become established and grounded in a love so perfect that no challenge or adversity will be able to knock you down. If you think that you've messed up, now is the time to turn to your Father. In His loving arms you will find hope, security, and refuge from any storm.

I love how the apostle Paul puts it: "Who shall separate us from the love of Christ? Shall tribulation, or distress, or persecution, or famine, or nakedness, or peril, or sword?...Yet in all these things we are more than conquerors through Him who loved us. For I am persuaded that neither death nor life, nor angels nor principalities nor powers, nor things present nor things to come, nor height nor depth, nor any other created thing, shall be able to separate us from the love of God which is in Christ Jesus our Lord" (Rom. 8:35, 37–39).

Beloved, *nothing* and *no one* can ever separate you from the love of your Father. Don't you just love that complete sense of assurance in the unshakable foundation of God's promise to you? There are no caveats or disclaimers when it comes to the love of your heavenly Father. The Bible plainly states that *nothing* shall be able to separate you from the love of your Father in heaven. It's an absolute declaration and promise. "Nothing" means *nothing*. As a believer, this means that even your mistakes, failings, and sins cannot separate you from the love of your Father. Hallelujah!

In fact, it is the Father's love for you that gives you the power to overcome every mistake, failure, and sin in your life. The Bible puts it this way: "For sin shall not have dominion over you, for you are not under law but under grace"(Rom. 6:14). What this means is that the more you experience the love and grace of your heavenly Father, the more you fall in love with Him and out of love with sin.

> *It is the Father's love for you that gives you the power to overcome every mistake, failure, and sin in your life.*

Like many of the testimonies we've read throughout this book, you will find destructive addictions losing their grasp over your life. I like how the New Living Translation translates Romans 6:14: "Sin is no longer your master, for you no longer live under the requirements of the law. Instead, you live under the freedom of God's grace." Isn't that beautiful? Today you are living under the freedom of God's amazing grace—His unmerited, undeserved, and unearned favor in your life. Grace gives you freedom. Freedom from lack, from fear, from addictions, from the torment of guilt, and from every curse and every sin!

Knowing Your Value Makes a Difference

Did you know that the enemy has no hold over people who know their Father loves them? If Adam and Eve had believed in God's love for them, the devil would not have been successful in tempting them. Unfortunately, they chose to believe the lie that the serpent had planted by portraying God as stingy and selfish, as if He was withholding something good from them.

That's why I want you to be anchored in the Father's love. You will be unshakable. You will have no desire to touch certain things, go to certain places, or be associated with certain people. You will keep away from negative influences because you trust your Father's heart for you and believe that He only wants what's best for you. You rest, knowing that He is watching out for you to protect you and insulate you from harm.

Be anchored in the Father's love. You will be unshakable.

I've seen that children who are secure in their father's love are able to say no to all kinds of temptations. This is because that vacuum in their lives is already filled. They don't have to do things to win the approval of their friends when they can find absolute security, identity, and approval in their parents' love for them and, most of all, in their heavenly Father's love for them.

In the same way, when we trust in our Father's love for us, we will have the power to say no to temptations. When you have an abiding revelation of just how valuable, precious, and righteous you are in Christ, it becomes increasingly easy to say no to sin.

Let me illustrate this. If you are wearing a nicely pressed white shirt, would you want to play in the mud? Of course not! Why? Because you are conscious that your dazzling white outfit and mud don't go together. Similarly, when you are cognizant of your righteous identity in Christ, would you want to wallow in the mud and filth of sin? The truth is, the more righteousness-conscious you are and the more conscious of how valuable and precious you are in Christ, the more you will know that your righteous identity in Christ and sin don't go together—and the more you will experience the power to say no to temptation.

You Are Beloved and Well Pleasing

When Jesus was baptized in the Jordan River, the Word of God records that as He came out from the waters, "the heavens were opened to Him, and He saw the Spirit of God descending like a dove and alighting upon Him. And suddenly a voice came from heaven, saying, 'This is My beloved Son, in whom I am well pleased'" (Matt. 3:16–17).

I love the way the Bible describes how the heavens opened to Jesus. I believe that whenever Jesus is preached, the heavens open to Him. This means that when we hear messages that are all about Jesus, we are really standing under an open heaven and all the blessings, favor, and goodness of God fall upon us.

After Jesus' baptism, the Spirit led Him into the wilderness, and the devil came to tempt Him saying, "If You are the Son of God, command that these stones become bread" (Matt. 4:3).

Many years ago when I was studying this, the Lord opened my eyes and showed me that the devil had subtly left out the word "beloved." Just moments ago, God the Father had just affirmed Jesus as His *beloved* Son at the Jordan River. However, when the devil came to tempt Jesus, he removed the word "beloved" and simply said, "If You are the Son of God…"

The Lord unveiled to me that if you are reminded that you are the beloved of the Father, you can never be successfully tempted! Even the devil knew this, and that's why he removed the word "beloved" when he spoke to Jesus. Now that's a powerful truth!

So every time you are tempted, just remind yourself, "I am God's beloved child, and my Father loves me." No temptation can triumph over you when you rest securely in your Father's love.

> *No temptation can triumph over you when you rest securely in your Father's love.*

I just want to say a quick word to all fathers reading this: it is the father's approval that will give a child the power to excel. Therefore, when you speak words of approval and affirmation to your children, you are really empowering them for success. They will meet every temptation head-on and will be victorious in life.

Observe Jesus' reply. He didn't have to prove to the devil that He was the Son of God. Secure in His identity as God's beloved Son, He simply replied, "It is written, 'Man shall not live by bread alone, but by every word that proceeds from the mouth of God'" (Matt. 4:4).

When I was studying this verse, the Lord said this to me: "Study the words that just proceeded from the mouth of God. These are the words that I want My people to live by."

Do you remember what words the Father just said at the Jordan River? That's right, He said:

"This is My beloved Son, in whom I am well pleased."

I want to encourage you to personalize this and meditate on it every day! That's how the Father sees you today. He sees you in Christ, and in Christ you are His precious, beloved child, in whom He is well pleased. Place your hand on your heart and hear your Father in heaven saying these words to you:

"You are My beloved child, in whom I am well pleased."

Would you believe that with all your heart today?

If you are struggling to overcome a disorder or addiction, close your eyes and hear your Father saying to you, "You are My beloved child, in whom I am well pleased." Every time you are fearful, every time you are consumed by worry, anger, or depression, hear your Father saying to you, "You are My beloved child, in whom I am well pleased."

Yes, right in the midst of whatever failures you may be experiencing, you are His beloved child, and He is well pleased with you because you are in Christ.

Keep hearing it and repeating it until you find rest, peace, and joy overflowing in your heart. If you feel like just crying in His presence, cry. He knows what you are going through and He understands—in a way that no one else can—the pain, hurt, suffering, and loss that you are experiencing.

You Are Accepted in the Beloved

But Pastor Prince, I have done nothing to make myself well pleasing to God!

Neither did Jesus. God called Jesus His beloved and said that He was well pleasing *before* He had even performed one miracle or act of service for Him. You see, Jesus is well pleasing to His Father not because of what He has *done*, but because of who He *is*. Did you get that? If not, please read the last sentence again.

Jesus didn't have to *do* anything or accomplish anything before He was considered beloved and pleasing to the Father. The good news for you and me today is that our Father in heaven has "made us accepted in the Beloved," and "in Him we have redemption through His blood, the forgiveness of sins, according to the riches of His grace" (Eph. 1:6–7).

This is true for any believer of Jesus. The moment you received Him into your life, God the Father made you accepted in the Beloved.

We know that the word "Beloved" here is in reference to Jesus. So why didn't God just say "accepted in Jesus Christ"?

That is because God wants you to be conscious that you are now part of the family and you are *beloved* to Him the same way that Jesus is. Furthermore, the word "accepted" in the original Greek is a word far richer in meaning than the English translation can convey. It's the word *charitoo*, and it means "highly favored."[1] This word is used only one other time in the Bible, when angel Gabriel appeared to Mary and said to her, "Rejoice, highly favored [*charitoo*] one, the Lord is with you; blessed are you among women!" (Luke 1:28).

So you and I are not just accepted in the Beloved, which is already fantastic, but we are more precisely *highly favored* in the Beloved, Jesus Christ. In fact, the Greek scholar Thayer says that *charitoo* also means we are surrounded by favor.[2] That's why in my church we like to proclaim and declare that we are *highly favored, greatly blessed*, and *deeply loved*. It's a powerful declaration and an important reminder that you are not alone and left to fend for yourself in life. You have a Father in heaven who loves you, favors you, protects you, and watches over you and all your loved ones.

> *You have a Father in heaven who loves you, favors you, protects you, and watches over you and all your loved ones.*

His Love Makes a Difference

I love this heartfelt praise report I received from Gina, who lives in Maryland. Listen to how she has been transformed by the love of the Father:

> *Dear Pastor Prince,*
>
> *I have been a Christian for about thirty-four years. Since discovering your teachings, I feel like I have been released from thirty-four years of being in a prison of Christian legalism, rules, and lists of things I had to do to get God to help and bless me.*
>
> *Before hearing the unadulterated gospel of grace, I had all but given up on my life as a Christian. Yes, I still believed that I would go to heaven, but just barely. I didn't even pray anymore because I felt I had so many problems that I would probably not be praying right anyway, so why bother? I hated reading the Bible because to me it was just a reminder of all the things I was doing wrong and all the stuff I had to do if I wanted God's help.*
>
> *But now I can't get enough of God's Word because I see it as a love letter from God rather than a book of rules that I can't keep. I also can't get enough of listening to the sermons that I get from you and feel like I have been given healthy, nourishing food after spending thirty-four years eating junk food. I listen to your sermons over and over again. I find myself spending more time in the Word because it is*

FINALLY really and truly GOOD NEWS that I am hearing. I want to know more about who God is for real.

For the first time in my life, my kids, who are in their twenties, are EXCITED about God too. We are all reading Destined To Reign *and constantly listening to teachings from your ministry. Recently I was thinking about the God whom I now know as my Abba Father, and I felt overwhelmed by His love for me. I started to say, "I love You." Suddenly I realized there are just no words to adequately convey the love I feel for Him now. Those three little words just don't cover it. Sometimes I feel like my heart will burst from the love I feel for Him now because I finally believe He feels the same way about me!*

Additionally, things that I have been trying to quit for DECADES are now beginning to just fade away as I rest in God knowing He's going to keep loving me no matter what. Who knew that NOT trying to "be good" would bring about a heart change and then change me on the outside too. I cannot believe all this has been available to me all along.

I am so happy now that I can't even describe it. Yes, I am still having my share of challenges, but things look so much different when you know that God not only CAN handle it, but He WILL handle it when you just rest and let Him be the Daddy to you that He wants to be.

I cannot thank you enough for your ministry and your obedience to God in bringing this life-changing Word to us, His children. I have been forever changed, and I tell everybody about the gospel of grace that you preach. God is so wonderful, and I look forward to the next seventy years of my life walking in His grace and sharing it with His people.

Don't you just love reading about how lives are changed and transformed when they encounter the love of the Father? I love what Gina shared about how she now knows God as her Abba Father. Isn't it amazing that you could have been a Christian for more than three decades and yet not have had the opportunity to encounter the Father's love? I am so grateful and humbled that God has given me the honor and privilege of unveiling the Father to this precious lady and her family. I pray that you too will experience what she has experienced. In her letter, she is literally brimming over with love and joy, and it warms my heart greatly to see her family touched by our loving heavenly Father too.

Believe the Father's love for you. See His grace. Come boldly into His throne room of grace and receive help in your time of need. In her praise report, Gina shared there were things that she had been trying to quit for DECADES but couldn't. However, the moment she began to find security in our Abba Father's love for her and had the revelation that God was going to keep loving her no matter what, transformation effortlessly began from within her and those things began to fade away.

> *Believe the Father's love for you and receive help in your time of need.*

When you see and believe the Father's love shining on you, darkness fades away. Depression fades away. Eating disorders fade away. Suicidal thoughts fade away. Fears fade away. Destructive addictions fade away. The more you place yourself under His grace, the more sin will have no dominion over you. Temptation will have no power over you when you are saturated with the Father's love, approval, favor, and acceptance. All this freedom can be yours when you truly believe that:

You are His beloved child, in whom He is well pleased.

Here is my prayer for you, my friend. I pray that you will begin to comprehend and believe the width and length and depth and height of your Father's unconditional love for you. Rest in your Father's love for you and not on your love for Him. And may you experience victory over every fear, every sense of guilt, and every addiction in your life.

CLOSING WORDS

Dear reader, thank you for taking this journey with me in *The Power of Right Believing*. You've been a wonderful and attentive travel companion, and I pray that you've been blessed by the truths shared in this book.

While there is so much emphasis on right living and right doing today, I trust you are beginning to see that the answer is really found in right believing. If you can change what you believe, you can change your life.

Right believing always leads to right living.

When you believe right, you will end up living right and doing right.

Through reading this book, I trust you have discovered that right believing is really all about the person of Jesus. When you believe in Him—in His love for you, His grace toward you, and the power of His finished work in your life—He will transform you from the inside out. And we know that real change and breakthroughs can only come from the inside out.

I encourage you to get ahold of *Destined To Reign* and *Unmerited Favor* and continue to establish yourself in right believing. *The Power of Right Believing* is built upon the foundation of these two books, and there are many truths that you will find in these books that will anchor your faith and propel you forward in right believing.

I also would like to hear from you if you have been blessed and impacted by this book. Please write to praise@josephprince.com.

Until then, do know that my love and prayers are with you and your family.

In His loving grace,
Joseph Prince

NOTES

CHAPTER 2 *The God Who Seeks the Shunned*

1. OT: 5911, *The Online Bible Thayer's Greek Lexicon and Brown, Driver & Briggs Hebrew Lexicon*. Copyright © 1993, Woodside Bible Fellowship, Ontario, Canada. Licensed from the Institute for Creation Research.

CHAPTER 3 *"Jesus Loves Me! This I Know"*

1. Cornwall, Judson, and Michael Reid. *Whose Love Is It Anyway?* Closter, New Jersey: Sharon Publications, 1991. pp. 58–59.

CHAPTER 4 *Play the Right Mental Movies*

1. NT: 342, *Thayer's Greek Lexicon*, Electronic Database. Copyright © 2000, 2003, 2006 by Biblesoft, Inc. All rights reserved.

2. Yong, Ed. "Snakes Know When to Stop Squeezing Because They Sense the Heartbeat of Their Prey." *Discover Magazine*. January 17, 2012. Retrieved January 18, 2013, from http://blogs.discovermagazine.com/notrocketscience/2012/01/17/snakes-know-when-to-stop-squeezing-because-they-sense-the-heartbeats-of-their-prey/#.UPin5Oh8Nyg.

3. Hardy, David L. "A Re-evaluation of Suffocation as the Cause of Death during Constriction by Snakes." *Herpetological Review*, 1994. p. 229:45–47.

CHAPTER 5 *See Yourself as God Sees You*

1. NT: 1343, *Vine's Expository Dictionary of Biblical Words*. Copyright © 1985, Thomas Nelson Publishers.

CHAPTER 11 *Victory over the Enemy's Mind Games*

1. Retrieved May 3, 2013, from www.biblestudytools.com/classics/bunyan-grace-abounding-to-the-chief-of-sinners/grace-abounding-to-the-chief-sinners.html.

2. Retrieved May 3, 2013, from www.biblestudytools.com/classics/bunyan-grace-abounding-to-the-chief-of-sinners/grace-abounding-to-the-chief-sinners.html?p=2.

3. NT: 3341, *Thayer's Greek Lexicon*, Electronic Database. Copyright © 2000, 2003, 2006 by Biblesoft, Inc. All rights reserved.

CHAPTER 12 *Beware of the Roaring Lion*

1. NT: 4991, *Thayer's Greek Lexicon*, Electronic Database. Copyright © 2000, 2003, 2006 by Biblesoft, Inc. All rights reserved.

2. Prince, Joseph. *Unmerited Favor*. Lake Mary, Florida: Charisma House, 2009. p. 201.

3. *The Truth about Ananias and Sapphira*, November 28, 2010, message CD by Joseph Prince. For more information, visit JosephPrince.com.

CHAPTER 14 *Jesus, Be the Center of It All*

1. NT: 453, *Thayer's Greek Lexicon*, PC Study Bible formatted Electronic Database. Copyright © 2006 by Biblesoft, Inc. All rights reserved.

2. NT: 3474, *Biblesoft's New Exhaustive Strong's Numbers and Concordance with Expanded Greek-Hebrew Dictionary*. Copyright © 1994, 2003, 2006 by Biblesoft, Inc. and International Bible Translators, Inc.

3. Retrieved May 6, 2013, from www.blueletterbible.org/lang/lexicon/lexicon.cfm?Strongs=G1695&t=KJV.

4. OT: 3070, *Biblesoft's New Exhaustive Strong's Numbers and Concordance with Expanded Greek-Hebrew Dictionary*. Copyright ©

1994, 2003, 2006 by Biblesoft, Inc. and International Bible Translators, Inc.

CHAPTER 16 *The Battle Belongs to the Lord*

1. NT: 1680, *Vine's Expository Dictionary of Biblical Words.* Copyright © 1985, Thomas Nelson Publishers.

2. OT: 2617, *Vine's Expository Dictionary of Biblical Words.* Copyright © 1985, Thomas Nelson Publishers.

3. OT: 1294, *The Online Bible Thayer's Greek Lexicon and Brown, Driver & Briggs Hebrew Lexicon.* Copyright © 1993, Woodside Bible Fellowship, Ontario, Canada. Licensed from the Institute for Creation Research.

CHAPTER 17 *God Loves It When You Ask Big*

1. OT: 3258, *The Online Bible Thayer's Greek Lexicon and Brown, Driver & Briggs Hebrew Lexicon.* Copyright © 1993, Woodside Bible Fellowship, Ontario, Canada. Licensed from the Institute for Creation Research.

CHAPTER 18 *Finding Hope When All Seems Hopeless*

1. Retrieved May 3, 2013, from www.nlm.nih.gov/medlineplus/ency/article/003647.htm.

2. OT: 2617, *Vine's Expository Dictionary of Biblical Words.* Copyright © 1985, Thomas Nelson Publishers.

CHAPTER 19 *Receive the Father's Love for You*

1. Retrieved April 5, 2013, from www.blueletterbible.org/lang/trench/section.cfm?sectionID=69&lexicon=true&strongs=G3338.

2. NT: 5206, *Vine's Expository Dictionary of Biblical Words.* Copyright © 1985, Thomas Nelson Publishers.

CHAPTER 21 *Find Rest in the Father's Love*

1. NT: 5487, *Biblesoft's New Exhaustive Strong's Numbers and Concordance with Expanded Greek-Hebrew Dictionary.* Copyright © 1994, 2003, 2006 by Biblesoft, Inc. and International Bible Translators, Inc.

2. NT: 5487, *Thayer's Greek Lexicon*, Electronic Database. Copyright © 2000, 2003, 2006 by Biblesoft, Inc. All rights reserved.

STAY CONNECTED WITH JOSEPH

Connect with Joseph through these social media channels, and receive daily inspirational teachings:

Facebook.com/Josephprince

Twitter.com/Josephprince

Youtube.com/Josephprinceonline

Prayer Request

If you have a prayer request, you can share it with our online community at Gracehope.com/Josephprince. Our prayer teams are on standby to pray with you.

Free Daily Email Devotional

Sign up for Joseph's FREE daily email devotional at JosephPrince .com/meditate and receive bite-sized inspirations to help you grow in grace.

SPECIAL APPRECIATION

Special thanks and appreciation to all who have sent in their testimonies and praise reports to us. Kindly note that all testimonies are received in good faith and edited only for brevity and fluency. Names have been changed to protect the writers' privacy.

DESTINED TO REIGN

This pivotal and quintessential book on the grace of God will change your life forever! Join Joseph Prince as he unlocks critical foundational truths to understanding God's grace and how it alone sets you free to experience victory over every adversity, lack, and destructive habit that is limiting you today. Bé uplifted and refreshed as you discover how reigning in life is all about Jesus and what He has already done for you. Get your copy today and start experiencing the success, wholeness, and victory that you were destined to enjoy!

UNMERITED FAVOR

This follow-up book to *Destined To Reign* is a must-read if you want to live out the dreams that God has birthed in your heart! Building on the foundational truths of God's grace laid out in *Destined To Reign*, *Unmerited Favor* takes you into a deeper understanding of the gift of righteousness that you have through the cross and how it gives you a supernatural advantage to succeed in life. Packed with empowering new covenant truths, *Unmerited Favor* will set you free to soar above your challenges and lead an overcoming life as God's beloved today.

100 DAYS OF FAVOR

(Containing 100 daily readings)

Dive headfirst into the vast ocean of God's favor and learn how it releases good success in your life! Taking key teachings from *Unmerited Favor* and turning them into bite-sized daily devotionals, Joseph Prince shows you how to develop favor-consciousness that releases the wisdom and blessings of God in everything you do, every day. With inspirational Scripture verses, prayers, and liberating thoughts on God's unmerited favor in each devotional, *100 Days of Favor* is a must-have resource that will empower you to overcome every challenge in your life and walk in good success. Be sure to order your copy today!

SALVATION PRAYER

If you would like to receive all that Jesus has done for you and make Him your Lord and Savior, please pray this prayer:

Lord Jesus, thank You for loving me and dying for me on the cross. Your precious blood washes me clean of every sin. You are my Lord and my Savior, now and forever. I believe You rose from the dead and that You are alive today. Because of Your finished work, I am now a beloved child of God and heaven is my home. Thank You for giving me eternal life and filling my heart with Your peace and joy. Amen.

WE WOULD LIKE TO HEAR FROM YOU

If you have prayed the salvation prayer or if you have a testimony to share after reading this book, please send us an email at praise@ josephprince.com.

Books By Joseph Prince

Destined To Reign

Destined To Reign Devotional

Unmerited Favor

100 Days of Favor

Healing Promises

Provision Promises

Health And Wholeness Through The Holy Communion

A Life Worth Living

The Benjamin Generation

Your Miracle Is In Your Mouth

Spiritual Warfare

Right Place Right Time

For more information on these books and other
inspiring resources by Joseph Prince, log on to
JOSEPH**PRINCE**.COM